– THE –
ARBITERS OF
REALITY

– THE –
ARBITERS OF
REALITY

HAWTHORNE, MELVILLE,
AND THE RISE OF
MASS INFORMATION CULTURE

Peter West

THE OHIO STATE UNIVERSITY PRESS
COLUMBUS

Library of Congress Cataloging-in-Publication Data
West, Peter, 1972–
The arbiters of reality : Hawthorne, Melville, and the rise of mass information culture /
Peter West.
  p. cm.
Includes bibliographical references and index.
ISBN-13: 978–0–8142–1088–8 (alk. paper)
1. Hawthorne, Nathaniel, 1804–1864—Criticism and interpretation. 2. Melville, Herman,
1819–1891—Criticism and interpretation. 3. Reality in literature. 4. Journalism—United
States—History—19th century. 5. Telegraph—United States—History—19th century. 6.
Narration (Rhetoric)—History—19th century. 7. Romanticism—United States. 8. Literature
and society—United States—History—19th century. I. Title.
PS1888.W47 2008
813.'3—dc22
                    2008005982

This book is available in the following editions:
Cloth (ISBN 978–0–8142–1088–8)
CD-ROM (ISBN 978–0–8142–9168–9)

Cover design by James Baumann.
Text design and typesetting by Jennifer Shoffey Forsythe.
Typeset in Times New Roman.

9 8 7 6 5 4 3 2 1

CONTENTS

ILLUSTRATIONS

PREFACE

WHEN I began this project, my aim was to understand how the narrative innovations of antebellum fiction responded to the practices of an emerging mass journalism. At a time when the popular conception of reality was being transformed by a centralizing and commercializing newspaper culture; by technologies such as the electromagnetic telegraph, the daguerreotype, and the moving panorama; and by savvy entrepreneurs such as P. T. Barnum, antebellum writers of fiction seemed to have an important argument to make about the dangerous mingling of information and entertainment taking place in the 1830s, 1840s, and 1850s. As part of this planned study, I would consider the work of Nathaniel Hawthorne and Herman Melville, whose approaches to storytelling seemed to respond to the various informational media and representational practices that defined early mass culture. Like many new historical scholars writing about these two authors in the first decade of the twenty-first century, I saw these two writers as astute cultural theorists who were concerned about the integrity of American democratic debate; and so, in my chapters on Hawthorne and Melville, the plan was to place their fictions in particular discursive contexts (the early days of the penny press revolution; the rise of telegraphy), thereby illustrating how the narrative strategies of these works exposed and combated the disturbing implications of the antebellum commercial revolution.

As I began digging into these rich contexts, however, and as I worked my way through each author's lesser-known writing (both public and private), it became increasingly clear that the romantic author's attention to what we today call the constructed nature of reality was something more complex than a cultural critique and would perhaps benefit from a more sustained and focused investigation. While I had initially assumed that these authors obsessively attended to the artifice of antebellum information culture to help their audience understand the implications of their superficial cultural practices, and while critics today often talk about romantic fiction as an attempt at refashioning the popular reader into a more engaged and reflective kind of citizen, this aspect of their writing seemed most meaningful to me as a language through which the literary artist invoked mass cultural practice as the antithesis of romantic belief. Though new historicism, in reconnecting the antebellum literary artist to the social, cultural, and political contexts of antebellum life, can now easily imagine the romancer as the engaged, even reform-minded critic of society, Hawthorne and Melville exhibited a relationship to their culture that I found conspicuously, well, romantic.

What eventually emerged out of these early findings is the following two-author study, an examination of how Hawthorne and Melville defined themselves and their art against the informational practices of an emergent mass culture. As my title suggests, I am arguing that these authors imagined themselves, in public and in private, as "arbiters of reality"—privileged seers who portrayed the antebellum commercial revolution as a threat to the very stability of truth. It is, of course, a cliché of postmodern culture to place the word "reality" inside scare quotes, to highlight how the various media that dominate our lives bombard us with images and words that construct not only particular truth claims but also the very category of the real. What Hawthorne's and Melville's writing suggests to us today is that seeing through the artifice of the media that surround us, and treating "reality" as a word that is always to be put inside of quotation marks, is a way of inventing and maintaining a particular kind of self. Amid a range of cultural forms offering highly contrived ideals of "authenticity," the romancer treated the critical ability to recognize the fraudulent surfaces of culture, and the artistic capacity to recast the authentic as that which resists linguistic and visual representation, as the defining achievements of autonomous, uncompromised selfhood.

My goal is to trace the emergence of this romantic logic in each author's writing and to illustrate how their narrative art was fundamentally dependent on the existence of a mass marketplace in which reality was very much for sale. As I will suggest, one danger of sharing with Hawthorne and Melville the view that blithely sees *through* those images and stories peddled as truth in the marketplace is that it renders us incapable of asking why (as consumers, artists, or critics; in the nineteenth century, or today) we are so preoccupied with the nature of reality in the first place. What makes these authors so relevant to our own reality-obsessed culture is that their vivid imaginations keep coming back from the boundless realm of romance to the *un*reality of popular journalism and those other textual surfaces of American mass culture. In essence, the goal of this study is not to unveil our current media age as the triumph of capitalism but to recast the persistent American belief in a reality uncorrupted by commercialization as the powerful legacy of romanticism.

ACKNOWLEDGMENTS

A small portion of chapter 2 was originally published, in an earlier form, as "Frames More Valuable Than the Pictures Themselves: Fiction and Journalism in Hawthorne's *The Story Teller*" in *ATQ*, Volume 16, No. 4, December 2002. Reprinted by permission of The University of Rhode Island. Sandy Crooms at The Ohio State University Press was helpful and encouraging from day one, and I am grateful to her, Maggie Diehl, and everyone else at the press for their patience, expertise, and professionalism. Thanks also to my two anonymous reviewers for the press, whose judicious and thoughtful readings were immensely valuable. Sean McCann, Claudia Stokes, and Anna Brickhouse kindly provided guidance in the early stages of the publication process. Thank you to Joe Parsons for his insight, honesty, and encouragement. And, of course, I owe a debt of gratitude to the many excellent scholars whose work I cite throughout the following chapters.

This study began as a dissertation in the English department at Emory University, where I was lucky to work with Barbara Ladd, Michael Elliott, and Cris Levenduski; their inspiring examples continue to shape who I am as teacher, advisor, and scholar. As my project evolved in more recent years into something very different from the dissertation, Michael continued to work with me while drawing on seemingly endless stores of patience and enthusiasm. Thank you for continuing to represent for me the full realization of what a professor of English can and should be. Both at Emory and at the University of Wyoming, I enjoyed the intellectual and emotional support of many colleagues and friends. Eduardo Paguaga, Scott Ellis, Beth Loffreda, and Peter Parolin have all read portions of this book, and all have helped me improve my work in significant ways; more importantly, they are also cherished friends. From outside of academia, David Ludmar has provided friendship and cheer, encouragement and understanding. I am grateful to the English department at UW for a research leave and to the UW School of Arts and Sciences for a faculty research grant. Thank you also to the wonderful staff at the American Antiquarian Society, the Interlibrary Loan Office at UW, and the New York Public Library.

My mother introduced me at an early age to the joys and rewards of teaching, my father to the philosophical and practical value of hard work; together they continue to model for me what it means to love and support one's child unconditionally. By far my greatest debt is to my wife, Laurel, for her wisdom and her faith. In a world of lies, you keep me connected to all that is true and unchanging. Finally, Josie, this book is for you—may you take it down from the shelf years from now, at a time when it might help to be reminded that your daddy, too, had mountains to climb. If the very existence of this book is a testament to the power of perseverance in the face of uncertainty, know that I drew all of my strength from the miraculous reality the three of us have built together.

INTRODUCTION

NATHANIEL Hawthorne's notebook from 1844 includes the following entry: "A dream, the other night, that the world had become dissatisfied with the inaccurate manner in which facts are reported, and had employed me, with a salary of a thousand dollars, to relate things of public importance exactly as they happen."[1] At first glance, this brief passage hardly seems noteworthy. As his numerous biographers tell us, and as his letters from this era vividly reveal, by 1844 Hawthorne was growing increasingly worried about financially supporting his expanding family, and so the dream's apparent preoccupation with the question of compensation affirms the long-standing view of an author struggling to navigate the vicissitudes of the marketplace. Read on another level, however, the notebook entry challenges the popular image of the quintessential American romancer, the writer of "fancy-pictures" whose fiction unapologetically leaves behind the mere "realities of the moment." Hawthorne's dream, as he recorded it, suggests a writer whose authorial identity is dependent not on his imagination but on his ability to relate important events "exactly as they happen." In a world riddled with inaccuracies, Hawthorne dreamed of himself as the privileged arbiter of the line between truth and lies.

Intriguingly, Hawthorne was not alone in imagining himself in such terms. In 1850 Herman Melville wrote (and anonymously published) "Hawthorne and His Mosses," a brilliant, rambling essay on the literary greatness of his fellow romantic author. Melville writes that great literary artists like Shakespeare—and, by implication, Hawthorne—probe at what he calls "the very axis of reality."[2] The essay goes on, in perhaps its most famous formulation, to define the genuine author as a truth-teller in an unreal world: "For in this world of lies, Truth is forced to fly like a scared white doe in the woodlands; and only by cunning glimpses will she reveal herself, as in Shakespeare and other masters of the great Art of Telling the Truth,—even though it be covertly, and by snatches" (244). Here Melville depicts "Truth" as something in danger and in flight, a "scared white doe" fleeing an encroaching "world of lies." If truth is forced to fly, as Melville tells us it is, such an articulation opposes the present day in which he writes with an implied past, a prelapsarian time (defined against "this world") when truth was presumably unthreatened. Most significantly, it is in the very act of telling this story about the contemporaneous status of reality that Melville reserves for the literary genius a singular cultural role: in Melville's essay, as in Hawthorne's dream, the true author enjoys a privileged access to an obfuscated "axis of reality" and a transhistorical awareness of the crisis posed by "this world of lies." Hence the contradiction at the heart of Melville's ideal of literary genius: while he invokes Shakespeare and "other masters" to distance his account of greatness from historical or cultural specificity, his description of "Truth" fleeing "this world of lies" situates the literary genius squarely within a particular historical narrative.[3]

As badly as Melville wants to define genius by its disconnection from any place or time, the story he tells in "Hawthorne and His Mosses" quietly marks him as a product of his cultural moment. For it is not hard to understand how Melville, writing in 1850, could imagine "reality" as a category that needed to be illuminated or clarified.[4] As Andie Tucher has written, "Antebellum America was a jamboree of ballyhoo, exaggeration, chicanery, sham, and flim-flam; [it] literally invented the word *bunkum*."[5] This was, after all, the era of both penny press journalism and P. T. Barnum's American Museum, two cultural forms that unapologetically, even gleefully, merged slippery ideals of authenticity with the goal of profit-making in courting their audiences. Indeed, according to scholars of both Barnum and the penny press phenomenon, during these years the consumption of highly unstable forms of authenticity emerged as a defining practice of a burgeoning mass audience. In his landmark discussion of Barnum's idiosyncratic art, Neil Harris famously illustrated that U.S. audiences in the 1830s, 1840s, and 1850s exhibited a "national tolerance for clever imposture."[6] And much more recently, James W. Cook has expanded this approach to antebellum culture in revealing that "artful deception was one of the main currents in American popular culture during the Age of Barnum." In other words, the criteria of authenticity signified during this era not merely as a question of fact and fraud but also "as a more slippery mode of middle-class play."[7] In the words of another critic, Barnum's exhibitions—such as his notorious "Feejee Mermaid," or Joice Heth, whom he promoted as a 161-year-old former slave of George Washington—depended "less on a massive duping of the public than on the mobilization of a dynamic in which deception and enlightenment operate together as inextricable complements."[8]

Like the example of Barnum, the story of the penny press suggests how the language of truth functioned in the antebellum marketplace as a salient and unstable feature of consumer culture. Beginning in the early 1830s, the first penny papers—cheap, daily productions that catered to the appetites of the masses—appeared in northeastern American cities.[9] James Gordon Bennett's *New York Herald*, first published in May of 1835, announced itself as a publication "equally intended for the great masses of the community—the merchant, mechanic, working people— the private family as well as the public school—the journeyman and his employer—the clerk and his principal."[10] In covering sensational stories such as the 1836 murder of New York prostitute Helen Jewett, "penny editors assured their readers again and again that they printed nothing but the truth and cared for nothing but the good of the public."[11] And yet even as such journalism was characterized by a grandiose commitment to unearthing "authentic facts," what made such news so popular was the vivid, highly readable style in which a good story was far more important than objectivity or verifiability. In the words of Ronald Zboray, who links the rise of penny press journalism to the demise of newspaper fiction, "fact often competed with fiction in the antebellum newspaper" to the point that "sometimes the distinctions between the two blurred."[12] By the mid-1840s penny press journalism would grow increasingly reliant on technologies such as the electromagnetic telegraph, steam power, and the expanding rail system. Bennett and *New York Tribune* editor Horace Greeley, for example, continually sought to outmaneuver one another by organizing rail expresses to carry "authentic news" received from European steamships as soon as they docked in places like Halifax. Thus, while the journalistic stories that penny-a-day newspapers presented to readers in the 1840s were often packaged in an emerging language of timeliness, reliability, and efficiency, this link to reality was becoming more valuable as an economic commodity.

The present study argues that the romantic author's claim to a more foundational understanding of reality was a by-product of both the increasingly mediated nature of antebellum life and the status of "reality" during these years as a constitutive category of mass cultural participation. My chapters situate the narrative idiosyncrasies of Hawthorne's and Melville's romantic fiction in specific cultural settings—Salem in 1830, for example, or New York City in 1846–47—to illustrate how the romantic "Art of Telling the Truth" was shaped by the representational technologies and practices of a nascent mass culture. As I hope to reveal, we can comprehend the romancer's self-invention as a more authentic kind of truthteller only if we read the storytelling machinery of romance against the kinds of truth claims it rejects as inauthentic. Paul Gilmore writes of the antebellum era, "If the market revolution meant, as Marx put it, that 'All that is solid melts into air,' many male authors positioned themselves as cultural authorities by promising access to a more solid ground beyond the market's illusions."[13] By recognizing how these authors invoked, refined, and critiqued a range of narrative practices and representational ideals that circulated during these years (including penny press and telegraphic journalism, moving panoramas, and daguerreotypy), we see the romance as one of many representational modes that emerged out of the antebellum commercial revolution—and we come to a clearer understanding of how the "very axis of reality" appeared to the romantic subject as a stable foundation on which to articulate a self.

To begin to understand how the dynamic conditions of antebellum culture shaped ideals of romantic authorship, chapter 1 takes us back to the early rumblings of the penny press revolution. The chapter describes the 1830 murder of Captain Joseph White of Salem, carefully interrogating the journalistic coverage of the murder and the ensuing trials in the local and regional press. As I reveal, Bennett traveled to Salem to capture, in his brilliantly lurid and dramatic manner, the details of the murder and trials for newspaper readers back in New York City. By highlighting how Salem's two newspapers responded to Bennett's presence, I argue that Salemites (including a young Nathaniel Hawthorne) were grappling not merely with the way their town was being represented in an urban-centered, nationalizing journalistic marketplace but also with what many considered a new type of reality. Using the dynamic example of the Salem Murder to illustrate the implications of the impending penny press revolution, I examine Hawthorne's idiosyncratic response to the murder scandal to locate the young author at a time and place where the very definition of reality was undergoing a cataclysmic transformation.

The second chapter moves from Hawthorne's hometown to the pages of his early fiction, where he rewrote the White murder in a little-known story that has a great deal to teach us about the philosophical preoccupations of his early career. Situating the narrative strategies of Hawthorne's early (and ultimately abandoned) *Story Teller* collection within the specific context of the Salem Murder and the nascent penny press phenomenon, I explore how his early writing claimed for its author a cultural authority as an arbiter of the line between truth and fiction. Many of the *Story Teller* pieces, I reveal, answered the sensationalistic practices of the newspaper—including "The Ambitious Guest," in which Hawthorne rewrote the true story of an avalanche that killed a New England family, changing important details so as to protect his fictional family from the grisly sensationalism that marked the journalistic coverage of the original catastrophe. The chapter suggests that the narrative concerns of Hawthornean romance found their first expression in this early fiction, where the romantic art of truth-telling was presented as an antidote to the fictions of a commercializing and nationalizing journalism.

Chapter 3 advances this sense of Hawthorne as an arbiter of the real by exploring how both his private and public writings continually redefine "reality" as that which cannot be contained or represented by contemporaneous media such as newspapers, panoramas, or daguerreotypic images. Encompassing a broad range of texts—including "The Old Manse," "Main Street," several of Hawthorne's notebook entries, and *The House of the Seven Gables*—the chapter treats the romance as a way of looking at mass culture, one that obsessively attends to its representational surfaces in order to oppose the transformation of the individual into a mass subject. While critics have long celebrated Hawthorne's sense of American public life as a realm of theatricality and spectacle, I highlight the rhetorical dimensions of such a mode of cultural witnessing by revealing how it afforded the author an imagined refuge from the otherwise inescapable process of modernization. Carefully examining the narrative techniques that appear in both his notebook writing and his published fiction, I argue that Hawthorne approached the practice of linguistic representation as a way of articulating a romantic consciousness undeluded by cultural fictions. Hawthornean romance thus emerges as an ongoing dialogue with contemporaneous representational practices, a means of self-invention that continually invoked and rejected the premises of mass subjectivity.

Turning to Melville, chapter 4 looks at the role played by the emergent ideal of telegraphic communication in the coverage of the Mexican War in New York from 1846 to 1848. At a time when American journalism was churning out broad and consequential myths about American expansion, Mexican inferiority, and racial heterogeneity as a threat to national cohesiveness—all under the aegis of a technology-based claim to infallible and instantaneous communication—Melville published a little-known series of satirical sketches that portrayed Mexican War journalism as a Barnumesque form of humbug. To comprehend Melville's relationship to the journalistic production of the Mexican War, this chapter examines how the coverage of the war in New York newspapers relied on a new telegraphic ideal to bring local readers in contact not only with the story of the war itself but also with a broader story about American identity and racial difference. By relocating Melville's "Old Zack" anecdotes in the periodical culture in which they first appeared, I suggest that Melville's ongoing sense of the true artist as a visionary in a "world of lies" was shaped in important ways by popular journalism's political and economic exploitation of new information technologies and by emergent forms of mass cultural participation.

Chapters 5 and 6 trace how Melville's critique of national and racial mythmaking are reworked in two of his better-known works, *Typee* and "Benito Cereno," treating the author's exposure of storytelling as a tool of racial and cultural exploitation as a by-product of his fraught relationship to mass culture. In *Typee,* for example, the ongoing attention to the surfaces of both American and Typee cultures is read not through the lens of postcolonial theory but as an attitude toward reality that reflected Melville's own location in an American information culture being redefined by both the emergence of a mass journalistic audience and the promise of national (and global) telegraphic connectedness. By attending to Melville's use of telegraphy as a crucial narrative symbol, I ask that we consider the text's refusal to penetrate into the secrets of Typee culture as a response to the telegraphic age Melville returned to, in 1844, after four years abroad. Ultimately, the author's use of telegraphic symbolism as a paradigm for seeing into Typee culture allowed Melville to keep both the American and Typee cultures of information in view and at a safe distance. Standing outside of each of these communication networks, the author of *Typee* claims to occupy a transcultural space that epitomizes the Melvillean self.

In turning to Melville's famous invocation of slavery, "Benito Cereno," chapter 6 explores how the author places the authentic reality of slavery beyond the reach of storytelling—at the very moment hundreds of thousands of American readers were encountering slavery in the pages of popular fiction. In attending to the ways in which Melville's "ruthless democracy on all sides" is fraught with a barely disguised hostility to "the tribe of general readers," I ask that we understand the narrative complexities of "Benito Cereno" as a vehicle for keeping these opposing forces in balance. By critiquing the racist logic of Delano's story-seeking mind, I argue, Melville opposes both slavery and the mass reading public and thus asserts his own idiosyncratic authority over the inauthentic surfaces of antebellum culture. At the same time, I juxtapose the narrative idiom of "Benito Cereno" alongside the narrative innovations of William Wells Brown, the ex-slave abolitionist author. Critics have long talked about Brown's formal idiosyncrasies—his evasion of a first-person autobiographical voice, his borrowings from various sources in the genre-defying *Clotel*—as an authorial reaction to the prefabricated "voice" imposed upon the black eyewitness by white abolitionism. By choosing not to approach "Benito Cereno" as a distinctly racialized response to the model of white authorship exemplified by Harriet Beecher Stowe—and instead reading the novella as a text that signifies Melville's moral outrage and his genuine concern for the fate of his country—we maintain a subtle but consequential double standard: Brown's narrative innovations have long been understood as a language of self-invention, shaped by Brown's racialized subject position as an ex-slave; "Benito Cereno," however, continues to serve as evidence of Melville's near-miraculous sensitivity to timeless epistemological, linguistic, and moral truths. Against such a view, I argue that "Benito Cereno" epitomizes a white model of romantic selfhood in which the fully realized human can be articulated only by disavowing the surface-oriented epistemology of the mass subject (Amasa Delano, the "blunt thinking American"), and probing into the "very axis of reality."

Throughout these chapters, I contrast the truth-telling claims of "romance" with the marketplace ideal of "authenticity," two terms that require clarification and context. Though I invoke the word "authenticity" in characterizing a range of antebellum forms and practices, in no way do I mean to imply that a deluded public naively believed it was purchasing unvarnished or antimarket truths from either an obvious humbug artist such as Barnum or an entrepreneurial journalist such as Bennett. Rather, I will be using the term "authenticity" to denote the way in which particular cultural forms sought to exploit the category of reality in the mass marketplace.[14] Whether or not audiences saw through the overwrought, sensationalistic postures of penny press writing, Bennett, like Barnum, courted an audience by claiming to capture the real world—so that the claim of authenticity, however suspect, nonetheless functioned as the basis of journalism's commercial appeal. At the same time, my use of "authenticity" refers to the way in which a product invites its consumer to participate in a "reality" shared with an imagined mass public—whether by following the story of an actual murder investigation in the *Herald*, by interrogating the "authentic" wooden leg of the Mexican general Antonio López de Santa Anna in the American Museum, by debating the portrayal of American slavery in Harriet Beecher Stowe's *Uncle Tom's Cabin*, or by participating in the virtual tourism offered by the Mississippi River panoramas of the late 1840s. Sometimes, as in the case of Barnum or Bennett, such "authenticity" was understood to be highly contrived; in other cases, as with daguerreotypy or telegraphy, a technology thrived precisely because it appeared to offer a lack of mediation and contrivance.

In the romantic mind, all of these practices and technologies were equally unreal, not simply because of their commercial nature but because they threatened to make reality the domain of the masses. Departing from current critical practice, my use of the term "romance" will refer to a particular mode of storytelling that carefully, even obsessively, invoked and rejected the truth claims of those cultural practices responsible for commodifying the real and peddling it before the mass public.[15] Of course, it is not that Hawthorne or Melville writes only about purely imaginative places or figures (see, for example, *The Blithedale Romance,* a roman à clef based on Hawthorne's time as a member of Brook Farm, the Utopian community) but that the romancer takes great pains, in his prefaces and within the complex machinery of his storytelling, to assure his audience that he enjoys a more rarefied and refined understanding of the nature of reality than is available in the popular marketplace, where claims of authenticity are mere commodities.[16] And so I read the romance as a reactive form, one that sought to protect reality from (what it portrays as) the fictionalizing forces of modernization by redefining the real as that which eludes specific technologies and modes of consumption.

When we recognize the romance as an attempt at negating the terms of antebellum culture, it comes as no surprise that romance often seems an almost perfect rhetorical counterpoint to that other controversial mode of mid-nineteenth-century truth-telling, the art of humbuggery. Indeed, nearly sixty years ago, Richard Chase noted the apparent symmetry between the showman and the romancer: "Looking back after one hundred years," Chase wrote, "we perceive a certain unity in American culture which embraces the kinds of thought and feeling represented by Barnum's scientific museum and Melville's *Moby-Dick.* Yet the difference is that most important of all differences: the one between art and other forms of organizing experience."[17] While Barnum's "operational aesthetic" invited his audiences to investigate the surfaces of his often carefully manufactured exhibits, an artist such as Hawthorne felt the need to warn his reader, as he does in the famous preface to *The House of the Seven Gables,* that "it exposes the romance to an inflexible and exceedingly dangerous species of criticism, by bringing his fancy-pictures almost into positive contact with the realities of the moment" (3).

And again we see the romancer invoking and rejecting the "inflexible" and "dangerous" practices of Barnum's America in "The Artist of the Beautiful," Hawthorne's famous tale of misread genius. At the conclusion of the story, Owen Warland presents his artistic masterpiece, a mechanical butterfly who appears as fluid and natural as nature itself, to the literal-minded Robert Danforth (a man "who spends his labor on a reality") and his bride, Annie. As if they are staring at Barnum's "Mermaid" or scrutinizing the notorious "Automaton Chess-Player" exhibited by Johann Nepomuk Maelzel in the early nineteenth century, Annie can only ask, "Tell me if it be alive, or whether you created it."[18] "Wherefore ask who created it, so be it beautiful?" the artist replies. Unable to categorize Warland's creation as either real or humbug, Danforth concludes, "That goes beyond me, I confess!" (928). Moments before the butterfly dies in the hands of Robert and Annie's child, Warland, in lieu of justifying his creation as "a gem of art" (928) to the couple, "smiled, and kept the secret to himself" (929). Of course, as the laboring author who *must* appear in the marketplace, Hawthorne does not keep the secret to himself but instead uses the shallow distinctions of the public to offset his depiction of the true artist—thereby finding for the romantic author a literary identity as the figure who can appear in the marketplace, but only as he who protects reality from the inflexible hands of the masses. As the story concludes, the reader is told that Warland "had caught a far other butterfly than this. When the artist rose high enough to achieve the Beautiful, the symbol by which he made it perceptible to mortal senses became of little value in his eyes, while his spirit possessed itself in the enjoyment of the Reality" (931). And so Hawthorne stands between the reader and what the artist considers to be the real, pointing outward at the public's superficial modes of consumption while nodding inward, beneath the surface of the printed page, to highlight for his readers what they can neither touch nor understand.

This sense of romantic fiction as a subversion of the specific authenticating practices of mass culture is also illustrated in the trajectory of Melville's early career. After publishing *Typee* and *Omoo,* the two fact-based accounts of his exploits abroad that launched his career, Melville grew increasingly frustrated with those readers who doubted the truthfulness of his narratives. In an 1848 letter to his English publisher, John Murray, Melville writes: "By the way, you ask again for 'documentary evidence' of my having been in the South Seas, wherewithall to convince the unbelievers—Bless my soul, Sir, will you Britons not credit that an American can be a gentleman, have read the Waverly Novels, tho every digit may have been in the tar-bucket?—You make miracles of what are commonplaces to us.—I will give no evidence—Truth is mighty & will prevail—& shall & must."[19] In the fall of 1846, following the publication of *Typee,* Melville responded to a similar request by Murray (seeking physical proof that he had spent time in the Marquesas) with the complaint, "how indescribably vexatious, when one really feels in his very bones that he has been there, to have a parcel of blockheads question it!"[20] But in the 1848 rejection, Melville goes further than he had before, defining his own ideal of "Truth" by rejecting the logic of documentation underlying his audience's requests.

The 1848 letter is noteworthy also for the way in which it formulates a theory of "romance" that unabashedly opposes an imagined popular audience who misunderstands the nature of reality. Describing his next project (which would end up as *Mardi*), Melville informs Murray: "My object in now writing you—I should have done so ere this—is to inform you of a change in my determinations. To be blunt: the work I shall next publish will [be] in downright earnest a 'Romance of Polynisian [*sic*] Adventure'—But why this? The truth is, Sir, that the reiterated imputation of being a romancer in disguise has at last pricked me into a resolution to show those who may take any interest in the matter, that a *real* romance of mine is no Typee or Omoo, & is made of different stuff altogether. This I confess has been the main inducement in altering my plans" (*Correspondence* 106). Here Melville envisions the genre of "romance" as both a confrontation of the literary marketplace's arbitrary practices of documentation and a path to artistic freedom. Indeed, "romance" functions in the passage as a literary form whose deeper understanding of reality is coextensive with an assertion of romantic autonomy: to see the Barnumesque dependence on "documentary evidence" as a hollow and misguided way of understanding truth is to locate an authorial identity apart from "the parcel of blockheads" who make up the imagined masses.

And, sure enough, when *Mardi* appeared in 1849, it included the following preface: "Not long ago, having published two narratives of voyages in the Pacific, which, in many quarters, were received with incredulity, the thought occurred to me, of indeed writing a romance of Polynesian adventure, and publishing it as such; to see whether, the fiction might not, possibly, be received for a verity: in some degree the reverse of my previous experience. . . . This thought was the germ of others, which have resulted in Mardi."[21] Critics often speak of works such as *The Confidence-Man* or "Benito Cereno" as hoaxes, as confidence games that Melville plays with his reader.[22] And yet to call one's novel *The Confidence-Man* is, I would argue, to define one's own mode of truth-telling *against* the con man's mode of trickery and deceit. In much the same manner, if this strange preface might seem to portray *Mardi* as a kind of hoax, to introduce one's work of fiction as a work of fiction is hardly to attempt to delude the public. Instead, Melville defines the "romance" that will follow against the slippery, even reversible ideals of a popular audience that loves to be humbugged; that is, he attempts to locate himself outside an entire marketplace of truth claims that he portrays as groundless fictions. Given that, as Neil Harris points out, the question of authenticity regarding *Typee* likely fueled its popularity in Barnum's America, it should not surprise us that Melville would come to equate (in works such as *Moby-Dick*, "Benito Cereno," and *The Confidence-Man*) the rejection of the very premises of authentication as a declaration of artistic and intellectual independence.[23]

Of course, Hawthorne and Melville were far from the only writers of the American romantic era to define themselves against the sham authenticities of the marketplace. Henry David Thoreau, for example, saw the newspaper as "the froth & scum of the eternal sea,"[24] a realm that (like the nearby town of Concord) afforded him a rhetorical counterweight for his own self-invention as arbiter of the line between "the mud and slush of opinion, and prejudice and tradition, and delusion, and appearance, that alluvion which covers the globe" and the "hard bottom and rocks in place, which we can call *reality*."[25] The language of reality that characterizes his romantic drive for individual autonomy suggests how deeply the romantic consciousness was indebted to the logic of authenticity that permeated so many cultural forms and practices. In one of many examples of Thoreau's rhetorical use of the newspaper, for example, he writes, "I am sure that I never read any memorable news in a newspaper. If we read of one man robbed, or murdered, or killed . . .—we never need read of another. One is enough. If you are acquainted with the principle, what do you care for a myriad instances and applications? To a philosopher all *news*, as it is called, is gossip, and they who edit and read it are old women over tea" (*Walden*, 64). Here Thoreau relies on the reading practices of the masses, and on the broader representative logic of mass culture (according to which characters and events stand in for types), to foreground his own location in the eternal realm of philosophy.

To further make his point, he elsewhere invokes Morse's famous invention as a way of asserting his own location outside the information network that was rapidly imagining the nation as a unified body, with telegraph wires serving as its metaphorical nervous system: "We are in great haste to construct a magnetic telegraph from Maine to Texas; but Maine and Texas, it may be, have nothing important to communicate" (*Walden*, 35). Of course, Thoreau's invocation of telegraphy, of information exchange, of the newspaper, complicates his very assertion of cultural autonomy. For Thoreau, to be a philosopher is to concern oneself with the kind of truths that are distinctly *not* merely informational and can*not* be contained by the technologies and practices of mass communication.

Admonishing his reader to "be your own telegraph" (*Walden,* 13), Thoreau transforms the very technology that (even more than the railroad) symbolized mass connectedness into a marker of authentic individualism.

In a somewhat different manner, Walt Whitman's 1855 "Song of Myself" (still untitled at that point) imagines "reality" as something comprising not only the kinds of representations available in the antebellum marketplace but also the less effable truths beyond the reach of commerce:

> My words are words of a questioning, and to indicate reality;
> This printed and bound book....but the printer and the printing-office boy?
> The marriage estate and settlement....but the body and mind of the bridegroom? also those of the bride?
> The panorama of the sea....but the sea itself?
> The well-taken photographs....but your wife or friend close and solid in your arms? (76)

Against the representations of the "printed and bound book," the panorama, and the photograph, Whitman defines the realm of romantic poetry as a way of indicating a "reality" that is—if not, like Thoreau's romantic reality, a negation of mass cultural terminology—able to embrace both the market's representations and the less effable sort of meaning that reproducible pictures and words can never contain. Whitman's famous career change from journalist to poet seems to quietly echo beneath the parallelism of the above lines: squarely at the left margin are books, panoramas, photographs; but as we move across the page, away from the artificial borders of the print shop and into the "organic" rhythms of his free verse, we get humanity—so that only in contrast to artifice do we get what the poet calls the "reality" that popular representations inherently fail to contain. As Mark Bauerlein argues, Whitman's goal is a poetic language in which "the word can be made contiguous or coexistent with the event . . . not distantly representational."[26] This desire to overcome the mediation of language reflects the increasingly mediated nature of antebellum life; for, as Whitman suggests, his writing must somehow overcome a culture of panoramas, photographs, and "printed and bound" books of poetry.

While Whitman's dialogue with the market's representations relies on a free-verse poetics, my project interrogates the work of two antebellum *storytellers* because I want to understand how the formal practices of romantic fiction relied upon *narrative* innovation to philosophically exploit the instability of the line between truth and fiction at a particular moment in time. Both theorists of the novel and critics of particular novelistic traditions have long recognized the dependence of fictional storytelling on the assumptions, postures, and conventions of information culture. Critics of the early English novel, for example, have shown how the novel invoked the contingent authority of journalism to carve out its unique cultural cachet. As Lennard Davis's account of the early English novel reminds us, the grand categories of literary taxonomy—fact/fiction, prose/poetry, printed/unprinted—are both subjective and subject to historical and cultural flux. My claim, then, is not that the antebellum era was the first moment in which fiction relied on the market-oriented nature of newspaper writing to articulate its own distinct literariness, for my own exploration of how antebellum information culture shaped the romantic imagination builds on Davis's great lesson that the novel can only be defined by its "unique and characteristic attitude toward fact and fiction, toward external reality and the nature of their own authenticity, and toward previous literary forms."[27] Rather than suggesting that the romance exhibits an unprecedented literary reliance on journalistic truth claims, I argue that the romantic storyteller was theorizing about the cultural fiction of authenticity because during these decades such a theoretical project promised these writers a critical (and mythical) distance from what Jonathan Elmer calls "the figure of the mass," an imaginary collective being that Elmer tells us is "posed over and against the self."[28] And so when we read the romance as an answer to the narrative practices of early mass culture, we see the romancer as a fragile discursive invention, a rhetorical being who must continually invoke and reject the economic roles of producer and consumer.

Perhaps more than anything else, it is this rhetorical distance from market practice that distinguishes Hawthorne and Melville from another canonical author of the American Renaissance, Edgar Allan Poe. As Terence Whalen has illustrated in his trenchant analysis of Poe's market-savviness, Poe invented literary forms such as the newspaper hoax and the detective tale that sought to capitalize on popular literary and journalistic practices.[29] Much like a patron of Barnum's museum, a reader of Poe's "Balloon-Hoax" experienced the slipperiness of the question of authenticity as it functioned in the antebellum marketplace—and as Poe's reader negotiated the line between truth and humbug, his innovative fictions would cash in (however modestly) on such a cultural practice. As I have already suggested, the two authors at the heart of my study devised literary forms that obsessively opposed, even confronted the economic exploitation of the question of authenticity. Thus, as we consider an early murder mystery tale of Hawthorne's, we will see how the tale's idiosyncratic narrative structure resisted the kind of closure that defined not only penny press journalism but also the tales of ratiocination that Poe would write a decade later. And so between Poe on the one hand and Hawthorne and Melville on the other, we have essentially two opposing kinds of exploitation: Poe's narrative innovations refine the logic of Barnum and Bennett without entirely rejecting the premise of salesmanship, while those of Hawthorne and Melville (though no less dependent on the contexts of mass culture) posit themselves, and imagine their authors, as the antithesis of such commercialism.

To further illustrate the romantic nature of Hawthorne's and Melville's relationship to the surfaces of antebellum culture, we can also consider the authorial self-invention carried out in one of the more popular novels of the 1850s, Fanny Fern's *Ruth Hall*. At the time that *Ruth Hall* appeared in 1855, Fanny Fern was a successful and well-known newspaper columnist—or, rather, Fern was the well-known alias of the writer Sara Payson Willis. The story of *Ruth Hall* traces the rise to prominence of the titular heroine (who writes under the pen name "Floy"), a character clearly based on Willis's own transformation into "Fanny Fern." After Ruth's husband dies, leaving her financially insecure with two young daughters, she comes face-to-face with the economic vagaries and political corruption of New York journalism. Over the course of the novel, Ruth comes to learn her economic value in the violent, sexist, and unpredictable marketplace—so that her emergence as "Floy" is directly linked to her achievement of economic independence and security. Less concerned with probing into the true nature of reality than with negotiating the arbitrary values of a world of surfaces, Fern embraces a model of identity that sees the self as a public construction unavoidably (and untragically) dependent on the terms that culture provides. As Michael Gilmore writes, Fern, like her fictional counterpart, "had become her public persona, and the only thing that existed behind her assumed identity was . . . her assumed identity as Fanny Fern."[30]

One antebellum commentator who was both impressed and taken aback at Fern's novel was Hawthorne, who wrote to his publisher, "The woman writes as if the devil was in her; and that is the only condition under which a woman ever writes anything worth reading. Generally women write like emasculated men, and are only distinguished from male authors by greater feebleness and folly; but when they throw off the restraints of decency, and come before the public stark naked, as it were—then their books are sure to possess character and value."[31] Hawthorne's rhetorical embrace of Fern's self-exposure is fascinating in part because, as I have just suggested, the novel is almost entirely preoccupied with the construction of its protagonist's public self. And yet, as Hawthorne's letter suggests, it was Fern's willingness to share vivid details of her private life that fueled its popularity: as Michael Gilmore notes, "the antebellum public scooped up the book because it told curious readers everything they could ever want to know about its celebrity author" (77).

Tellingly, though Hawthorne claims to admire the starkness of Fern's self-revelation, his own "Custom-House" preface to *The Scarlet Letter* is far more interested in opposing the romantic author's "inmost Me" from his "figurative self"—that is, he carefully distinguishes between the genuine humanity beyond the reach of the reader's gaze and the minor celebrity whose exploits as the recently deposed customs inspector were "careering" through the press.[32] As I suggest in chapter 3, by depicting himself as "decapitated" by the sensationalistic journalistic coverage of his politically motivated dismissal, Hawthorne locates his own literary artistry in a realm of romantic selfhood that the scandal-mongers can never reach. As in his earlier short fiction, the logic of romance as a storytelling ideal functions in his preface as a way of inoculating the artist against the empty commercialism that pervades the penny papers, the custom house, and antebellum society in general. Ultimately, then, the "stark" nakedness he praises in Fern's novel is a distinctly gendered literary ideal, one that, in assigning the goal of self-revelation to the female writer, reserves for the male author the romantic ideal of self-preservation.[33]

In portraying the romance as a genre that eschews the surfaces of American culture for a more philosophical interrogation of the nature of reality, I am corroborating a long-standing critical account of both Hawthorne and Melville as deeply theoretical writers. For well over half a century, literary critics have tended to define the fiction of these authors by its attention to what Lionel Trilling called "the problem of reality." In "Reality in America" (1940), Trilling attacks the critical approach taken by V. L. Parrington to American literature, stating that Parrington's "errors are the errors of understanding which arise from his understanding about the nature of reality." To Parrington, "there exists . . . a thing called *reality;* it is one and immutable, it is wholly external, it is irreducible." Against such a view, Trilling argues in "Manners, Morals, and the Novel" (1947) that the goal of the novel has always been "to try to penetrate to the truth which, as the novel assumes, lies hidden beneath all the false appearances." Though Trilling bemoans the fact that American romancers like Hawthorne and Melville have "not turned their minds to society," diverging too often from "the problem of reality beginning in the social field" and moving toward the airier concerns of romanticism, he nonetheless suggests that these authors understood reality as a problem, as something that is never perfectly known in any objective way, never adequately contained or represented. While Parrington's Hawthorne is "forever dealing with shadows" and therefore never able to "establish contact with 'the Yankee reality,'" Trilling's Hawthorne is most in touch with reality at the very moments when he struggles to find it: "The man who could raise those brilliant and serious doubts about the nature and possibility of moral perfection, the man who could keep himself aloof from the 'Yankee reality' and who could dissent from the orthodoxies of dissent and tell us so much about the nature of moral zeal, is of course dealing exactly with reality."[34]

Writing after Trilling, in a landmark account of the contrast between the novel and the romance in the United States, one that has defined the terms for a half-century of critical debate, Richard Chase famously described the latter as a "broken circuit," a distinctly American genre that eschews the quest for unity found in European novels in favor of depicting the "anomalies and disorders" of the American experience. Echoing the terms of Trilling, Chase argues that the novel and the romance differ "in the way in which they view reality."[35] Hawthorne, Melville, and other writers of romance, Chase suggests, are defined by their privileged and nuanced understanding of the deeper realities that lurk far beneath the mere surfaces of American culture. Throughout the numerous disagreements and controversies that have followed in the wake of Chase's account, the problem of reality has survived as a way of talking about the philosophical project of romantic fiction. Over the past several decades, Michael Davitt Bell has defined the romance by its "sacrifice of relation," its "fear of the artifice and insincerity of forms"; Evan Carton has described it as "a specific and urgent kind of rhetorical performance, a self-consciously dialectical enactment of critical and philosophical concerns about the relation of words to things and the nature of the self"; Walter Benn Michaels has suggested that "the romance represents nothing" as a way of recasting "representations [as] unrealities produced by mirrors"; Emily Miller Budick has argued that the romance exhibits a "double consciousness of interpretive processes" and an "awareness of the unknowability of material reality"; G. R. Thompson and Eric Carl Link have described the romance's "almost obsessive concern for experimental form, linguistic play, indeterminism, and self-reflexivity"; and Peter J. Bellis has written that "the romance's historical and rhetorical self-consciousness works . . . to resist co-optation by any hegemonic discourse or totalizing representation."[36] While these scholars disagree about the nature of romance—and while many scholars continue to read Chase's "romance thesis" as a function of mid-twentieth-century "cold war consensus-making"[37]—these and many other readers define the fiction of Hawthorne and Melville by its philosophical stance regarding the capacity of language and storytelling to access and lend meaning to reality.

As new historical modes of reading romantic fiction have predominated in recent decades, critics have often interpreted the romance's theoretical dimensions as a language of social critique and (symbolic) political action. Indeed, perhaps more than any other writers of the so-called American Renaissance, Hawthorne and Melville are often celebrated by late twentieth- and early twenty-first-century scholars for their insightfulness as social and cultural critics. While important readings of romantic fiction have exposed the sexist implications of Hawthorne's sense of authorship and the imperialist assumptions of Melville's literary imagination, just as often the new historicist sees the romancer as, well, a new historicist—a reform-minded analyst whose deconstruction of cultural facades was civic-minded and progressive. In the case of Melville, a text such as *Typee* "destabilizes our very processes of understanding 'other' people,"[38] while "Benito Cereno" exposes "sentimental modes of reading and response" to be "*civic* maladies" that threaten the integrity of the American republic.[39] Hawthorne, similarly, "wanted his readers to consider how barbarism took the form of 'culture'—not only as cultural 'documents,' but as structures of daily life, customs, premises."[40] And so the same writer who was once seen as the archetypal "citizen of somewhere else" is now routinely held up as "a cultural analyst of extraordinary acuity, ambitious . . . to reshape—in a sense, to cure—the community he addresses."[41]

Such a scholarly view seems grounded in part in the way romantic fiction echoes new historicism's own sense of reality as a category constantly being shaped by social, economic, and psychological conditions. Consider, for example, Millicent Bell's introductory essay to *Hawthorne and the Real,* a recent volume marking the bicentennial of Hawthorne's birth in which several important scholars reexamine the question of the romancer's relationship to history. In a thought-provoking essay, Bell verbalizes a longstanding assumption, held by countless readers of both Hawthorne's and Melville's fiction, that the romancer's theoretical perspective was both forward-thinking and miraculous: "Somehow [Hawthorne] foresaw a 'postmodern' way of thinking that 'reality' is a word always to be set in quotation marks as a part of the mind's figuration. . . . Hawthorne himself sometimes seems to make an ironic mockery of our search for stable meanings."[42] For Bell, as for many critics before her, "Hawthorne's notorious cultivation of ambiguity in his stories seems to mean that he, like ourselves, longed vainly for the classic realist's confidence in the singularity and accessibility of meaning . . . the solidity of a world which is not undermined by doubt of our perceptions. But his fiction does not

grant to our perceptions an indissoluble bond with unquestionable reality"
(19–20).

While my own study upholds Bell's claim, its greater aim is to reveal
that this romantic embrace of ambiguity was also a means of protecting reality from the masses—a reading of my authors that is somewhat
out of step with contemporary critical practice. Because new historical
treatments of Hawthorne and Melville aim, often explicitly, to correct
the earlier views of these writers as disconnected from place and time,
each author now regularly (though by no means always) appears as the
antithesis of the "citizen of somewhere else"—that is, as the engaged and
well-intentioned citizen of the American republic. But, of course, to histo-
ricize romanticism one need not deny the romantic flight from society as
a powerful and consequential drive. After all, in some of the most rigorous
and influential readings of canonical antebellum fiction (those by Walter
Benn Michaels, Myra Jehlen, Wai Chee Dimock, and Sacvan Bercovitch,
to name just a few) the historically minded critic takes as a subject the
romantic imagination's impossible quest for a space outside of ideology,
a space beyond history. For when we attend to the rhetorical dimensions
of the romancer's theoretical beliefs, Hawthorne's and Melville's shared
sense of "reality" as a word to be placed in scare quotes seems less a
vehicle of social critique than a language for imagining and communicating a self beyond the threat of collective identity-making.[43]

Consider the following excerpt from a letter that Melville wrote to his
brother, in which he announces the birth of his son, Malcolm:

> He's a perfect prodigy.—If the worst comes to the worst, I shall let him
> out by the month to Barnum; and take the tour of Europe with him. I
> think of calling him Barbarossa—Adolphus—Ferdinand—Otho—Gran-
> dissimo Hercules—Sampson—Bonaparte—Lambert. . . . There was a
> terrible commotion here at the time of the event.—I had men stationed
> at all the church bells, 24 hours before hand; & when the Electric
> Telegraph informed them of the fact—such a ding-donging you never
> heard. . . . Of course the news was sent on by telegraph to Washington
> & New Orleans.—When Old Zack heard of it—he is reported to have
> said—"Mark me: that boy will be President of the United States before
> he dies"—In New Orleans, the excitement was prodigious. Stocks rose &
> brandy fell.—I have not yet heard from Europe and Pekin. But doubtless,
> ere this, they must have placed props against the Great-Wall.—The harbor
> here is empty.—all the ships, brigs, schooners & smacks having scattered
> in all directions with the news for foreign parts.—The crowd has not yet
> left the streets, gossiping of the event.[44]

In linking the telegraph with the humbuggery of P. T. Barnum, money-hungry speculators, and the gossiping masses, Melville's letter mocks the commingling of information, entertainment, and capitalism that characterized antebellum culture. But if the twenty-first-century reader might celebrate Melville's awareness of the cultural fictions of a modernizing America, the above passage also suggests the extent to which this culture had successfully infiltrated the romantic mind. As Melville writes beyond the gaze of the public's eye, the symbols of mass culture have been so internalized within the author's consciousness, so woven into his very sense of what is real, that the significance of his son's birth can only be communicated by recasting Morse's technology and Barnum's humbugs as ironic symbols of his own joy; Melville's identity as a new father here can only be verbalized by invoking the *unreal* world of commerce, spectacle, and gossip in which the unseen masses live.

Just as these symbols of antebellum information culture continually appear in the romantic consciousness, so, too, does the subtle cultural logic that obsessively sees the world through the categories of truth and humbug. In the love letters that Hawthorne wrote to Sophia Peabody in the months and years leading up to and following their marriage in July 1842, for example, we see the author's ongoing struggle to find a refuge from the threat of collective identity. The Nathaniel and Sophia of these letters reside (with the literary geniuses of "Hawthorne and His Mosses") in a rhetorical space that exists outside the "unreal" world in which others live, work, and gossip. In September of 1841, the author writes to his fiancée, "If it were not for my Dove, this present world would see no more of me forever. . . . Once in a while, people might discern my figure gliding stealthily through the dim evening—that would be all. I should be only a shadow of the night; it is thou that givest me reality, and makest all things real for me."[45] Later in the same letter, Hawthorne describes his time at Brook Farm, the Utopian community from which he was temporarily away at the time of writing:

> I should judge it to be twenty years since I left Brook Farm; and I take this to be one proof that my life there was an unnatural and unsuitable, and therefore an unreal one. It already looks like a dream behind me. The real me was never an associate of the community; there has been a spectral Appearance there, sounding the horn at day-break, and milking the cows, and hoeing potatoes, and raking hay, toiling and sweating in the sun, and doing me the honor to assume my name. But be not thou deceived, Dove of my heart. This Spectre was not thy husband. Nevertheless, it is somewhat remarkable that thy husband's hands have, during this past

summer, grown very brown and rough; insomuch that many people per-
sist in believing that he, after all, was the aforesaid spectral horn-sounder,
cow-milker, potatoe-hoer, and hay-raker. But such a people do not know
a reality from shadow. (566)

Here we see Hawthorne move from describing the unsuitability of the
environment of Brook Farm to defining such an environment as "unreal"—so that the language of reality emerges as a way for the author to
evade the "spectral" identities ("horn-sounder, cow-milker, potatoe-hoer,
and hay-raker") Brook Farm threatens to impose upon him. More than
merely a philosophical category, the word "reality" allows the author to
contrast the integrity of his own identity with the marketplace's superficial
view of the individual as simply a source of labor.

   The passage is typical of Hawthorne's private writing in its distinguishing between the "reality" in which others live and the deeper, more
genuine reality that only the two lovers have access to. In other words,
"reality" seems to function in Hawthorne's imagination as a signifier
that carries with it a powerful distinction between romantic integrity and
an imagined mass of humanity that dwells amid inauthenticity. Another
letter from October of 1841, for example, claims that until "the heart is
touched" Nathaniel and Sophia "are not endowed with real life, and all
that seems most real about us is but the thinnest substance of a dream. . . .
That touch creates us—then we begin to be—thereby we are beings of
reality, and inheritors of eternity."[46] And in yet another correspondence,
Nathaniel tells Sophia, "Thou art my only reality—all other people are
shadows to me; all events and actions, in which thou dost not mingle, are
but dreams."[47] Similarly, in describing the blissful summer of 1842 the
author and his new wife spent at the Old Manse, Hawthorne wrote in his
notebook that "it might be a sin and shame, in such a world as ours, to
spend a lifetime in this manner; but, for a few summer-weeks, it is good to
live as if this world were Heaven. And so it is, and so it shall be; although,
in a little while, a flitting shadow of earthly care and toil will mingle itself
with our realities."[48] In Hawthorne's mind, he and Sophia lived in a reality that offset the shadows of the outside world; for even when his bride
suffered a miscarriage early the next year, Hawthorne would write that the
grief did not "penetrate to the reality of our life. We do not feel as if our
promised child were taken from us forever; but only as if his coming has
been delayed for a season" (American Notebooks 366).

   While Hawthorne's letters seem merely to epitomize the platonic language of romantic love, a realm from which two lovers look down on the
world of shadows in metaphysical union, we must recall that the unreal

world to which his love letters refer was always a historically specific place defined by the always-looming (and often united) threats of commerce and collective identity. After all, many of the letters to Sophia were written in settings that the author associated with the drudgeries of labor—the Boston custom house where he worked as a measurer for most of 1839 and 1840; Brook Farm; and the Salem "chamber" in which he wrote much of his early fiction. Writing by moonlight to Sophia about his days in the custom house, for example, Hawthorne defines his very humanity against the sort of work he performs during daylight hours: "Now, my intellect, and my heart and soul, have no share in my present mode of life—they find neither labor nor food in it; every thing I do here might better be done by a machine. I am a machine, and am surrounded by hundreds of similar machines;—or rather, all of the business people are so many wheels of one great machine—and we have no more love or sympathy for one another than if we were made of wood, brass, or iron, like the wheels of other pieces of complicated machinery."[49] If the deeper, more genuine "reality" to which his letters refer was thus a language for resisting the identity forced upon Hawthorne by the particular social and economic contexts in which he lived and wrote, it should not suffice to theorize that Hawthornean reality merely provided a forum in which to resist and critique the cold commerce of New England life. Rather, the above critique of the Brook Farm project suggests that Hawthorne's dependence on the language of reality was ontological—in that it offered the romantic mind a model of being apart from the logic of community that Brook Farm shared not only with other reform movements but also with what he considered the "one great machine" of American capitalist culture. By recasting the world of social intercourse, gossip, labor, political reform, and economic exchange as an unreality, Hawthorne could exist apart from any political party, reform movement, or social class, and beyond the shaping logic of mass identity.

In much the same way, the 1844 dream account from Hawthorne's notebook relies on the implied context of corrupt information to foreground the artist's capacity to see through the lies that define "the world" as a collective presence. And so it is no doubt significant that Hawthorne had his dream within months of one of the most consequential events of the nineteenth century: the May 1844 installation of Samuel Morse's electromagnetic telegraph, a moment that transformed the typical American's conception of reality. Although Morse's technology was initially seen as a supernatural curiosity, in the wake of its successful installation it quickly came to symbolize the promise of an instantaneous and unmediated link to distant places and events. "Professor Morse's is not only an era in the transmission of intelligence," the *Albany Weekly Herald* wrote, "but it has originated in the mind an entirely new class of ideas, a new species of consciousness. Never before was any one conscious that he knew with certainty what events were at that moment passing in a distant city—40, 100, or 500 miles off."[50] As we shall see, American commentators suddenly were able to imagine the entire nation sitting around an imaginary table, in a realm of informational purity and linguistic transparency. When considered in such a context, Hawthorne's recording of his dream positions the romantic author as a gatekeeper of reality, maintaining a firm hold on the criteria of truth-telling in the face of a potentially democratizing technology. At the same time, however, Hawthorne's description of his dream appears to co-opt the telegraphic ideal: as a truth-teller for hire, Hawthorne writes, he will "relate things of public importance *exactly as they happen.*" Like the myriad paeans to Morse's "miraculous" invention that appeared in 1844 and soon after, the final four words of Hawthorne's notebook entry quietly merge objective reliability and simultaneity, reimagining these telegraphic ideals as the shared criteria of perfect communication and romantic integrity.

All of these moments—Hawthorne's letters to Sophia, his dream, Melville's invocation of a foundational "axis of reality," his announcement of Malcolm's birth—rail against inauthenticity to invoke the imagined figure of the mass as the foil of the romantic self. In the following chapters, I develop this argument by approaching the deconstructive worldview of romance as both historical (shaped by particular discursive and material contexts) and rhetorical (employed by its practitioners as a means of negotiating such contexts). Perhaps, in privileging the romance as a meaningful and distinct category of American literary writing, and in upholding what has recently been called the "hoary notion" of romance as a form of escapism, my treatment of these authors seems like a return to the long-abandoned premises that shaped Americanist scholarship in the 1950s, 1960s, and 1970s.[51] In fact, what I hope these chapters offer is not a return to an earlier way of reading but an account of the romantic flight from contingency that has been informed by the insights and priorities of new historicism, a reading of antebellum literature and culture that sees the romancer's desire for a different kind of reality as a dream that was firmly grounded in place and time.

CHAPTER 1

FOREVER STAINED WITH BLOOD, BLOOD, BLOOD!

MURDER AND MASS JOURNALISM IN HAWTHORNE'S SALEM

Salem is a town obsessed with itself.
—Brenda Wineapple,
Hawthorne: A Life, on the town
as it was at the time of Hawthorne's birth

URING the night of April 6, 1830, Captain Joseph White of Salem, an elderly and wealthy retired merchant, was viciously stabbed and bludgeoned to death in his home. The crime and ensuing investigation and trials captivated Salem and much of New England in the months that followed, in part because two brothers from a very well-respected family, John Francis and Joseph Jenkins Knapp, were ultimately found guilty and hanged for the murder. In the days following the discovery of White's body, before any suspects had emerged, a group of Salem men organized a "committee of vigilance" to solve the mystery. The committee claimed an almost unmitigated authority, "with full power to search every house, and to interrogate every person."[1] Eventually the committee became a controversial subject in neighboring towns, and even as far as New York City, where James Gordon Bennett (the future editor of the *New York Herald,* who traveled to Salem in August of 1830 to report on the first trial) was publishing regular stories about the case in the *New York Courier.*

Adding to the drama and controversy of the "Salem Murder" (as it quickly became known) was the fact that the local man allegedly responsible for the actual killing, Richard Crowninshield, committed suicide in jail after Joseph Knapp confessed to plotting the crime and hiring Crowninshield to carry it out. In the cases against the Knapps, Senator Daniel Webster argued for the prosecution. Crowds gathered in the courthouse, even on treetops outside the courtroom windows, to catch a glimpse of the proceedings. As was often the case at such trials, pamphlets began appearing in town and around Boston promising authentic details of the crime—including maps of White's property, biographical sketches of the criminals, and drawings of the murder weapon. In addition to the significant concerns raised over the unchecked authority of the committee of vigilance, rumors spread about the "bloodthirsty" Salemites celebrating and drinking at the executions of the Knapps. Furthermore, many outside of Salem believed that Frank Knapp (as John Francis was known) was executed not because of his role in the killings but merely to satisfy the town's wrath. It is not difficult, in reading the extant newspaper editorials that raise such objections, to see Salem's notorious reputation as the town of the witch trials lurking beneath every word.

The Salem Murder survives as a compelling episode in New England history because of the complicated role played by newspapers in the events of the investigation and trials. The judge barred reporters from transcribing any of the court proceedings, and lawyers on both sides made repeated references to the "innuendo" and "gossip" that had slipped into the public consciousness through the newspaper coverage of the case. In addition, as the editors of Salem's papers fought back and forth in print with editors from neighboring areas to clear the town's name, they denounced the "profit-seeking" city publishers whose cheap trial pamphlets had arrived on the scene. What was at stake in the local papers was not merely the town's image as either "peace-loving" or "bloodthirsty"; with New England information culture teetering on the very precipice of a market revolution, local writers were grappling with the threat that an increasingly national and commercial journalistic culture posed to Salem's control over its own identity. As Bennett published his sensational stories in New York, as Boston publishers quickly manufactured their pamphlets for local circulation, as rival towns accused Salem of unprincipled vengeance, what was the real story of the murder, and whose public account of the town still haunted by witches would carry the day?

While Benjamin Day would not establish the *New York Sun* (the country's first penny paper) for another three years, Bennett's controversial presence in Salem in August of 1830 highlights many of the cultural tensions that would mark the penny press revolution: the conflict between local and national print cultures; the dual status of authenticity as marketplace commodity and informational ideal; the ways in which journalistic storytelling quietly imposed its narrative logic on the popular understanding of reality in antebellum America. Bennett's sensationalistic, story-driven mode of reporting placed the entire city of Salem on display for readers throughout the region. As nearby and not-so-nearby newspapers attacked Salemites not only for the murder and the committee of vigilance but also for the rapacity with which they devoured the latest facts of the investigation and trials, local commentators and editors fought desperately to correct the image of Salem that circulated around New England and beyond. Editorials defending the "natural" human appetite for sensationalism appeared in local papers. And to combat the widely circulating story of Salem as a morally depraved community, local writers argued that an emergent culture of sensationalism was distorting the typical reader's understanding of Salem by portraying the present day in the language of drama and intrigue. As we shall see, the journalistic frenzy that overtook Salem for much of 1830 transformed the way in which the city talked about the nature of reality.

Of course, if readers in Boston and New York considered themselves outside the culture of sensationalism that plagued Salem, they were themselves consuming a broader but no less sensational story about a town scandalized and stirred by the violent murder of one of its most prominent citizens. The newspaper coverage of the Salem Murder thus helps us understand the far-reaching implications of the antebellum journalistic revolution. Readers across the Northeast participated in the events in Salem by consuming the latest stories written by the dozen different journalists who had traveled to the town. The presence of this larger journalistic culture meant that the real story of the murder—and the real nature of Salem's people—was being debated far beyond the city's borders. While Salemites whispered among themselves about who might be arrested next, Boston and New York readers devoured the vivid narratives promising the "real story" left out of the formal legal proceedings. The question of authenticity was both a powerful engine for selling newspapers and a mode of consumption that helped characterize a developing mass audience.

As the penny press revolution fueled the emergence of this mass reading public, it also, much more quietly, shaped the literary imagination of Nathaniel Hawthorne. For Hawthorne, whose appetite for newspapers lasted his entire life, and whose letters from these years reveal an intense curiosity about the case, was among the countless Salemites following the story of the murder and the ensuing investigation and trials. In the young author's reactions to the murder and its aftermath, Hawthorne distanced himself from the popular obsession with the real story of the crime. But, as these letters reveal, he was as preoccupied with the scandal as the rest of Salem. As chapter 2 will show, Hawthorne eventually fictionalized the murder of Joseph White in a way that told a multilayered story about the changing nature of reality in the earliest days of the penny press era. If debating what the real world looked like was a practice of both local and national spectatorship, Hawthorne's early fiction relied on the newspaper to carve out an imaginary space from which the romantic author could look down upon the writerly and readerly practices of early mass culture. Ultimately, two decades after the Salem Murder, Hawthorne's view of reality as an economic, social, and narrative construct consumed by the masses would flower into the romance, a fictional form that claimed for its author a privileged understanding of American culture unmarred by the delusions of mass subjectivity. As a first step toward understanding how the romance's manner of representing reality came to represent, in Hawthorne's romantic consciousness, an autonomy from American culture, let us investigate the Salem Murder—not as an actual crime but as a window into the journalistic revolution that was transforming the popular conception of reality at the very moment when Hawthorne was embarking on his literary career.

FROM the moment Joseph White's body was discovered by his housekeeper on the morning of April 7, local newspapers invited the town to participate in the investigation of the crime. As one early story put it, "we deem . . . it our duty to lay before our readers every particle of authentic information we can obtain, respecting the horrible crime which has so shocked and alarmed our community"—a duty that included, for example, a careful and gruesome description of the coroner's report. Soon after White's body was put on display for the reading public ("upon removing the breastbone [. . . one sees] the cellular membrane beneath it"), the local editors challenged the town to solve the mystery, linking the very reputation of Salem to the resolution of the crime.[2] Two weeks after the murder, before any suspects had been apprehended, the *Gazette* reminded its readers that "the Murder remains shrouded in mystery," before going on to lay out precisely what was at stake: "A principal cause of the immunity we have hitherto enjoyed from gross crime has been the well-founded impression that escape was impossible, from the vigilance of our sharp sighted citizens. This safeguard is now, in a degree, removed,—its power has diminished in a ratio corresponding with the time that has elapsed since the bloody deed was done; and nothing can restore it but the detection and punishment of the offender."[3] The paper employs a logic here that clearly aligns the resolution of the "mystery" with the town's ability to reclaim its reputation as vigilant and respectable. Even more significantly, the *Gazette* links the future safety of Salem to the reestablishment of such a reputation—in other words, by solving the mystery the town essentially could protect their "Salem" from an alternative, externally imposed narrative. What is at stake in the above passage is not simply the town's understanding of what happened two weeks before but also its ability to determine the meaning of this past event within a narrative of their own construction. Unsolved, the murder signifies Salem's vulnerability; resolved, it rescues the town's upright reputation. And by June 1, after the Knapps had been apprehended and Joseph had confessed, the *Gazette* announced which story had prevailed: "The mysterious and horrid Murder, that has so long perplexed and agitated the public mind, is at last brought to light. The circumstances, that at first seemed inexplicable, are at length made clear and plain."[4]

To make sense of Salem's obsession with the crime, one must keep in mind the symbolic significance of a small city jointly following the story of a murder. The popular appetite for true stories in a murder case such as this was more than simply a question of public entertainment. As Karen Halttunen has convincingly argued, by the early nineteenth century public accounts of murders were increasingly presented within the framework of narrative mystery—so that the story told would be one each reader could participate in by attempting to put all of the pieces together.[5] Understanding the Salem Murder as both a real event and a journalistic narrative gradually being unfurled before the eyes of readers across New England and the Northeast suggests that this journalistic print culture quietly determined how Salemites conceptualized the shape of reality: after all, the very project of searching for "the real story," while implying that the truth has yet to be found, defines reality according to a narrative logic. In such a context, the ongoing attempt by the Salem papers to make concessions to the "human" desire for stories appears as a means of naturalizing journalism's version of reality: the truth is a story, and people have always loved a good story. And yet, as the town demanded the next chapter in the story, they were essentially calling for more arrests—demanding more blood, as it were. In other words, the same popular sentiment that lent its weight to the committee of vigilance—allowing its members to stop people on the street and question them, even to search houses without a warrant—implicitly sanctioned the journalistic storytelling that appeared with each new issue of the local papers. If nineteenth-century print culture framed murder as a mystery tale (which the local newspaper coverage of the Salem Murder undoubtedly did), it was the cultural force of storytelling as a method of interpreting the world that was partly responsible for blurring the line between local realities and the murder's status as a media event.

As the Knapp trials dragged on for most of the year, and as it became increasingly apparent that at least the people most immediately responsible for the murder were either dead or awaiting trial, the Salem papers found a new justification for the town's intense curiosity with every detail of the case. In August, by which time the piecing together of the conspiracy and the murder itself was the responsibility of Webster and the rest of the prosecution team (and thus the papers could no longer frame the town's obsession with the case as a matter of moral necessity), the *Gazette* took great pains to explain that such a curiosity was not unique to Salem: "The very great number of respectable strangers and professional gentlemen, who have continually attended from distant places, proves that the circumstances and incidents of this tragedy intrinsically possess a deep interest, not engrossing the attention or affecting the feelings of us who reside in this vicinity, more than those who dwell at a great distance. . . . The same eager curiosity to learn the details of this sad narrative, that is manifested here, extends to the remote regions of our country, and with nearly the same degree of intenseness."[6] Carefully pointing to the respectability of the visitors who have frequented the court proceedings, the paper uses the "professional" status of these "gentlemen" to ease the town's anxieties about following such a sensational story. One can easily see in such an argument the editor's need to identify the trial as a respectable mode of behavior suitable not to those on the margins of society but to what we might call an emerging middle class. As the above editorial continues, it becomes clear that one key to the carving out of such middle-class respectability is the idea of a normalized human appetite for stories:

And that all should feel this eager curiosity and deep interest, or as some denominate it, "excitement," is perfectly natural as well as innocent. The same principles of our nature that give interest to scenes of fictitious distress and horrors in dreams and romances, operate to chain attention to the history of this murder, the atrocity of which is not equal to its strangeness. It furnishes another example to illustrate the force of Lord Byron's remark that "*Fiction* is not so strange as *Truth.*" The circumstances that led to the crime were so unnatural and improbable, that without *confession* it could never have been detected. . . . That a trial in which so much of the strange and the marvellous is developed should excite deep interest in the public mind, is natural, and is independent of prepossessions against, or in favor of the persons implicated.

To follow the story for its interest in no way compromises the impartiality or respectability of the Salem public. In fact, the "public" being shaped in the above excerpt is one that is defined precisely by the ability to balance a republican disinterest with the natural appetite for narrativity. The paper, of course, rather than describing some preexistent group of respectable curiosity-seekers, participates in the carving out of the image of a middle-class readership that would fuel the penny press revolution.

As the *Gazette* and other papers continued to legitimize the public's curiosity about the trial, the town's editors gradually lost their grip on the very identity of "Salem." Rumors began swirling in nearby (and not-so-nearby) cities that Salem was exhibiting an uncomely vengeance in tracking down and punishing those responsible for the White murder. The *Herald* of Newburyport, Massachusetts, published a letter claiming (among other allegations) that many Salemites were drunk at the September execution of Frank Knapp. In answer to such a charge, the *Gazette* reported that "[a] more orderly, a more solemn assemblage, was never seen anywhere on any occasion, even those expressly dedicated to devotional excesses."[7] When Joseph Knapp was executed at the end of the year, the paper, to forestall such charges the second time around, pointed to "the deportment of the assembled multitude, as on the former occasion, being that of a people conscious that they had character at stake, and determined to preserve that of good citizens."[8]

A letter published in the *Essex Register* in June, as the facts were still being sorted out in the case, provides an early glimpse into the struggle among local editors to define the relationship between the public appetite for more information and the difficulty of locating the line between fact and fiction. In attacking other local papers (including the *Gazette*) the letter's author bemoans that fact that "every late paper has been more or less filled with *en parte* statements, calculated to prejudice the public against the accused."[9] After excerpting a number of newspaper stories, the writer concludes the following: "Now, it appears to me it would be as well to let 'particulars' alone till *after the trial,* for the old adage is sometimes true, that 'one story is good till another is told; and that there *may* possibly be two sides to the question.'" Indeed, the *Register* took an impartial-sounding approach in presenting the latest details from the murder and its aftermath. In attempting to resolve the question of the behavior of Salemites at the first execution, the *Register* published testimonials from a variety of people claiming to be eyewitnesses—some claiming to have witnessed public drunkenness, and others agreeing with the writer who claims, without irony, "I have attended many Executions, and say, that I never attended any one where it was conducted with more propriety than the one referred to."[10]

While Warwick Palfray's *Register* staked its journalistic authority on a model of reporting that juxtaposed competing claims about their town, the paper advanced such a claim of impartiality by attacking the cheap pamphlets that appeared during the trials of the Knapp brothers. These pamphlets preyed upon the popular appetite for authentic details having any relation at all to the crime by including features such as a floor plan of White's home, a map of the local streets ("accompanied with a key"), and a sketch of the bludgeon used in the murder that was found under the steps of a local church (see figure 1). Seeking to exonerate the town itself from any role in the success of such publishing ventures, the *Register* reported, "Great numbers of these trashy and spurious publications were sold to the strangers in town, and even to our own inhabitants, who were ignorant of their contents."[11] Using explicitly economic language, the papers condemned the "pamphlet pedlars parading through all our streets, and amidst the spectators at the place of execution, vending a pamphlet consisting of a farrago of monstrous lies and absurdities." While the political rivalry between Caleb Foote's *Gazette* and Palfray's *Register* is everywhere evident in each of these papers, the publications seem to have agreed on the necessity of protecting Salem from charges of a disreputable fascination with the more lurid details of the crime. On the one hand the *Gazette* formulated its theory of the universal appetite for storytelling; on the other, the *Register* pointed to the scandalous lies of the Boston publishers looking to capitalize on innocent Salemites as the real source of the sensationalism.

Between the pamphlets that circulated across the region and the newspaper interest in the crime itself, Salemites were undoubtedly aware of how their town was being transformed into a spectacle. The local *Gazette,* for example, reprinted a piece in August from the *Boston Courier* that described the "melancholy interest excited by viewing the mansion of the murdered Joseph White" and carefully detailed the victim's yard, house, and possessions.[12] In fact, by August of 1830, as the first Knapp trial began, a story about the town itself had already begun to take shape outside of Salem. The *Register* of Marblehead, Massachusetts, was one of the first papers to publicly attack the committee of vigilance, a hostility that emerged in response to the arrest and imprisonment of two Marblehead citizens early in the investigation. In writing of the first of these two arrests in early May, the *Register* states the following: "With infinite regret, we perceived the indictment of a citizen of this town, and one too, from whose general character and amiability, we could not, and do not for an instant allow ourselves to suspect."[13] While the paper initially asked its readers "to suspend their opinion in this matter, until its final adjudication," the release of both people, nearly three months later, was met with a harsh critique of the Salem committee: "Thus have two innocent individuals suffered all the ignominy and deprivation of three months imprison-

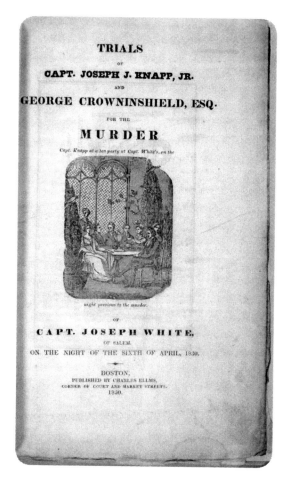

FIGURE 1. DETAIL FROM "TRIALS OF CAPT. JOSEPH J. KNAPP
AND GEORGE CROWNINSHIELD." BOSTON: CHARLES ELLMS, 1830.
(COURTESY AMERICAN ANTIQUARIAN SOCIETY)

ment and, through the unwarrantable organization and officiousness of a
self-constituted body, called 'Committee of Vigilance.' We protest against
all such associations of individuals; they are incompatible with personal
security and civil freedom."[14] The editors go on to reveal that "we prepared an article some months since, on the inexpediency and dangerous
tendency of raising 'Committees of Vigilance,' but forbore its publication,
through fear of adding to the public excitement, which was then too great
to yield to the control of sober reason." One week later, in responding to
a piece in the *Newburyport Herald* (the same paper that would accuse
Salem less than two months later of reveling at the first Knapp execution)
questioning the above article, the editors clarified the nature of their pro-

test. Contrasting the "personal responsibility" of an individual magistrate to the committee of vigilance, in which individuals lose such responsibility "by acting in the mass," the editors used the authority of the Salem committee to give a shape to anxieties about the dangers of mob rule.[15] Furthermore, in contrasting their own forbearance with the rashness of their neighboring town, the Marblehead paper initiated a public narrative that portrayed Salem as an unruly town driven by vengeance.

Once the Knapp trials began, much of the journalistic coverage of the cases made Salem itself an actor in the drama that was being played out in the courtroom. In describing the scene of Frank Knapp's first trial, a writer from the *Boston Courier* makes the crowd in the courtroom as important as the proceedings themselves:

> It is always painful to enter a court of justice where a fellow creature is on trial, and observe, as one not particularly interested cannot help observing, the indifference of the gaping crowd swayed hither and thither by the anxiety of those without to learn something, they know not, and care not what, of that which is passing within; the silent dignity of the Court whose province it is to mete out "even-handed justice," and the parade of authority in the minor officers of the law, who keep uncovered the heads of hydra the crowd. But when the crime for which the prisoner is on trial is one of such peculiar atrocity, exciting terror and a loud cry for justice by its enormity, and commiseration for the respectable connections of those implicated, when the amount of the connection of the prisoner with the crime becomes a delicate point, not to be found except by evenly balancing the cry for blood, between the law on the one side, and testimony on the other, it becomes doubly painful to watch the progress of the proceedings, and the alternations of the case, as perceptible in the faces of the Jury, as in those of the most indifferent persons in the Court. The effect of this trial, whatever may be its result, will, for years to come, be perceived and felt in Salem.[16]

In order to understand the implications of this description, one must remember that Frank Knapp's relationship to the murder was murky at best. Only after Crowninshield killed himself did the prosecution draw up new charges for the brothers in which each was charged for the murder itself. In fact, the first trial (the one described here) ended in a hung jury, as jurors were not able to agree that Frank was directly involved in the killing. Thus the *Courier* writer implies that the "delicate point" of the "connection of the prisoner with the crime" is a product of the "cry for blood" on the part of "hydra the crowd." By adopting a perspective on the courtroom that depicts the crowd within the courtroom as part of the spectacle, the author of the above piece implicates Salem in the trumped-up charge against Frank Knapp. The concluding sentence above suggests that the piece's real subject is not the defendant, nor even the trial itself, but the town of Salem, who sat on a public stage for Boston's reader-spectators. When the coverage of the case is read in such a way, the Salem papers seem to be fighting for the right to define their own town against (what they call) the profit-seeking city publishers.

By far the most dominant presence of all the city writers attending the trials was Bennett's. In his own accounts of the investigation and trials that were being published back in New York, Bennett was far more willing than the Salem editors to challenge the story being constructed by Webster and the prosecution inside the courtroom. Reading his stories, one sees ample evidence of his interest and skill in bringing out the full dramatic force of events: "Joe Knapp, as he is called, was not exactly counted on as one of the confederacy headed by Crowninshield. He was jealous of the popularity of Dick among such men as Palmer, Hatch, &c. &c. He managed his criminal concerns on his own hook, and it was merely the case that made him apply to the leader of the execution of a plan, from which through his connections, he expected to reap the full benefit. Knapp possesses, it is said, much vanity and superciliousness. His wife is considered one of the handsomest females in Essex county."[17] By using the nicknames of those accused in the crime, by sprinkling in local gossip, by relying on colloquial phrases like "on his own hook," Bennett provided an aura of authenticity that was defined against the accounts that appeared both in the legal proceedings and in competing newspapers. Little of Bennett's reporting appeared in the Salem papers (though his stories were often quoted in the Boston papers), presumably because his accounts of the conspiracy repeatedly sought to open up more and more narrative threads, instead of merely sanctioning the story being pieced together in court. Indeed, Bennett was repeatedly reprimanded by the judge who presided over the case. As one Boston paper covering the first trial reported, "The New York reports of this trial were to-day brought up, and severely censured, as characterised with incorrectness and stupidity."[18] The judge's hostility toward "the New York Press" even led him to warn that "if any one person was detected . . . taking notes of the evidence in the Court House, for the purpose of sending them without the state for publication, previous to the conclusion of the trial, he would be proceeded against by the Court, as for a contempt."[19] Such threats led Bennett to respond that "it is an old, worm-eaten, and Gothic dogma of the Courts, to consider the publicity given to every event by the Press, as destructive to the interests of law and justice." In defending the importance of his brand of journalism, he concludes, "The honesty—the purity—the integrity of legal practice throughout this country, are more indebted to the American Press, than to the whole tribe of lawyers and judges who issue their decrees. The Press is the *living* jury of the nation."[20]

In such a role, Bennett repeatedly gave voice to the concerns about the abuses of power by the committee of vigilance.[21] In addition, his paper was apparently the only paper covering the Joseph Knapp trial to report that one potential juror was disqualified because he expressed significant doubts that Frank Knapp (who had already been executed by the start of his brother's trial) was treated fairly by the courts. Like the Boston piece excerpted above, Bennett's coverage of the trials put Salem and its citizens on display for the New York audience, transforming the "quiet town" into a media-manufactured spectacle. After the first jury returned without a verdict against Frank Knapp, for example, Bennett wrote the following: "The result of this trial has produced a great excitement in Salem. No one who has not been present during these trials, and observed the tone and current of conversation in that town, can imagine the feelings with which the people of Salem have viewed every event connected with the singularly atrocious murder of Captain White. Before any discovery was made tending to fix the murder upon its perpetrators, such was the excitability of the public mind in Salem, that many individuals of standing in society talked of emigrating from the place altogether—of removing from a community containing characters so dangerous and fearful."[22] Such a description reveals how the public identity of Salem was being shaped by competing print media. As the local *Gazette* used the murder and subsequent investigations to uphold the town's reputation before its own citizens, writers such as Bennett defined Salem as potentially "dangerous and fearful" by placing it within their own sensational narratives. When a Boston-published pamphlet called "A Biographical Sketch of the Celebrated Salem Murderer" described a secret meeting place in the forest outside of Salem where the conspirators would assemble, Salem editors fought back by attacking the piece as "lies and plagiarisms," even taking the time to deny the existence of such a spot.[23]

In the days leading up to the execution of the second Knapp brother, as the drama seemed to be coming to an end, the local opinion that White's housekeeper (whose daughter was married to Joseph Knapp) knew about the murder plot made its way into the *Gazette,* though the editors stopped short of naming any names. Editors at the *Rhode Island American* responded by republishing the piece, along with the following commentary:

One would suppose that the Salem people were glutted with blood, and yet their editors are crying for more. Three lives for one would not satisfy them, and they really seem to long for a female subject to harrow up the public feeling with. The Salem Gazette, in an article which we publish today, has let slip the dogs of suspicion against some one bearing the form of woman. . . . The fact is that an attempt is making to damn the house keeper of Mr. White in public opinion, and drag her before the gaping multitude; and all because Joe Knapp wishes to save his own life by taking that of a woman. In God's name let us be spared this horror in the Salem tragedy. Even if the woman be guilty, let her go and sin no more. We do not believe it, we will never believe it, even of the vilest population of Salem, where they seem to have acquired an extraordinarily high relish for public executions. . . . Must we on opening their papers forever find them stained with blood, blood, blood.[24]

The editors of the *American,* in describing the accused woman "[dragged] before the gaping multitude" by a town "forever . . . stained with blood, blood, blood," link the Salem Murder with the town's infamous witch trials. Such a move by the paper's editors reveals that from the first discovery of White's body to the above attack on Salem's native thirst for blood, the story of the Salem Murder changed dramatically—from a murder mystery whose resolution would vouchsafe Salem's solid reputation to a larger narrative about the town in which the committee of vigilance served merely as the latest chapter in the ongoing story of a cursed and depraved community.

While the *Gazette* initially sought to counteract this story of Salem by attempting to legitimize the public's intense preoccupation with the case, the paper gradually came to recognize that the definition of "Salem" was no longer simply a product of the town's own self-authored history. An article that appeared in November of 1830, about a month before the execution of the second Knapp brother, betrays the paper's anxiety regarding such a development. In a piece titled "The Times We Live In," the anonymous writer addresses "the general, but very erroneous notion, that there must have been a great deterioration of the public morals."[25] While the writer cites the White murder as the cause of this public opinion, the deeper implication is that nostalgia has effaced the unseemly realities of Revolution-era Salem, where "more riot, debauchery, and vice, obtruded themselves upon the sight in a week than could now be discovered by diligent search in a month." Most importantly, the author argues that the "dreadful tragedy" of White's murder kept "the thoughts and conversations of the community continually directed to that enormity," and thus fueled the false impression of the town's moral decline.

Of course, what kept the town's focus continually directed on the case was a months-long journalistic narrative that unfurled before readers the latest news on the murder, investigation, and trials. The *Gazette* implies that the open-ended story that began in April, whose resolution promised to save Salem's reputation, has in fact reconfigured the town's own understanding of themselves. The paper seeks to remind its audience that what has changed more than their neighbors' behavior is the way in which they have become accustomed to reading about their world—and thus the article undercuts the story that has been concocted about Salem's moral decline by highlighting the enormous and delusive power of storytelling. While the popular opinion cited in the article held to a story about the town's fall from innocence, and while accounts of the murder such as that of the *Rhode Island American* privileged one that depicted Salem's innate and unchanging depravity, local editors formulated a story of their own, one in which the popular appetite for news had given rise to a false sense of an idyllic past. Ultimately, the *Gazette* seeks to combat the transformation of their town by pulling the rug out from under all the stories that circulated about Salem, in Marblehead and Providence, Boston and New York. Facing a network of stories about Salem that they could no longer control, the *Gazette* claimed, paradoxically, that the ultimate story about Salem could only be understood by recognizing how a new journalistic culture had transformed the city's very sense of what was real.

In biographies of Bennett, and in historical accounts of the penny press era, the Salem Murder warrants at most a passing mention.[26] And yet in many ways the months-long spectacle anticipated the journalistic revolution that would take place throughout the 1830s and 1840s. In the urban centers of the North, daily newspapers would quickly become commonplace, and readers would grow accustomed to following sensational stories on a daily basis. Patricia Cline Cohen has examined the newspaper coverage of the 1836 murder of Helen Jewett, for example, to illustrate how New York's penny papers manufactured the crime into an ongoing narrative that fed a new kind of reading public. Similarly, scholars have revealed how the penny press revolution facilitated the spectacular showmanship of P. T. Barnum, who famously manipulated local papers to drum up business for his museum exhibits and hoaxes.

On a much smaller scale, this realization would also shape the career of Edgar Allan Poe. Poe's "Balloon Hoax," which appeared in the *New York Sun* on April 13, 1844, was published as an actual news article describing the crossing of the Atlantic by eight men in a large "steering balloon" inflated with coal gas. In ways that we have only recently come to appreciate, Poe was an attentive, if not often successful, businessman whose fiction, nonfiction, and poetry reveal the author's career-long quest for a model of cultural authority indebted to the marketplace. Hoaxes like the balloon story thus capitalized, à la Barnum, on the instability of authenticity as a valuable commodity in a newspaper climate that privileged a great story over anything else. Terence Whalen has shown that Poe's writing was profoundly shaped by the economic conditions of antebellum America, especially after the financial panic of 1837. In the wake of the panic, Whalen suggests, Poe became "painfully aware of the need to satisfy both elite and common readers *with a single text.*" His response was to merge his literary ambitions with the terms of the marketplace—thereby constructing "a self purged of unprofitable romantic tendencies and recast in the furnace of entrepreneurial capitalism." Connected to the market revolution, of course, was the information revolution; and so for Poe, "[t]he rise of information as a dominant form of meaning induced him to reject the old profundities, first by redefining literary creation as the combination of already existing ideas, and then by relocating literary meaning to the surfaces of culture."[27] In Whalen's reading, C. Auguste Dupin's mastery of these surfaces in the detective tales reflects Poe's own capitulation to the ways in which meaning is produced in capitalist culture.

Barnum's, Bennett's, and Poe's varied though related attempts at mastering the antebellum culture of authenticity are easily seen as a new mode of cultural production made possible by the market revolution. By returning to Salem in 1830 with the above discussion in mind, we can also elucidate Hawthorne's relationship to the material conditions of antebellum life. The Salem Murder is a small, mostly forgotten moment in local New England history, but one that brings into focus Hawthorne's preoccupation with the unreality of American culture as a by-product of the complex developments that gave rise to Barnum's and Bennett's careers. Indeed, one readily sees the young author's desire to fashion his own identity against the popular obsession with the real story of the crime in his recorded reactions to the murder. While I would not suggest that this event somehow gave rise to Hawthorne's preoccupation with a public deluded by false realities, interrogating his relationship to this most sensational example of popular storytelling unveils the author's preoccupation with the meaning-making power of stories as a way of defining himself against the gossip-hungry mob.

In a long letter to his cousin's new husband, John S. Dike (who had recently moved from Salem to Steubenville, Ohio), Hawthorne describes the circulating gossip about the murder and the ensuing trials. What is perhaps most significant about the young author's account of the sensational events is the relationship he carves out to his fellow townspeople. I quote the entire portion of the letter that pertains to the murder in part to illustrate how intensely Hawthorne was following the story:

> The town now begins to grow rather more quiet than it has been since the murder of Mr. White, but I suppose the excitement will revive at the execution of Frank Knapp, and at the next November term of the Court. Frank Knapp's situation seems to make little or no impression on his mind. The night after his sentence, he joked and laughed with the men who watched him, with as much apparent gaiety as if he had been acquitted, instead of condemned. He says, however, that he would rather be hung than remain a year in prison. It is reported, also, that he declares that he will not go to the gallows, unless two women go with him. Who those women are, must be left to conjecture. Perhaps you have not heard that many people suspect Mrs. Bickford and her daughter, Joe Knapp's wife, of being privy to the whole affair before the murder was committed. I cannot say whether there are good grounds for these suspicions; but I know that it was daily expected, during the trial, that one or both of them would be arrested; and it is said that they were actually examined at the house of Mr. Brown the jailer. It is certain that Joseph Knapp's wife has twice attempted to hang herself. The first time was soon after her husband's arrest, and the second immediately after Frank was found guilty. Old Captain Knapp also made a similar attempt, a little while ago, and was cut down by his son Phippen. The poor old man is entirely broken in mind and almost crazy; and it is no wonder that he should be so, when all sorts of trouble have come upon him at once. He and his son Phippen have injured their reputation for truth, by the testimony they gave at their trial; but I have little doubt that they believed what they said; and if not, they had as much excuse as there can possibly be for perjury. There seems to be an universal prejudice at present against the whole family;—I am afraid Captain Knapp himself meets with but little real pity, and I believe every body is eager for the death of his two sons. For my part, I wish Joe to be punished, but I should not be very sorry if Frank were to escape. It is the general opinion, however, that Joe will not live to be brought to trial. He contrives to obtain spirituous liquors in his cell, and is in a state of intoxication almost all the time. He is utterly desperate, and will not even wash and dress himself, and at one time he made a resolution to starve himself to death. I do not wonder that he feels unpleasantly, for he can have no hope of mercy, and

it is absolutely certain that he will not be alive at the end of six months from this time.[28]

Hawthorne writes here from the perspective of one who is fully apprised of the latest gossip and yet can still refer to a "universal" opinion with which he disagrees. As a resident of "the town" he describes, the authorial persona of the above letter resides somewhere outside the town's "prejudice," even as he shares in their knowledge of recent events and innuendo. Such a narrative perspective should be familiar to any reader of Hawthorne, as it appears in works as obscure as "Sights from a Steeple" (an early sketch in which the nameless narrator has climbed up a church steeple and looks down at his village) and as well known as *The Scarlet Letter*, in which Hawthorne's romantic narrator first describes for us Hester walking out of the prison-house from the perspective of the Puritan crowd gathered outside, only to then turn the narrative lens on the crowd itself—as if our narrator were hovering somewhere above the scene.

Scholars have long noted how Hawthorne often distances himself from an imagined public that serves as the antithesis of romantic identity, but we seem far less curious about his reliance on the language of reality as a strategy for making such a distinction. In a sense, Hawthorne's response to the Salem Murder brings together these two preoccupations that would in many ways define his career. His account of the Knapp trials addresses the public skepticism regarding the completeness of the official story authorized by the legal proceedings. In fact, while the guilt of both Crowninshield and Joseph Knapp was beyond public doubt, a great number of suspicions toward other Salemites remained even after the last trial. Margaret Moore explains that after the execution of the Knapp brothers, many locals believed that the true story of the White murder never appeared anywhere in the newspaper version of events. Despite the conviction and execution of the Knapps in the case, she writes, "the end of the trial left unanswered questions." While the editorial that drew the ire of the *Rhode Island American* argued that "the facts had not been fully ascertained," the editor of the *Gazette*, "fearful of libel . . . did not give names to his suspicions."[29] The story of the Salem Murder was thus unfinished in the journalistic coverage that captivated readers for the better part of a year. When the mystery tale sanctioned by the legal proceedings and the Salem papers ended with the execution of the second Knapp brother, popular opinion in town was defined in large part by the sense that the full truth was absent from the official story. As Hawthorne wrote to his cousin, "it was daily expected" that further arrests would occur, and yet they never did—presumably because a murder, a suicide, and two executions made the town both weary from the four deaths and wary of perpetuating their reputation as bloodthirsty. In Hawthorne's town, the public narrative of events was recognized, even by those who paid to consume it, as a fabrication. As it would throughout his career, here the claim that reality existed somewhere outside of print allowed the author to undercut the modes of truth-telling consumed by an imagined public that Hawthorne sought to keep at a distance.

Instead of participating in the public debates over the real story, then, Hawthorne carves out an imagined autonomy from public opinion by pointing to a "universal" sentiment that he finds inadequate, at once invoking and eluding the question of authenticity. Unlike the editors of the *Gazette* and the *Register*, Hawthorne's own account does not involve replacing one narrative with another—he does not, for example, refute the story of Mrs. Bickford's guilt by suggesting a more accurate account of the crime. In a sense, his narrative is something of a counternarrative; in lieu of engaging directly in a debate about the reliability of the rumor ("I cannot say whether there are good grounds for these suspicions"), he will comment only on the very narrative about which he has no opinion ("I know that it was daily expected . . . that one or both of them would be arrested") by addressing its very status as a narrative. Furthermore, his letter's use of passive voice in phrasings such as "it is reported" or "it is said" shapes an idiom that both communicates a story and foregrounds its story as the product of popular opinion. Hawthorne's interest in exposing the narrative logic that determines the popular conception of reality provides the author with a rhetorical space outside of the simple act of telling stories—a space that would soon find a literary form in the narrative innovations of his early fiction: carving an authorial space outside the stories he recounts, Hawthorne's letter anticipates the authorial persona of *The Story Teller* by looking down on a "public" that produces, consumes, and debates stories.

As Hawthorne would write to Sophia more than a decade later: "Every day of my life makes me feel more and more how seldom a fact is accurately stated; how, almost invariably, when a story has passed through the mind of a third person, it becomes, so far as regards the impression that it makes in further repetitions, little better than a falsehood, and this, too, though the narrator be the most truth-seeking person in existence. How marvellous the tendency is! . . . Is truth a fantasy which we are to pursue forever and never grasp?"[30] The distance between story and fact is what fascinates him, he tells Sophia; both unavoidable (even to "the most truth-seeking person in existence") and marvellous, this distance allows

Hawthorne to formulate a conception of truth as fantasy, as something that can only be imagined through the rejection of perfect fidelity as a linguistic and narrative possibility. If the 1830 letter seeks a distance from the particular story being constructed by his fellow townspeople, the Brook Farm letter portrays the fictionality of *all* stories. In fact, the letter relies on the failure of storytelling to advance a definition of romantic truth—as that which storytelling can never contain. This, in turn, defines the romantic artist as the intellect who recognizes the delusions of those (at Brook Farm, presumably, but also in the world more generally) who seek reality in narrative form.

The value of digging into the journalistic origins of romance, as my next chapter will seek to do, is that it exposes the romance as one half of a dialogue with competing accounts of the real. As critics such as Michael Gilmore and Walter Benn Michaels have revealed, much of Hawthorne's corpus is marked by a sense of the marketplace as a looming menace threatening to transform local realities into capitalist spectacles. The case of the Salem Murder reminds us that Hawthorne's view of commerce as an invading and fictionalizing force reflected his own geographical location vis-à-vis the market revolution. The debates about the murder and its aftermath reveal that an urban-centered commercialization arrived in Salem in the form of a new mode of journalistic writing, and thus carried with it a new discourse about the capacity of language to represent the real world. In 1830 Salem was at the very nexus of a commercializing city journalism and a less urban newspaper culture that was still primarily localized and party-run. As the next chapter will suggest, the continual presence of the newspaper throughout his early fiction reminds us that Hawthorne's obsession with the problem of reality was shaped by the local print conditions amid which he wrote his first significant works of fiction.

CHAPTER 2

THE JOURNALISTIC
ORIGINS OF ROMANCE

OUR years after the murder of Joseph White, and only months after the penny press era officially began, Nathaniel Hawthorne invented a murder scandal of his own. In "Mr. Higginbotham's Catastrophe," Squire Higginbotham's murder is graphically described in a fictive town's local newspaper in ways that clearly echo the coverage of the White murder. But there was a crucial difference between the original crime and Hawthorne's rewriting of it: the reader of "Mr. Higginbotham's Catastrophe" ultimately learns that, despite the detailed account of the crime in the local paper, Higginbotham *was never murdered.* The newspaper's sensationalistic descriptions of Higginbotham's corpse, and its melodramatic account of the victim's grieving niece, are nothing more than the fictions of an overzealous journalistic culture eager to feed the public's appetite for authentic-seeming stories. When read in light of the changes in American journalistic practices taking place in the early 1830s, the story's humorous invocation of journalistic sensationalism has a serious point to make about how the popular demand for scandal and authenticity was conspiring with market-savvy newspaper editors to rewrite the line between fact and fiction.

Hawthorne originally wanted to publish "Mr. Higginbotham's Catastrophe" as part of a collection called *The Story Teller,* a series of tales linked via the framing device of an itinerant storyteller traveling across the New England countryside and sharing his stories with local audiences. The narrative frames that were intended to introduce each of Hawthorne's tales (which would have been presented as the inventions of the titular storyteller) reveal the careful process by which the storyteller pieced together his stories to meet what he perceived to be the particular tastes of each audience. The collection was therefore singularly meaningful as a collection—for it was in the very dialogue between stories and frames that Hawthorne portrayed all narrative production as a question of supply and demand. Though he apparently wrote a number of tales intended for *The Story Teller,* only the Higginbotham story was published in its intended frame. As I hope to illustrate, in overlooking the narrative innovations that defined *The Story Teller* as Hawthorne envisioned it, scholars have missed a rich site for exploring the formal and philosophical preoccupations of Hawthorne's early career.

In what follows, I connect *The Story Teller* to Hawthorne's quest for an authorial identity outside the terms of a commercializing print culture. In the literary marketplace of early-1830s New England, as new print technologies and an expanding mass readership were making magazine and book publishing increasingly profitable, Hawthorne was forced to confront the practical demands of the emerging profession of authorship. Like other authors working in these years, he faced the paradoxical challenge of courting an audience for his fiction while simultaneously protecting the artistic integrity of his literary creations. In a sense, the narrative machinery of *The Story Teller* was his response to such a dilemma: by making a storyteller both the subject and source of his fiction, Hawthorne defined the romantic artistry of the genuine "author" against the practices of those who simply peddled stories to the masses. To write stories is to serve the public, Hawthorne's collection implied, but to expose the economic forces of supply and demand that shape all acts of storytelling, to bemoan the commercialization of writing, is to be an artist.

Out of this complex authorial self-invention emerged the romantic theory of reality that would largely determine the shape of his literary career. While Hawthorne's fictional storyteller is the principal producer of narrative in the *Story Teller* pieces, in as many as a third of the stories likely to be from the collection, newspapers show up within and around the tales, positing an alternate mode of storytelling to that presented by the author's fictive raconteur. In its original form, *The Story Teller* argued that while journalism claimed merely to represent in gritty detail the truths of American life, it took its shape from invisible forces of market demand— particularly the demand for entertaining stories. Like the Salem editors who attacked the sensationalistic practices of Bennett, Hawthorne betrays an anxiety regarding the contemporary move toward a more national and more commercial print media. By portraying journalistic narratives as no more factual than his storyteller's fictions, by revealing the ease with which such stories travel as fact across the country, and by depicting the eagerness with which such stories were consumed by American and foreign readers, Hawthorne's early fiction argues that antebellum newspapers were enjoying an unprecedented power to write a new modern world. As we shall see, this was more than simply the warning of an engaged citizen concerned for the fate of his society: Hawthorne's self-invention as the author operating outside the unrealities of the marketplace required the newspaper—and its treatment of reality as something that could be authentically captured in print—as a rhetorical protection from the commercial world the author both needed and loathed.

I N "The Seven Vagabonds," which appears to have been intended as an opening sketch to the collection, Hawthorne introduces his storyteller as a huckster looking to make an easy living. The "vagabonds" of the title refers to the titular storyteller and six other characters—a showman, a book peddler, a couple traveling with a show-box, a fortune teller, and an Indian archer who performs for a living—who meet one another and then travel together to a camp meeting, each intending to make money off the "poor souls" they find there. Importantly, our hero is not yet a storyteller when the group decides to head to the meeting. As the showman reminds him, "All of us here can get our bread in some creditable way. Every honest man should have a livelihood. You, sir, as I take it, are a mere strolling gentleman."[1] Only in response to the necessity pointed out by the showman does our narrator decide he will tell stories for a living. So while the showman is preoccupied with the problem of earning a living "in some creditable way," Hawthorne looks down on the inartistic mode of entertainment that these "vagabonds" trade in.

By portraying the vagabond storyteller as a type of showman looking to make a profit off of an unsuspecting public, Hawthorne locates the author squarely outside such economic concerns. Consider the following description of the book peddler, in which our narrator imagines that the peddler's "completest glory" would come when he stops for the night and brings his library into a crowded bar: "Then would he recommend to the multifarious company, whether traveler from the city, or teamster from the hills, or neighbouring squire, or the landlord himself, or his loutish hostler, works suited to each particular taste and capacity; proving, all the while, by acute criticism and profound remark, that the lore in his books was even exceeded by that in his brain. . . . Thus happily would he traverse the land; sometimes a herald before the march of Mind; sometimes walking arm in arm with awful Literature, and reaping every where, a harvest of real and sensible popularity, which the secluded book worms, by whose toil he lived, could never hope for" (143).

The job of the bookseller, not surprisingly, is to read the customer and match his supply with their demand.[2] Authors, on the other hand, are "secluded book worms, by whose toil [the book peddler] lived." In truth, of course, such a formulation could just as easily be reversed: the author, after all, could never make a living *without* the salesmanship that helps find an audience. And so this moment suggests that Hawthorne responds to his artistic predicament by defining the author as both the ultimate creator of real value and a "secluded" figure who toils at a distance from the vagaries of the marketplace. By placing the author outside the forces of supply and demand, Hawthorne makes the author's seclusion visible to his reader, articulating a public identity defined against the storyteller's reliance on spectacle and showmanship—so that the author is connected to a more foundational kind of value.

The Story Teller further distances the author from the commercial realm by aligning the jobs of book peddler and storyteller. In the slightly later "Passages from a Relinquished Work," Hawthorne's storyteller describes the craft of narrative-making as merely another case of supply and demand. "Passages" comprised a longer portrayal of the young narrator growing into the role of storyteller and included a final section, "The Village Theatre," which was the frame in which "Mr. Higginbotham's Catastrophe" first appeared. In "Passages" Hawthorne's storyteller similarly makes his story to order, infusing the product he manufactures himself with the autonomy of those books described in "Vagabonds." While the book peddler's salesmanship allows the author to remain secluded, the storyteller is both the producer and the peddler of his tales. Indeed, it is on the storyteller's ability to make his tales appear as if they were someone else's—as if they were products upon a shelf—that his success depends: "No talent or attainment could come amiss; every thing, indeed, was requisite; wide observation, varied knowledge, deep thoughts, and sparkling ones; pathos and levity, and a mixture of both, like sun-shine in a rain-drop; lofty imagination, veiling itself in the garb of common life; and the practiced art which alone could render these gifts, and more than these, available. . . . I manufactured a great variety of plots and skeletons of tales, and kept them ready for use, leaving the filling up to the inspiration of the moment; . . . But my best efforts had a unity, a wholeness, and a separate character, that did not admit of this sort of mechanism" (183–84). If the invocation of book peddling introduces the problem of authorship in the literary marketplace, the collection's story/frame machinery, by revealing how stories are manufactured to appease the particular demands of an audience, was Hawthorne's response. The author's frame asks that we recognize the stories that will follow as a negotiation between teller and audience, a product whose "separate character" is a mirage fabricated in response to specific expectations.

Just as the showman travels around with a "mimic world"—a sort of puppet show in which "a multitude of little people [were] assembled on a miniature stage" (140)—from which he earns his living, Hawthorne's storyteller invents his own fictions simply as a way of making money. And so we are asked by Hawthorne to treat his narrator with suspicion. If, as the storyteller confesses in the above excerpt, all literary products are tailor-made in the storyteller's formulation, it would seem that even the collection's frames must be read as giving the audience what it expects. But while setting up the framed narrative structure on which the collection would rely, Hawthorne's storyteller stops short of acknowledging this fact. In contrast to the above excerpt, where he describes for us the mechanisms that drive his stories, here we are merely on the receiving end of his sales pitch: "With each specimen will be given a sketch of the circumstances in which the story was told. Thus my air-drawn pictures will be set in frames, perhaps more valuable than the pictures themselves, since they will be embossed with groups of characteristic figures, amid the lake and mountain scenery, the villages and fertile fields, of our native land" (177).

The reader learns that the "value" of the storyteller's collection rests not in the fanciful tales themselves—there is nothing substantive in such "air-drawn" sketches, this passage implies—but on the materiality of the frames. If the "air-drawn" sketches are mere inventions aimed to please an audience hungry for certain kinds of stories, the storyteller implies that the frames are more valuable because they are "characteristic"—that is, because they capture the real New England in a pleasant, picturesque manner. In fact, neither frames nor sketches lie outside the market's expectations as the storyteller envisions them; Hawthorne posits a fictive storyteller who devises both story and frame to appease the readerly market as he envisions it. Hawthorne's storyteller fabricates the value of his literary productions (his picturesque frames) by distancing them from a competing mode (his entertaining stories) that he confesses to be somewhat groundless.

When read as a unified whole, Hawthorne's collection reminds his reader that, the storyteller's claims notwithstanding, this entire economy of narrative modes exists on the page solely as a product of clever salesmanship: the reader, we are told, can enjoy a more authentic New England by recognizing the stories as the fictions that offset the reality of the frames. Significantly, the storyteller's account of his frames' "characteristic figures, amid the lake and mountain scenery," sounds a lot like the "mimic world" of the showman and the show-box of the young couple from "Vagabonds"—all products whose value relies upon the audience's willingness to pay to experience "characteristic" displays of actual places. Outside of the collection's economy of story and frame sits the author himself, who reveals all literary value to be the product of narrative posturing. Hawthorne's focus on the act of framing itself suggests that narrative modes are shaped by their creator's preoccupation with the expectations of those readers who will ultimately consume his work; in doing so, *The Story Teller* recasts the line between fiction and reality as a source of value in the marketplace—that is, as something to be manipulated by the savvy salesman.

This desire to recast storytelling as an economic venture reflects Hawthorne's own struggle at negotiating a respectable public identity as an author. In a letter he wrote at age sixteen to his mother, while he was living in Salem and preparing for college, he first gave voice to his desire to write for a living:

> I have not yet concluded what profession I shall have. The being a Minister is of course out of the Question. I should not think that even you could desire me to choose so dull a way of life. Oh no Mother, I was not born to vegetate forever in one place, and to live and die as calm and tranquil as— A Puddle of Water. As to Lawyers there are so many of them already that one half of them (upon a moderate calculation) are in a state of actual starvation. A Physician then seems to be "Hobson's choice," but yet I should not like to live by the diseases and Infirmities of my fellow Creatures. . . . Oh that I was rich enough to live without a profession. What do you think of my becoming an Author, and relying for support upon my pen. . . . But Authors are always poor Devils, and therefore Satan may take them.[3]

To be an author, it seems, is to come before the public seeking recompense but to be without a true profession. More than a decade after he wrote this, he placed his fictional storyteller in a remarkably similar predicament. In describing his fundamental disagreement with his guardian, Parson Thumpcushion, the narrator of "Passages" tells us the following:

> Our chief and final dispute arose from the pertinacity with which he insisted on my adopting a particular profession; while I, being heir to a moderate competence, had avowed my purpose of keeping aloof from the regular business of life. This would have been a dangerous resolution, any where in the world; it was fatal in New-England. There is a grossness in the conceptions of my countrymen; they will not be convinced that any good thing may consist with what they call idleness; they can anticipate

nothing but evil of a young man who neither studies physic, law, nor gospel, nor opens a store, nor takes to farming, but manifests an incomprehensible disposition to be satisfied with what his father left him. (175)

Rejecting the same three options for the educated man that the author-to-be had already rejected as a teenager, Hawthorne's storyteller answers the above need only after falling in with a band of less-than-respectable vagabonds. For the author, formulating the category of storyteller afforded him the means of "keeping aloof from the regular business of life"—that is, he could at once come before the public with the stories that constituted his attempt to make a living and maintain the very respectability that eludes the storyteller: he was not a salesman but a critic; not a purveyor of stories but an arbiter of value.

"Mr. Higginbotham's Catastrophe," the tale told by the narrator of "Passages from a Relinquished Work" near the end of that framing sketch, illustrates how Hawthorne's narrative strategies keep the "public" and its appetites in critical view. But even more significantly, the story expands the above critique of the marketplace into an argument about the nature of reality in a profit-driven print culture. When read in its original frame, "Mr. Higginbotham's Catastrophe" explores a community's eagerness to digest true stories and illustrates that such a demand is ultimately appeased not through accurate reportage but through the interplay of a reader's uncompromising appetite for true stories and a text's careful maintenance of its narrative postures. By distancing his fictive audience (the crowd of "The Village Theatre" who sits listening to the story of Higginbotham) from those characters in the story proper—by separating frame from tale—Hawthorne seems to imply that the frame's fictive readers more capably understand the line between fictional and nonfictional narrative than do the story's characters. When read closely, however, the frame complicates Hawthorne's project considerably. The audience that sits listening to "Mr. Higginbotham's Catastrophe" laughs at the storyteller's characters for mistakenly reading a fictional newspaper story as truth itself. Yet the same audience in "The Village Theatre" never learns the deeper lesson that the author's story and frame together convey: that even their own conception of reality is based upon the stories they consume.

"Mr. Higginbotham's Catastrophe" follows the travels of a storyteller, Dominicus Pike, a gossipy tobacco peddler. When we first meet Pike, he is walking through the woods on his way to the town of Parker's Falls, "as eager to hold a morning gossip, as a city shopkeeper to read the morning paper." The young peddler, we are told, is "inquisitive, and something of a tattler, always itching to hear the news, and anxious to tell it again" (188). Upon encountering a traveler heading in the opposite direction, Pike learns of the murder of Squire Higginbotham of Kimballton, on the other side of Parker's Falls. Higginbotham, the reader and Pike learn, was reportedly hanged from a pear tree "by an Irishman and a nigger" (189).[4] When Pike later repeats the rumor to a farmer outside Parker's Falls, the farmer questions its reliability, telling Pike he has seen the squire only that morning. The remainder of the narrative follows our hero's repeated attempts to get to the bottom of the story. After spreading the rumor throughout town only to find its veracity brought into serious question, the confused, ostracized Pike decides to visit Higginbotham's home, where he finds an Irish servant about to hang the gentleman from a pear tree. Pike saves Higginbotham from certain death and is rewarded with a betrothal to the squire's beautiful niece. Importantly, Hawthorne does not end his tale until Pike and his reader know exactly what led to the story's climactic scene: three men—the stranger (who first told Pike of Higginbotham's murder), a mulatto (whom Pike met the next day, and who tells him Higginbotham had in fact been murdered only the night before), and the Irishman—initially plotted to murder Higginbotham, but on successive days the first and second men lost courage, each delaying the attempt by twenty-four hours. Thus Pike could learn of the "event" before it actually happened.

As the storyteller of "Passages" confesses, tales such as "Mr. Higginbotham's Catastrophe" emerge out of the audience's appetite for certain narrative conventions and for a narrative style that subtly weaves these features together without revealing any sort of machinery.[5] In the story, the author connects the storyteller's ability to satisfy such demand with a competing mode of information exchange—the newspaper. After hearing only a few details of the murder, Pike "could not avoid filling up the outline, till it became quite a respectable narrative" (190). Upon entering Parker's Falls he quickly spreads word of the event, until "the story ran through the town like fire among girdled trees" (192). It is not long before Pike's manufactured narrative becomes journalistic fact: "Such was the excitement, that the Parker's Falls Gazette anticipated its regular day of publication, and came out with half a form of blank paper, and a column of double pica, emphasized with capitals, and headed HORRID MURDER OF MR. HIGGINBOTHAM! Among other dreadful details, the printed account described the mark of the cord round the dead man's neck, and stated the number of thousand dollars of which he had been robbed; there was much pathos, also, about the affliction of his niece, who had gone from one fainting fit to another, ever since her uncle was found hanging on the St.

Michael's pear-tree, with his pockets inside out" (193). Here, in the figure of Mr. Higginbotham's niece and in the grisly description of the murder scene, are the pathos and varied details Hawthorne's narrator described as central to his project in the "Passages" frame. More significantly, we see in the Gazette's account a story whose history—whose mechanism, to use one of Hawthorne's favorite terms—is entirely hidden from view.

If the storyteller and the journalist are each defined by their unwilling-ness to acknowledge the narrative machinery of their stories, the author of *The Story Teller* eagerly exposes what these other writers keep out of view. As Hawthorne shows us, the newspaper's account of the murder is the product of Pike's own investigation and, just as importantly, of the false consensus on which the story's verifiability is founded. Pike invents his "respectable narrative," we are told, because he "found himself invariably the first bearer of the intelligence, and was so pestered with questions" (190). The story of Higginbotham's murder was thus produced in response to audience demand. But when he begins to circulate the details of Mr. Higginbotham's death, he is careful to leave the *origin* of the story invis-ible—to leave its status as story and not information as entirely irrelevant. As he promulgates the tale, he does not "profess to relate it on his own authority, or that of any one person; but mentioned it as a report gener-ally diffused" (192). Thus when it is reported in the local paper, it is not as a narrative with an author and with specific circumstances leading to its production. It appears as vivid as material reality itself: the rhetoric of newspaper journalism, with its reliance upon detail and drama, creates out of thin air its claims to reality. What is entirely absent from the account is precisely what Hawthorne is careful to include in his own narrative: the fact of Pike's hunger for the news—the invisible truth of readerly demand—that led to the story being written.

Within the frame provided by "Passages" (in which Hawthorne's storyteller makes his narratives to order), the newspaper writing of "Mr. Higginbotham's Catastrophe" looks a lot like fiction. Indeed, the tale links newspaper writing with a readerly appetite for vivid, sensational stories and suggests that factual accuracy is entirely irrelevant to such writing. It is significant, then, that in the *New-England Magazine,* where most of the stories that were to be part of *The Story Teller* first appeared (including "Mr. Higginbotham's Catastrophe" and all sections of "Passages from a Relinquished Work"), writers routinely argued that newspaper reading was the prime means through which citizens gathered their information and formulated their opinions about the world in which they lived. And like Hawthorne's *Story Teller,* these articles describe the fictionality of newspaper writing as a dangerous by-product of the market revolution.

The magazine sought to expose how newspaper writing was too often founded solely on the goal of entertaining and was in fact often devised merely to appease public appetites for sensational stories. In a satiric article of 1832, the editors facetiously provide newspaper editors with various bits of advice, including the suggestion that the most successful editors "fail not to insert in [their] columns all the bloody murders and executions [they] can find." As in "Mr. Higginbotham's Catastrophe," newspaper journalism in the article is said merely to give the appearance of objectivity, while actually striving solely for popularity. Furthermore, the key to such popularity is to provide all the sensational details that the reader craves, for "the sole end of your creation is to eat, drink, and make money."[6]

In a piece titled "Story-telling," published in January 1835, only a month after the second installment of *The Story Teller* appeared (which included "Mr. Higginbotham's Catastrophe"), John Neal wrote that "story-telling would appear to be the great business of life with a majority of mankind, the chief purpose of language almost everywhere."[6] Neal goes on to link such storytelling skills to the "newspaper transmutations" undergone by "the oldest and commonest Joe Millers" in the hands of newspaper writers who have "a knack at the business."[7] Neal further remarks that "whole races are addicted to story-telling," (2), as if Neal, like Hawthorne, sits outside the very public that is their subject. The magazine's editors believed that "the mere entertainment of a day or an hour should not be the principal object of the writer, or the reader."[8] In another issue, they depict the typical newspaper editor as "a man, whose scissors are in his hand—a man who lives by cutting, and cabbaging."[9] He is, like Dominicus Pike, hungry for gossip, and always willing and eager to steal information from other papers.

While "Mr. Higginbotham's Catastrophe" enacts a project similar to these pieces from the magazine that attacked newspapers as profit-driven, Hawthorne's frames reveal more clearly than the pieces outlined above what precisely was at stake in such a discourse. When the story first appeared in the *New-England Magazine,* the reader returned from "Mr. Higginbotham's Catastrophe" to "The Village Theatre," a framing device that illuminates those demands that shape literary production. As Hawthorne's storyteller describes (in "The Village Theatre") the advertisements announcing his performance that night in a rural town of "his famous tale of 'Mr. Higginbotham's Catastrophe,'" he confesses that the story was "as yet an unfilled plot; nor, even when I stepped upon the stage, was it decided whether Mr. Higginbotham should live or die" (184). The storyteller, as he warned us earlier, relies upon maintaining in his work the facade of "a unity, a wholeness, and a separate character, that did not admit of this sort of mechanism," even as he invents his tale onstage.

Central to the audience's faith in "Mr. Higginbotham's Catastrophe" as an autonomous, preexisting text, we are told, is how written texts capitalize upon their reader's hunger for stories about the world outside. Though the tale will not exist until it is spoken that night, playbills written "in the hugest type that the printing-office could supply" claim that what we know to be a nonexistent tale "had been received with rapturous applause, by audiences in all the principal cities" (184). This focus on type echoes the erroneous report of the Parker's Falls Gazette and its "column of double pica," thus underscoring the importance of the relationship between story and frame. In the frame, writing creates the idea of a world outside, and the storyteller capitalizes on this: "The good people of the town, knowing that the world contained innumerable persons of celebrity, undreamt of by them, took it for granted that I was one, and that their roar of welcome was but a feeble echo of those which had thundered around me, in lofty theatres" (186).

While the line between fiction and fact survives in the fictive world of Dominicus Pike—Higginbotham lives and the newspaper is proven wrong—the equally fictive audience that hears his story from Hawthorne's storyteller never learns that the world of rapturous audiences has been fabricated by their printing office. As in the coverage of the Salem Murder, writing here has created distant realities, and thus the crowd laughs at Pike's narrow-minded delusions without recognizing their own. To the audience that sits listening to the story of Higginbotham, the story enacts an assault upon the fictionality of newspaper journalism already being waged by periodicals such as the *New-England Magazine*. Within its original frame, however, Hawthorne's story mocks the very assumption that writing could ever overcome realities of space and time. Just as the Parker's Falls Gazette describes a murder that has not yet occurred (and in fact never occurs), the frame's printed advertisements extol an unwritten tale. And as in the young author's letter to his cousin, in which he posits himself outside the narrative contrived by his community about the scandalous murder of one of their neighbors, here the author sits beyond both fictional towns, laughing at their faith in the written word. The reader is invited to join him in the rhetorical space afforded by his text, outside story and frame alike, in the realm that can only be defined by its imagined distance from the practice of authentication.[10]

By juxtaposing newspaper journalism and fictional storytelling, Hawthorne implies that a contemporary print culture was conspiring to manufacture a new understanding of reality. As Pike walks through the woods after being shunned for his false story (before he heroically saves Higginbotham's life), he remembers that the printed word will vindicate him—that it will turn fiction into fact: "The handbills of the select-men would cause the commitment of all the vagabonds in the State; the paragraph in the Parker's Falls Gazette would be reprinted from Maine to Florida, and perhaps form an item in the London newspapers; and many a miser would tremble for his money-bags and life, on learning the catastrophe of Mr. Higginbotham" (196). As technology renders written communication more rapid and reliable, Hawthorne implies, it becomes easier for writing to reshape, even invent reality. The untrue story of Mr. Higginbotham's death emerges out of one consumer's appetite for gossip, a detail utterly absent from the newspaper account that races across the continent. Hawthorne's frame reminds us how easily storytelling keeps its machinery out of view, and thus Pike's realization that the newspaper account looks true enough connects the storyteller's fictional tale (with all of its improbable coincidences) with the real world of a nationally, even globally connected print media. The eventual unveiling of what almost happened to Higginbotham becomes irrelevant to the report that crosses the Atlantic. Writing has created a new reality, leaving truth far behind—and it is the layered narrative approach of *The Story Teller* that allows its author to point out precisely where fiction becomes fact. Such a seemingly minor moment in a largely forgotten story anticipates Melville's description of his fellow romantic author: Hawthorne here defines himself, more than fifteen years before the major romances, by his ability to see through a fictional world, into "the very axis of reality."

But we can also look retrospectively from this moment, to the debates that took place in the months following the murder of Joseph White. While the editors of the Salem papers combated the promulgation of (what they termed) an inauthentic picture of their town, the author of *The Story Teller* looks down on the entire print culture depicted in the collection's stories and frames. Using a broad, almost panoramic perspective, and echoing Neal's discussion of the "whole races of people" that consume stories, Hawthorne points out to his reader where fiction (the untrue story of Higginbotham's murder) becomes fact (in the nationalizing and global-izing journalistic culture that connects Maine to Florida, and the United States with England). As in the newspaper coverage of the White murder, in Hawthorne's collection replacing the inauthentic story with the authen-tic is the job of the storyteller. Above such a project, Hawthorne shapes a dialogic narrative that affords the reader a distance from the audience depicted in his frame and thus a rhetorical identity apart from the masses. While the mob digests the work of storytellers, while his neighbors share the latest rumors about the murder conspiracy, Hawthorne exists outside the very act of storytelling—looking down not only on a specific crowd but also on the imaginary "public" that was quickly expanding to include vast amounts of geography.

Another useful touchstone for Hawthorne's invocation of journalistic storytelling is the similar treatment of newspaper sensationalism in the fiction of Edgar Allan Poe. We have already seen how Poe's newspaper hoaxes exploited the instability of authenticity in penny press culture in much the same manner that Bennett and Barnum capitalized on the appetites of the masses. But in many ways the treatment of the newspaper in "Mr. Higginbotham's Catastrophe" is more closely related to Poe's tales of ratiocination, specifically "The Murders in the Rue Morgue" and "The Mystery of Marie Rogêt." In each of these stories, after all, Dupin must negotiate the sensational depiction of a crime in the newspaper, seeing through the lies of popular journalism so that he can access what truly happened. As Terence Whalen writes, "Dupin makes sense out of a conflicting mass of information and thereby leads the city out of confusion and impending chaos." If Dupin's authority over mass culture here stands in for Poe's quest for a related mastery, we must recall that such an authorial identity unapologetically privileged the terms of a marketplace. Like Dupin, Poe sought to make money off of the obfuscated nature of reality in early mass culture. Whalen, for example, reveals how Poe capitalized on the popular interest in the real-life murder of Mary Cecilia Rogers to stir up interest in his fictional retelling of the murder in "The Mystery of Marie Rogêt." Just as he had done in attempting to sell *The Narrative of Arthur Gordon Pym,* a work of fiction peddled as fact, Poe carefully "emphasized fact over fiction" in selling his story to the masses.[11]

In Poe's detective stories, as in the newspaper hoaxes, the rise of information brings with it a new realm of cultural fictions that can be mastered only by a new kind of cultural elite. For Dupin, as for the author of the balloon hoax, such mastery afforded its practitioner a control over the means of production through which a mass audience was exploited. If this mode of control was valuable to Poe partly for the kind of autonomy it represented, Whalen's work reminds us that the author never even came close to renouncing the goals and practices of the literary marketplace. Using the vocabularies of Hawthorne's early fiction, Poe was both author and book peddler, always keeping his eye on the reading practices of the masses as a way of maximizing his financial success. In *The Story Teller,* however, Hawthorne builds into his narrative the added layer of a storyteller who, like Dominicus Pike, peddles his wares to a paying public. Poe's willingness to capitalize on the slipperiness of authenticity thus brings into striking relief the distance Hawthorne attempts to place between such showmanship and his own authorial persona.

While Dupin's success at unveiling the real story behind scandalous crimes ultimately privileged the criteria of journalism, the invocation of the newspaper throughout the *Story Teller* pieces allowed Hawthorne to reject the very premise of seeking out authentic information. In "Old News," another sketch apparently intended for the collection (and one that, like "Mr. Higginbotham's Catastrophe," also appeared in the *New-England Magazine*), Hawthorne's narrator peruses newspapers from various moments in eighteenth-century New England.[12] "Old News" explores how the nineteenth-century newspaper reader's hunger for authentic stories was at once transforming the very sense of historical reality and shaping how New Englanders thought about their own social world. Like the 1830 *Salem Gazette* piece that warned its readers against inventing too bleak a story about their town, "Old News" uses history to illustrate the power of storytelling in defining present-day New England. The narrator's need to make a story out of eighteenth-century New England life makes the past deceptively, even violently picturesque—for the narrator uses his nostalgic account of eighteenth-century life as a justification for nineteenth-century American slavery. After reflecting on the relatively small number of ads for "these human commodities" in the old newspapers, the narrator concludes that the slaves "were the merriest part of the population—since it was their gift to be merry in the worst of circumstances; and they endured, comparatively, few hardships, under the domestic sway of our fathers" (*Tales,* 256).

We soon learn that our reader-narrator knows this to be the case simply because slavery *appears* innocuous in the newspapers before him. Throughout the first half of the paragraph on slavery in New England before the Revolutionary War, the narrator's hunger for an authentic story about eighteenth-century New England compels him to invent historical reality out of bits of factual details: "When the slaves of a family were inconveniently prolific, it being not quite orthodox to drown the superfluous offspring, like a litter of kittens, notice was promulgated of 'a negro child to be given away.' Sometimes the slaves assumed the property of their own persons, and made their escape: among many such instances, the Governor raises a hue-and-cry after his negro Juba" (256–57). Once the reader-narrator has gotten going on the topic, he moves from creating particular stories grounded in the advertisements he reads to speaking about slavery in general. So while early on in the paragraph he assumes an insight into the past based on a pile of old newspapers, by the end he is casually authoring social myths: "Without venturing a word in extenuation of the general system, we confess our opinion, that Caesar, Pompey, Scipio, and all such great Roman namesakes, would have been better advised had they staid at home, foddering the cattle, cleaning dishes—in fine, performing their moderate share of the labors of life without being harassed by its cares" (257). He goes on to argue that "the sable inmates of the mansion were not excluded from the domestic affections," finally concluding with a grandiose vision of slavery in America as not just tolerable but downright *picturesque:* "Slave labor being but a small part of the industry of the country, it did not change the character of the people; the latter, on the contrary, modified and softened the institution, making it a patriarchal, and almost a beautiful, peculiarity of the times" (257).

By creating a narrator who takes scenes and characters fixed in the pages of particular newspapers and invents detailed stories about their lives, Hawthorne focuses on the way in which the narrator's hunger for an authentic story about the past shapes the logic by which he moralizes on his own world. Like Hawthorne's hometown *Gazette* in the wake of the White murder, the narrator of "Old News" attempts to define Salem by telling a story about its past. Hawthorne, however, frames such an attempt at storytelling by linking it to the narrator's preoccupation with the materiality of the newspapers, an attraction that borders on the fetishistic. In doing so, the author invites us to view the narrator's hunger for historical truth as a desire for a specific type of object. The sketch opens with the narrator carefully describing the look and feel of the documents he peruses: "Here is a volume of what once were newspapers—each on a small half-sheet, yellow and time-stained, of a coarse fabric, and imprinted with a rude old type. Their aspect conveys a singular impression of antiquity." Next, our narrator connects their physicality to the time and place from which they survive: "Ephemeral as they were intended and supposed to be, they have long outlived the printer and his whole subscription list, and have proved more durable, as to their physical existence, than most of the timber, bricks, and stone, of the town where they were issued." Finally, in introducing the reflections that take up the rest of the sketch he tells us, "It is pleasant to take one of these little dingy half-sheets between the thumb and finger, and picture forth the personage, who, above ninety years ago, held it, wet from the press, and steaming, before the fire" (251). Such a progression connects the narrator's focus on the materiality of the newspapers with his desire to produce a meaningful sense of the past, as if "history" here is the story that answers the reader's appetite for authenticity. Telling stories, then, is understood as the means by which the narrator manufactures a reality to answer his appetite for the authentic. By invoking newspapers from a bygone era, Hawthorne's sketch can distance the items in the paper from the chronological setting to which they refer. In a sense, this chronological distance underscores the fictionality of the narrator's sense of history: instead of getting closer to historical truth, he uses the newspaper's status as truth-teller to authenticate his own fictions—thereby making a mockery of the process of authentication. From the very title of "Old News," Hawthorne was flaunting the fact that his own work had no new piece of authentic information to report.[13]

Reading "Old News" as part of *The Story Teller* warns against a celebratory reading of the text's invocation of slavery. Though we might like Hawthorne to be assaulting slavery here by recasting apologist defenses of the institution as the product of an easy nostalgia, one cannot understand the appearance of slavery in "Old News" apart from the collection's ongoing attempt to keep the question of authenticity at arm's length. Seeking to rise above the popular debate over what the real South looks like, the sketch relies on slavery as a textual marker by which Hawthorne could place himself above the fray. As in the young author's letter to his cousin, in which he reports on circulating rumors about the Knapp brothers without deigning to share his own opinion, the author of "Old News" points to a specious defense of slavery that is nothing more than the product of the narrator's hunger for a pleasant and appealing story. Rather than replacing this view with a competing account of slavery, Hawthorne portrays the debate itself as another example of how the desire for authentic information determined the value of antebellum texts.

In fact, Hawthorne wrote "Old News" at the very moment that southern slavery was indeed encroaching into Salem's public consciousness. An 1830 editorial in the *Salem Gazette* treats slavery as a distant reality that is both distasteful and entirely divorced from New England life. "We, whose good fortune it is to be removed from the sight of that wretched race," the paper wrote, "cannot, without an effort of imagination, conceive of all the numerous ills of servitude."[14] But only four years later, a writer in the *Gazette* announces that "it is with unspeakable pleasure that I perceive the people of Salem and its vicinity, at length arousing from their apparent apathy on the subject of slavery; and that a society has been formed for the promotion of all rational measures towards its total abolition."[15] An article in the paper two months later describes the first meeting of the Anti-Slavery Society of Salem, at which C. P. Grosvenor attacked the northern myth that slaves are treated kindly by their masters. The reader learns that a Boston minister "exhibited an overseer's whip, which was made in New-York, not only to show the kind of instruments of punishment used, but also to show that New-York has *something* to do with slavery."[16] It was also pointed out at the meeting "that these instruments of torture were manufactured in New England, thus taking away at once from the North the specious plea, which has been industriously trumpeted from Maine to Connecticut, that she has nothing to do with the slavery of the South." In the early years of the 1830s, which saw the first major strides of the abolitionist movement in New England, slavery was no longer simply an institution defined largely by its distance from New England life. A burgeoning antislavery movement tried to highlight the economic and social (and, of course, moral) connectedness of New England to the "southern institution." Hawthorne's invocation of slavery, written just as abolitionism was bringing slavery as a virtual reality into Salem life, responded to such a development by carving out a rhetorical space within which the author and reader could imagine themselves gazing down at an emerging public debate about the "real" South.

In the better-known "Wakefield," another tale likely intended for *The Story Teller,* Hawthorne again invokes the newspaper to contrast his own mode of fiction against the journalistic ideal of informational writing. As in the frames of *The Story Teller,* where all textual production is portrayed as essentially economic in nature, here the narrator's unapologetic invention of his story ultimately reveals reportage as just another kind of storytelling. After the narrator begins with a brief mention of an article he recalls from some years ago, this half-forgotten reading experience fuels both the story's entire narrative and its conspicuous, easily moralizing tone. Hawthorne's story opens, "In some old magazine or newspaper, I recollect a story, told as truth, of a man—let us call him Wakefield—who absented for a long time from his wife." Upon recounting those circumstances of the story that he recalls, the narrator tells us, "This outline is all that I remember. But the incident, though of the purest originality, unexampled, and probably never to be repeated, is one I think, which appeals to the general sympathies of mankind" (*Tales,* 290). Sounding like the storyteller-protagonist of "Passages from a Relinquished Work," Hawthorne's narrator outlines what makes the story attractive to the reader and then tells us he will fill in the rest of the details as his fancy dictates: "If the reader choose, let him do his own meditation; or if he prefer to ramble with me through the twenty years of Wakefield's vagary, I bid him welcome" (290). As in "Old News," the casual, easily moralizing tone of "Wakefield" is defined against the newspaper's claim to authenticity, as if the story's reading experience were valuable precisely because no claim to accurate representation is at stake. Indeed, our narrator's way of telling his story values the deeper truths—those that appeal "to the general sympathies of mankind"—over the mere facticity of journalistic writing.

Once again, truth is too elusive, too complex for the newspaper-devouring public. Like many of the other *Story Teller* pieces, "Wakefield" explores the human hunger for narrative; it is, after all, the product of a reader making a story out of one near-forgotten fact. But if the stories of "Old News" emerge out of our narrator's desire for an authentic history, the narrator of "Wakefield" takes great care to remind us that his narrative is mostly invention. Adopting a narrative technique by which this story is not "told as truth" (as the original story was), the author seeks to redefine "truth" as a product of how stories are told. While the relationship between frame and story in "Mr. Higginbotham's Catastrophe" suggested that all writing—newspaper journalism and fictional storytelling alike—seeks ultimately to satisfy audience demand, "Wakefield" again juxtaposes fiction and fact to recast these as merely two ways of telling a story. The "Wakefield" to whom our narrator refers, after all, becomes more real to the reader than the faceless, nameless man our narrator once read about.

In order to understand the kind of critical authority sought by Hawthorne's *Story Teller,* it is worth considering the collection alongside a work that shares its name: Walter Benjamin's essay, "The Storyteller." In describing the threat posed to "the art of storytelling" by the emergence of "information" as a new, modern form of communication, Benjamin argues that the reliance of information on verifiability "proves incompatible with the spirit of storytelling" (84, 89). Because "no event any longer comes to us without already being shot through with information," the openness of storytelling—its stubborn insistence on keeping its stories "free from explanation"—has no place in an information age (89). In discussing the novel, Benjamin privileges the "unattained and therefore inexpressible meaning of life" (a phrase he borrows from Lukács) and the capacity of novels to communicate how this unity is comprehended within the individual life. The story, though, seeks no such closure—and this is the loss that the ascension of information brings with it.

While Hawthorne's definition of storyteller differs from Benjamin's use of the term, what their work shares is the commitment to locating a form of narrative art that is meaningful and valuable for the alternative it provides to the threat of information. In a sense, Hawthorne merges the role of storyteller into the realm of information by portraying the eponymous hero of his collection as a market-minded showman. In doing so, the author reserves for himself Benjamin's role as the one who theorizes the line between information and truth. If Benjamin claims to place the storyteller among "the ranks of the teachers and sages" (108), his essay asserts the ultimate authority of its own theoretical mind as the arbiter of various forms of truth; it is Benjamin himself, after all, who decides the timeless value of the storyteller's art (108). His essay thus exemplifies how the act of theorizing the line between information and artistry produces cultural capital. And Hawthorne's own narrative manipulations show us how this capital shapes the profession of authorship: in the very act of framing both storytelling and journalism, Hawthorne asserts his own ability to distinguish between two types of textual value.

Though most of the works that would have appeared as part of *The Story Teller* would seem to have nothing direct to say to the newspaper, the collection as a whole seeks a kind of authority that was modeled against the truth-telling claims of journalism. In fact, "The Ambitious Guest," an account of a New Hampshire family killed by an avalanche, was actually a fictional rewriting of an event that received significant coverage in Salem newspapers in the late 1820s. Hawthorne changed a few minor details of the 1826 catastrophe that killed the entire Willey family, along with two hired men: among other changes, he made the oldest daughter seventeen (instead of twelve) and he introduced the figure of a visiting stranger who died with the family (in truth, this visitor arrived on the scene the next day). But when we read "The Ambitious Guest" alongside the newspaper coverage of the event, these modifications are far less striking than the dramatic contrast in narrative approach. While the newspaper accounts provided as many authentic details about the family as possible, Hawthorne's mode of telling continually acknowledges its own fictionality. After they first hear the rumblings of an impending slide, Hawthorne writes, "Let us now suppose the stranger to have finished his supper of bear's meat; and, by his natural felicity of manner, to have placed himself on a footing of kindness with the whole family" (*Tales,* 301). As in "Wakefield," Hawthorne's approach to the story is to interpolate the facts, leaving behind the goals of informational reportage to transform the event into an allegory of human nature. Of the guest we are told, "The secret of the young man's character was, a high and abstracted ambition. He could have borne to live an undistinguished life, but not to be forgotten in the grave" (301).

When the mudslide arrives, Hawthorne rejects graphic sensationalism in favor of an approach that foregrounds the impossibility of description: "The simplest words must intimate, but not portray, the unutterable horror of the catastrophe" (306). When read as an echo of Higginbotham's "catastrophe," Hawthorne's retelling of the mudslide relies on that story's use of the fiction of sensationalistic reportage—Higginbotham, after all, is never even murdered—to prop up the romantic fiction of "The Ambitious Guest" as more authentic precisely because it rejects sensationalism. Indeed, perhaps the most significant modification that Hawthorne made in fictionalizing the White Mountain Disaster (as newspapers called it) was the decision to keep the victims' dead bodies out of view. "Long ere the thunder of the great Slide had ceased to roar among the mountains," Hawthorne writes, "the victims were at peace. Their bodies were never found" (306).

In reality, however, newspapers in Boston and Salem and throughout New England were filled with graphic depictions of the unclothed and mutilated corpses of the Willey family: "Mr. W when found, had both of his legs and both arms broken, and was otherwise bruised. His wife was most horribly mangled—nearly half her head, from the forehead to the back part, was gone, literally torn off! And there she lay, naked, with her brains scattered around, a most hideous spectacle. The hired man [who lived with the family] was also much bruised. I am this evening informed that the entrails of one of the children have also been found."[17] Hawthorne's authorial relationship to the catastrophic event is to protect the family from the gaze of the public eye, and from the sensationalism and spectacle-making of the newspaper. In doing so, the story adopts a narrative stance that treats its reality as something that could never be contained by mere words. Though the newspaper is nowhere present in the work, the very assumption that the horror of the family's deaths is incommunicable was made possible only by the journalistic exploitation of the catastrophe as a public spectacle.

It is thus significant that Hawthorne's story ends with a refusal to divulge any new information, or even to speculate about the real story of this mysterious guest: "His name and person utterly unknown; his history, his way of life, his plans, a mystery never to be solved; his death and existence, equally a doubt! Whose was the agony of the death-moment?" (307). Consider such a refusal to solve the mystery of this stranger with the following excerpt from a piece that appeared in a Salem newspaper in the wake of the tragedy: "Every appearance of the house indicated that the family had fled from it in the night, in the moment of alarm. Their clothes were on the floor nigh the beds where they had lain down for the last time to sleep. . . . The Willey family had probably after the rain had ceased, retired to rest; but awakened and alarmed by the crash of the barn, they rushed out of doors, and were flying for the Camp, (which Mr. Willey, after the slide of the 18th of June last, had built as a place of refuge,) in the extreme darkness, they ran directly into one of the avalanches, and were swept into the flood below, to instant destruction."[18] Like many of the newspaper accounts of the incident, the writer here frames the scene of the Willey home as part of a mystery to be solved by writer and reader alike. Anticipating the coverage of the White murder, the journalistic coverage of the White Mountain Disaster was defined by the narrative quest for the authentic story of what happened inside the Willey home. In light of this journalistic approach, a crucial part of Hawthorne's rewriting of the event was his introduction of a stranger who was not in the home at the time of the accident, and his foregrounding of the impenetrable mystery of his identity.

More than simply an allegory of human ambition, the story takes as its subject an event that had already been sensationalized and speculated about and retells it by loudly rejecting these objectives and ideals of journalism. In opposition to the narrative trajectory shared by both the White murder mystery and Poe's later detective fictions, Hawthorne stubbornly concludes with indeterminacy—even accenting such a refusal with an exclamation mark, as if getting off one final dig at the melodramatic scandal-mongering of the newspaper. The story's narrative approach must be considered in light of the other *Story Teller* works discussed above—both the frames that reveal the market-oriented nature of literary creation and the tales and sketches that explicitly invoke the newspaper as the rhetorical antithesis of romantic fiction. In "The Ambitious Guest" we encounter an authorial stance that treats reality as something beyond the reach of linguistic or narrative representation. When we consider the idiom of "The Ambitious Guest" as part of *The Story Teller,* when we recognize how Hawthorne's envisioned collection distanced its own artistic ambitions from the commercial ambitions of the newspaper, Hawthorne's notorious suspicion toward the act of linguistic representation emerges as a response to the material conditions of antebellum New England: by writing against the aims of reportage, Hawthorne seems to believe he was protecting reality from an encroaching culture of spectacle and sensationalism.

In order to protect reality, his early fiction continually assailed the commercialization of information. We see this not only in the invocation of the newspaper in a work like "Mr. Higginbotham's Catastrophe" but also in the "Village Theatre" frame that originally surrounded it. Following the storyteller's resoundingly successful performance of the Higginbotham story, he explains that "the success of the piece was incalculably heightened by a stiff queue of horse-hair" that someone had fastened to his collar (which, unknown to him, had delighted the audience during the show). Our storyteller uses this scene to make the following point about his sudden notoriety: "How much of fame is humbug, how much the meed of what our better nature blushes at, how much an accident; how much bestowed on mistaken principles; and how small and poor the remnant. From pit and boxes there was now a universal call for the Story Teller" (186). As our storyteller walks offstage for the very first time, recognizing his own arrival in the spectacle-laden world of show business, the local postmaster hands him a letter "with the postmark of my native village, and directed to my assumed name, in the stiff old hand-writing of Parson Thumpcushion" (187). The letter forces him to come to grips with the unreal world he has just joined: "I seemed to see the puritanic figure of my guardian, standing among the fripperies of the theatre, and pointing to the players,—the fantastic and effeminate men, the painted women, the giddy girl in boy's clothes, merrier than modest—pointing to these with solemn ridicule, and eyeing me with stern rebuke. His image was a type of the austere duty, and they of the vanities of life" (187). In the eyes of Parson Thumpcushion, the storyteller's success is connected to spectacle, costumery, and humbug. And yet, crucially, our storyteller informs us that the letter affected him "most painfully" even though *he never reads it.* After returning to his chamber, he tells us, the storyteller "strode twice across the chamber, then held the letter in the flame of the candle, and beheld it consume, unread." Afraid that his benefactor's loving and forgiving tone would convince him to give up his newfound profession, he destroys the letter, making "an irrevocable choice between good and evil fate" (187).

Using the burning of an unopened letter as a way of announcing the storyteller's arrival in the marketplace, Hawthorne invokes the private exchange of information between two individuals as the antithesis of spectacle and humbuggery. Such a moment is most fully understood in the context of the tale just performed by the storyteller, where information is aligned with the unreal world of commerce. The "news" of Higginbotham's death, we recall, has nothing to do with reality and everything to do with dramatic, sensational storytelling. According to this logic, a letter that is destroyed without being read is a most fitting symbol of the storyteller's surrender to the superficialities of the commercial world. And even more intriguingly, the scene anticipates the most famous unopened correspondence in all of American literature: Poe's "The Purloined Letter." In both works, the letter functions as a symbol without its actual contents ever being divulged—so that the ideal of two individuals exchanging information privately is overwhelmed by the surface-oriented world of reputation and fame.[19] The purloined letter, we recall, has no meaning in the story other than its "certain power in a certain quarter where such power is immensely valuable."[20] The narrative structure of Poe's detective story, by emulating Dupin's skill at reading this world of surfaces, implicitly condones the commodification of information. The idiom of *The Story*

Teller, however, bemoans the protagonist's transformation from a moral and emotional being connected to his childhood to a mere manipulator of surfaces with neither a name nor a meaningful history. In Hawthorne's imagination, the integrity of the self depends on one's understanding of reality: in joining the world of celebrity and spectacle, the storyteller loses what makes him human; the only thing protecting Hawthorne from the surface-oriented world that consumes his fiction, it seems, is his ability to see through its artifice.

To escape the fate of his storyteller—to authenticate his own self, we might say—Hawthorne invents the character of Oberon, an author figure who appears in two of the later works from the collection. In "The Devil in Manuscript," our narrator visits "an intimate friend, one of those gifted youths who cultivate poetry and the belles lettres" (*Tales,* 330). The narrator tells us that "Oberon" is not his friend's actual name but rather "a name of fancy and friendship between him and me" (330). As other critics have noted, Hawthorne often signed his letters to college friends with the name Oberon, and he used the name again as a byline for some of his early fiction. Instead of simply pointing out the parallels between the fictive and the real author, though, I want to conclude my discussion of *The Story Teller* by highlighting how the invention of Oberon charted for Hawthorne a way out of the unreal world in which the storyteller and journalist peddle their wares. By relying on the question of reality as a way of defining the romantic artist's autonomy, the invention of Oberon anticipates the creation of that famed citizen of somewhere else: the romancer.

"The Devil in Manuscript" presents Oberon complaining about the business of publishing as he burns all of his unpublished manuscripts. Hawthorne, of course, destroyed many of his own early manuscripts, and so here we have yet another parallel between the author and his character. But *depicting* an author burning a pile of unpublished manuscripts is a very different thing from destroying one's own work. Instead of eschewing publication, Hawthorne argues in "The Devil in Manuscript" that works of the imagination lose their authenticity at the very moment they appear in printed form. As in "The Ambitious Guest," Hawthorne defines the true romantic artist as the figure who redefines reality in the face of the fictionalizing threat of the marketplace. Soon after our narrator arrives, Oberon points to a stack of manuscripts and tells him that "there is a devil in this pile of blotted papers," the material embodiment of his attempt "to embody the character of a fiend, as represented in our traditions and the written records of witchcraft" (330, 331). As Oberon devoted himself to this attempt at capturing the nature of the fiend, he tells the narrator, he retreated further into his own imagination: "You cannot conceive what an effect the composition of these tales has had on me. I have become ambitious of a bubble, and careless of solid reputation. I am surrounding myself with shadows, which bewilder me, by aping the realities of life. They have drawn me aside from the beaten path of the world, and led me into a strange sort of solitude—a solitude in the midst of men—where nobody wishes for what I do, nor thinks nor feels as I do" (331). As Oberon retreats inward, his own imagination moves further and further away from reality. The "solitude in the midst of men" that defines his own isolation is, it seems, exacerbated by a literary marketplace that has no demand for his works of imagination. "Nobody wishes for what I do," Oberon laments, and so his solitude only deepens.

Over the course of the story, however, Oberon's sense of the unreality of his imagination is reversed. After telling his friend of the seventeen booksellers who have rejected his work, Oberon recalls the moments of inspiration that led to his imaginative works. Though written at least two years before the appearance of Emerson's *Nature,* the passage calls to mind that work's famous description of the transcendental experience: "This scene came into my fancy as I walked along a hilly road, on a starlight October evening; in the pure and bracing air, I became all soul, and felt as if I could climb the sky and run a race along the Milky Way. Here is another tale, in which I wrapt myself during a dark and dreary night-ride in the month of March, till the rattling of the wheels and the voices of my companions seemed like faint sounds of a dream, and my visions a bright reality" (333). Here Oberon's fancy is no longer a distraction from what is real but the reality against which the outside world is defined. In choosing to burn his own creations, he is making his decision to escape the fate of authorship—"Would you have me a damned author?" he asks his friend, who is trying to talk him out of setting the works on fire (334). Finally, only as the papers burn do the stories become real to him: Oberon tells his friend he sees "my lovers clasped in each other's arms . . . the features of a villain, writhing in the fire [. . . and] my holy men, my pious and angelic women" (335).

As a work that did appear in print, "The Devil in Manuscript" saves itself from the oblivion to which Oberon's work is fated by defining its own romanticism against the unreality of the book trade. Though far less successful than the prefaces to the later romances, this early sketch anticipates these later moments by presenting its author as the gatekeeper standing between the romantic imagination and the unreal world of publicity and mass consumption. In a sense, the romances would need prefaces for the same reason that Hawthorne's early fiction required the figure of the storyteller: if appearing in public was tantamount in the romantic imagination to losing one's humanity, he would have to continually find new ways of publishing his fictions while vouchsafing his integrity as an artist.

While "The Devil in Manuscript" is no doubt a minor work, when read as part of *The Story Teller* its account of the romantic authorial imagination speaks to the competing depictions of reality that circulate throughout the collection. Oberon's authorial posture in the story, as I have already suggested, echoes Hawthorne's refusal to graphically describe the death of the Willey family in "The Ambitious Guest." But I have also revealed that the romantic protection of reality enacted in "The Ambitious Guest" was in direct counterpoint to the sensationalistic practices of journalistic storytelling. In such a context, the figure of Oberon is more than simply Hawthorne's fictive alter ego; he is a rhetorical invention that allowed Hawthorne to formulate a model of romantic authorship opposing not only the commercializing literary culture of antebellum America but also the commodification of reality that characterized antebellum information culture. In the figure of Oberon, Hawthorne begins moving beyond the negative ideal of authorship (in which the author was largely the inverse of the market-obsessed storyteller and journalist) that marks the earlier *Story Teller* pieces, for "The Devil in Manuscript" depicts the romantic author as the artistic figure whose literary inventions are somehow more "real" than the world that fails to appreciate them. When read as a culminating work of *The Story Teller,* this assertion of authenticity is both a way for Hawthorne to negotiate his own predicament as an artist and a by-product of the journalistic commodification of the real: to escape the fate of his storyteller, Hawthorne wrote his way into a more genuine reality.

To most fully comprehend Oberon's burning of his unpublished writing, one should consider that "The Devil in Manuscript" was Hawthorne's apparent response to a piece that appeared in the *New-England Magazine* in March of 1833. "The Devil Among the Books," published anonymously but written by John H. Warland, is little more than an inelegant echo of Washington Irving's *Sketchbook.* Warland's sketch depicts a printer-book-seller, named Timothy Folio, who falls asleep and dreams that the long-forgotten books sitting on shelves in his shop's attic ("these abortions of the press," our narrator calls them) come to life and quarrel among themselves. A novel complains that he has been relegated to a life of oblivion because of a string of bad reviews: "My author's brains were squeezed into my pages," the novel cries. Similarly, a book of poems laments a negative review and reveals that the book's author "was found dead in his chamber, with the review in his hand" (104). While the *New-England Magazine* piece merely advances the typical complaint that reviewers and "puffers" held an inordinate amount of sway in the literary marketplace, the sketch brings into focus the implications of Hawthorne's response, which would appear in the same magazine two years after Warland's work. Hawthorne was not simply complaining, like Warland was, about the economic contingencies that shaped the profession of authorship. While Warland's sketch depicts how books already in print suffered from the vagaries of literary culture, Hawthorne's piece rejects the very premise of publication; in lieu of distinguishing between popular success and popular failure, "The Devil in Manuscript" depicts the act of bookmaking as the moment when the truths of the imagination become the surfaces of the marketplace.

As with so many other moments from *The Story Teller*, such a claim echoed the language of reality from the journalistic culture the collection so adamantly claimed to be rejecting. At the same time, my reading of *The Story Teller* also suggests that the cultural and theoretical authority claimed by Hawthorne's early fiction was connected to a developing periodical culture that opposed itself to the rise of mass journalism. Like Hawthorne, the *New-England Magazine* sought a certain type of readership by castigating newspaper editors who simply pandered to audience demand. As entrepreneurial publishers such as Day and Bennett changed the vocation of writing, literary magazines pointed to newspaper journalism as a realm in which the quest for profit was complicating the relationship between fact and fiction. In the *New-England Magazine* writers such as Park Benjamin and John Neal waged a critique of the increasingly market-driven nature of newspaper writing, pointing specifically to the distasteful manner in which journalists preyed upon the popular addiction to storytelling in peddling a "reality" that was carefully produced. It was amid this literary discourse, in a magazine that regularly assaulted the economic pandering of journalistic storytelling, that Hawthorne's public career as romancer took shape.

Finally, Hawthorne's inability to find a publisher willing to keep his collection together underscores the link between the framing device of *The Story Teller* and the market conditions that these frames sought to oppose. While the collection as a whole attempted to differentiate between authorship and salesmanship, Hawthorne was forced to break up *The Story Teller* and publish most pieces independently of one another—a development that essentially relegated Hawthorne to the role of storyteller. His inability to publish the collection together echoes Hawthorne's conception of a reading public hungry for stories that appeared as vivid as reality itself (with no frame, no acknowledgement of its own status as product). In a sense, the collection was destroyed by the very thing it sought to expose. That Hawthorne believed it was Park Benjamin himself who broke up the collection reminds us that the *New-England Magazine*'s theories of literary artistry and journalistic truth were always in the quest for financial viability: the self-styled literariness of the magazine, though modeled against the commercialism of the newspaper, was simply another kind of market commodity.

Hawthorne's struggles with the financial dimensions of publishing would continue in the years following the breakup of *The Story Teller*. In 1836 he took over the editorship of the *American Magazine of Useful and Entertaining Knowledge,* a project that was both ill-fated and short-lived. In the wake of the panic of 1837, he found it harder and harder to support himself and his family by writing for magazines. Though he would grow increasingly reliant on the language of reality and authenticity as a way of communicating his distaste for the world of commerce, the newspaper would largely disappear as a presence in his fiction. And yet the dialogue between the frames of *The Story Teller* and the newspaper fictions they surround makes it possible to trace the development of a Hawthornean logic that equated the rejection of authenticity with an escape from the marketplace back to the journalistic reliance on sensationalism and linguistic transparency in the years that saw his first major strides as an author. In the next chapter, we leave behind the specific context of this journalistic revolution as we head through the 1840s and into his major phase. But the rejection of authenticity at the heart of the *Story Teller* fictions would not only survive as a preoccupation of Hawthorne's career; it would also evolve into a defining obsession of romance, a way of seeing that would again locate the romantic author somewhere outside the contrivances of the antebellum social world.

CHAPTER 3

HAWTHORNE'S
CITY OF REFUGE

"THERE is at least no flattery in my humble line of art," Holgrave, the young daguerreotypist, tells Phoebe Pyncheon in the sixth chapter of *The House of the Seven Gables*.[1] If the daguerreotype relied on this public claim of a new type of representational ideal—objective, scientific, unmediated—behind the camera an emerging class of amateur and professional daguerreotypists turned to handbooks, instruction manuals, and journals that described how to manufacture the "perfect picture": "Select the view of the face most favorable for the just delineation of lights and shadows,—having placed the seat and chosen the most graceful and becoming position for the body, draperies, &c. . . . These with the easy natural position, and the artistical arrangement of all the accessories, make up the perfect picture; and should be decided upon without apparent reflection or hesitation."[2] As Holgrave tells Phoebe, it is the sunlight itself that "brings out the secret character with a truth that no painter would ever venture upon." And yet the above excerpt from an 1851 daguerreotypy manual is typical in its careful focus on the ways in which the camera operator could *make* a picture that flattered its subject while appearing to humbly capture nature itself. In another treatise on the new medium, George Dewy claimed that the "embodiment of character" exhibited in the most successful pictures is made by "the taste and skill of the operator." Like Prometheus, Dewy wrote, "true artists . . . are not satisfied with the mere imitation and resemblance of life, but seek to impart the divinity of the soul to their productions."[3]

As these writers attempted to define daguerreotypy as an art (Dewy himself was the secretary of the Philadelphia Arts Union), their ongoing attention to the more commercial aspects of daguerreotypy reminds us that it was also very much a trade. Claiming that "our 'great secret' lies in our generally having a gratifying amount of business," M. A. Root admonished aspiring daguerreotypists to wait upon visitors promptly, to give them pictures to take away ("instead of the promise to 'send them'"), and to exhibit a "uniform politeness to all, whether they wish pictures or not" (187). Of course, the ideal of a carefully contrived but natural-seeming authenticity was deeply connected to this sense of daguerreotypy as a business. In railing against those inartistic pictures that lack the proper "elegance of composition," Dewy keeps his focus on the bottom line: "Such pictures," he tells aspiring operators, "are valueless" (179).

Apparently unconcerned with these "great secrets" by which the daguerreotypist quietly manufactures his pictures of reality, Hawthorne's novel would seem to privilege Holgrave's disingenuous claim that his art is free from the taint of contrivance. Except that the daguerreotypist's assertion must be read in light of the novel's preface, where Hawthorne tells an entirely different story about the truths of photographic representation. After his famous discussion of the differences between the novel and the romance—in which the former "is presumed to aim at a very minute fidelity, not merely to the possible, but to the probable and ordinary course of man's experience," and the latter is linked with "the truth of the human heart" (1)—Hawthorne turns to the new art of daguerreotypy to further distinguish the technique of the romancer. If he wishes, Hawthorne explains, the romancer "may so manage his atmospherical medium as to bring out or mellow the lights and deepen and enrich the shadows of the picture."

While it is easy to see the parallel Hawthorne draws here—the romancer, like the daguerreotypist, is allowed to carefully manipulate atmosphere to bring out a desired picture—the novel's depiction of Holgrave implies a crucial distinction between the romance and the daguerreotypic image: the daguerreotype produces carefully manufactured representations that claimed an unmediated relationship with reality, while the romance willingly exposes its own pictures as the product of artistic manipulation. Hawthorne thus defines the self-consciously fictional romance against a medium whose own fictionality (in *Seven Gables* and in an emerging professional discourse) was the great secret that must remain hidden from the public.[4]

As in the earlier *Story Teller* pieces, where Hawthorne seeks to frame the market forces shaping all narrative acts, the above dialogue between romance and daguerreotypy allows the author of *Seven Gables* to high-light both the surface illusions of his own fiction and those produced by daguerreotypy. That is to say, the explicit and self-referential fictionality of his narrative idiom in both cases defines itself against a cultural realm where inauthenticities masquerade as truths. While critics have long celebrated the romance's sense of the theatricality and spectacle of public life, such a perspective sounds so much like the prevailing new historical understanding of capitalist culture here in the early twenty-first century that it is all too easy to simply accept Hawthorne's critique of American commercialism as impartial, even forward-looking. In order to more thoroughly understand such a perspective as a worldview grounded in place and time, this final chapter on Hawthorne's career will highlight how carefully his narrative strategies speak to a range of competing representational modes—daguerreotypy, moving panoramas, even the very act of linguistic description—so that we can better understand the romance as a reactive literary form, one that obsessively countered the truth claims of (what it portrays as) more market-oriented cultural practices. As I hope to reveal, the romance's preoccupation with the construction of reality in antebellum life, more than simply a way of critiquing capitalist culture, was the product of Hawthorne's ongoing attempt at keeping the epistemology of the mass subject at a conspicuous distance. Thus, while my account of Hawthorne's career began in the material conditions of Salem in 1830, the "city of refuge" to which my chapter title refers is neither an actual city nor the mythical "somewhere else" of romance; rather, it is Hawthorne's singular mode of cultural witnessing, his celebrated attention to the spectacular aspects of antebellum life, that promises the romantic subject a philosophical inoculation from the otherwise inescapable process of modernization.

"THERE is no such thing as a true portrait," Hawthorne wrote in his notebook in 1850. "They are all delusions."[5] Of course, to reject all portraits as "delusions" is to redefine the human subject as that which no representation could ever contain—and so such a statement, much like his depiction of daguerreotypy in *Seven Gables,* must be read in light of a society in which portraits were "more accessible to the same middle class that was enjoying increased access to books and magazines."[6] If Hawthorne's rejection of portraiture attributes to humanity an essential nature no image can capture or reproduce, and if portraiture was an increasingly prominent marker of middle-class identity, Hawthorne's ideal of humanity, here and elsewhere, can be understood as a rhetorical counterproduction, one that defined the contours of the human by negating the representational practices and assumptions of the consumer class: to recognize the inherently delusional nature of portraiture, Hawthorne continually seems to imply, is to be an uncompromised self.

This rhetorical understanding of Hawthorne's representational ideals clarifies the apparent effort he makes, in both his notebooks and in his published writing, to draw attention to his own privileged understanding of American society as a kind of spectacle manufactured for public consumption. A notebook entry from 1842, which served as the foundation for "The Old Apple-Dealer," describes a gingerbread vendor at a railroad station and attempts to access what it is about the vendor that resists a hastily composed linguistic portrait: "At times, by an indescribable, not striking, but perfectly quiet movement to his features, the expression of frost bitten, patient despondency becomes very touching" (223). As Hawthorne again points to the presence of something "indescribable in the vendor," he further defines the vendor's real self as beyond linguistic representation, and, in turn, safely out of reach of the gaze of the marketplace. Here his own unwillingness to portray the seller lies at the heart of the notebook passage's self-portrait of Hawthorne as author—for, as he reminds us, only one who was looking at more than the vendor's wares would pick up on what others have no need to see: amid the noise and movement of trains and travelers, Hawthorne writes that "his quietness is what strikes me," as if only a true author could recognize and resist the commodifying impulse of all that surrounds them. He needs his subject both to reveal one way out of the market, and to perform the author's own capacity for inventing an idiom that can serve as such an exit.

In the version of "The Old Apple-Dealer" that was ultimately published in *Mosses from an Old Manse,* Hawthorne tells us that "in order to invest my conception of the old man with a more decided sense of reality, I look at him in the very moment of intensest bustle, on the arrival of the cars" (*Tales,* 719). Reality, then, is both equated with economic activity and revealed to be the product (as opposed to the subject) of Hawthorne's description—that is to say, Hawthorne's writing describes as it acknowledges description to be an act of "investing" a subject with what we call "reality." If in Hawthorne's sketch such description takes various narrative forms, such an approach celebrates that mode of writing capable of revealing description as invention, treating reality as both a narrative and economic construct. As Dana Brand writes of the sketch, "the language of the narrator makes us aware that virtually all of his 'perceptions' are essentially acts of creation. . . . [The narrator] is painting, he is not seeing."[7] The narrative idiom of "The Old Apple-Dealer," marked by a casual and self-conscious style, epitomizes Hawthorne's project of making the description of reality into art—what Melville would later call "the great Art of Telling the Truth"—by contrasting his own word painting with the market-minded approach of straightforward mimesis. In presenting his various portraits of the apple-dealer on the heels of failed attempts to describe his subject directly, Hawthorne relies upon the failure of traditional mimesis to define his own narrative idiom. As in *The Story Teller,* such artistry relies on the careful exposure of "reality" as a relational value of the marketplace, for the old man's portrait can only be nailed down by resorting to the language of contrast: "He and the steam-fiend are each other's antipodes; the latter is the type of all that go ahead—and the old man, the representative of that melancholy class who, by some sad witchcraft, are doomed never to share in the world's exulting progress. Thus the contrast between mankind and this desolate brother becomes picturesque, and even sublime" (719). "The Old Apple-Dealer" communicates by placing its subject in a marketplace of subjects, where the vendor finally becomes meaningful only in dialogue with other presences—a younger vendor who stands nearby, the railroad, the narrator's own expectations.

Hawthorne's notebooks contain numerous descriptions that read much like the apple-dealer passage, including several where the author's integrity as a cultural witness depends on the salient presence of an actual audience who delights in theatricality and artifice.[8] After visiting a show of wax figures in July of 1838, for example, Hawthorne wrote a long entry in his notebook describing the exhibit, the showman, and the crowd. The wax figures, Hawthorne reports, were representations of famous murderers and their victims. He writes, "the showman seemed very proud of Ellen Jewett, and spoke of her somewhat as if this wax-figure were a real creation" (177).[9] After spending many sentences describing the showman's salesmanship—"he invites his departing guests to call again and bring their friends" (177)—Hawthorne turns his attention to the audience. A list of every member of the crowd, along with brief descriptions of their appearance and demeanor, concludes with, "myself, who examine[s] wax faces and faces of flesh with equal interest" (178). Neither showman nor customer, the author of the passage can only be sketched by first depicting the representations that appear in the marketplace and then the (equally unreal) public that consumes them. Two months later, in September of 1838, Hawthorne recorded in his notebook a visit to an exhibition of wild animals. As in the earlier entry, Hawthorne focuses briefly on the showman's manner of presentation: "He gave a descriptive and historical account of them, and some fanciful and jocose &c" (140). Quickly, though, his attention turns to "all the spectators looking on, so attentively that a breath could not be heard" (140–41). In the eyes of the romantic artist, "That was impressive—its effect on a thousand people, more than the thing itself" (141).

A much later entry (dated May 8, 1850) describes a visit the previous night to the National Theatre, where Hawthorne saw a "pantomime" of "Jack and the Giant Killer": "The audience was more noteworthy than the play. The theatre itself is for the middling and lower classes; and I had not taken my seat in the most aristocratic part of the house; so that I found myself surrounded chiefly by young sailors, Hanover-street shopmen, mechanics, and other people of that kidney. It is wonderful the difference that exists in the personal aspect and dress, and no less in the manners, of people in this quarter of the city, as compared with others" (501–2). The entry goes on to depict in great detail two girls who sat next to him, along with a third who "was so dark I rather suspected her to have a tinge of African blood" (503). After devoting several notebook pages to the girls, Hawthorne writes, "I should like well to know who they are—of what condition in life—and whether reputable as members of the class to which they belong." Finally, after briefly describing the drunken sailors who shouted and sang throughout the performance, Hawthorne concludes, "It was a scene of life in the rough" (504). These notebook sketches suggest an author working out strategies for portraying American life in a manner that could also keep the spectatorial practices of the masses in clear view—as if Hawthorne imagined that by seeing reality as a form of theater he could accomplish both of these ends. Significantly, the audience members in each of these scenes participate *en masse* in the same kind of unreal world conquered by Hawthorne's storyteller; and, as in "The Village Theatre" frame, Hawthorne resides in a rhetorical space that is defined against the showman and the representative types the author is able to identify in the audience.

Hawthorne again invokes the theatricality of antebellum culture in "The Old Manse" (the sketch that he wrote to introduce his 1846 collection, *Mosses from an Old Manse*), in which the author positions himself between the gated manse property and the "public highway" that sits just beyond. The manse, of course, belonged to Emerson's family, and as Hawthorne tells us, "A priest had built it; a priest had succeeded to it; other priestly men, from time to time, had dwelt in it; and children, born in its chambers, had grown up to assume the priestly character" (*Tales*, 1123–24). But Hawthorne's role in the sketch is not to simply dwell in the religious atmosphere of the manse property; he stands conspicuously between the manse environment and the cold commerce of the world beyond the gateposts, almost as if he were positioned on the proscenium of a theater. After describing the "many strangers" who visit the property each summer to view the Revolutionary War battleground, for example, he claims that "I have never found my imagination much excited by this, or any other scene of historic celebrity" (1129). Instead, "there is a wilder interest in the tract of land . . . which extends beyond the battlefield." There, encouraged by Thoreau, Hawthorne finds relics from an Indian village that stood "in some unknown age, before the white man came." Of these relics he writes, "Their great charm consists in [their] rudeness, and in the individuality of each article, so different from the productions of civilized machinery, which shapes everything on one pattern" (1129).

Against the outside world's obsession with "historical celebrity," the manse property stands like a bastion of romantic individualism, but one in which the public's appetite for celebrity has transformed the thinkers inside the gates into little more than caricatures of themselves. For Hawthorne's descriptions of these relics, in echoing his own culture's fetishization of the authentic, seem to suggest that the line separating the cloistered philosopher from the practices of the masses is yet another cultural fiction. Indeed, "The Old Manse" later contrasts the "real and tangible existences" of his own "kitchen vegetables" against what he calls the productions of "the market-gardener." "If there be not too many of them," Hawthorne tells his reader, "each individual plant becomes an object of separate interest" (1131). At each of these moments, Hawthorne portrays the genuine individualism cherished on the manse property as both authentically antimarket and already fetishized by the threat of public consumption that lurks saliently outside the gateposts of the manse property.

Another moment describes Hawthorne wandering with the younger William Ellery Channing across the grounds: "Strange and happy times were those, when we cast aside all irksome forms and straight-laced habitudes, and delivered ourselves up to the free air, to live like the Indians or any less conventional race" (1138). As they talk together, their conversation gushes up "like the babble of a fountain," and Channing's words are "lumps of golden thought" (1141). Hawthorne writes, "Could he have drawn that virgin gold, and stamped it with the mint-mark that alone gives currency, the world might have had the profit, and he the fame." Finally, the reader learns that "the chief profit of those wild days . . . [lay] in the freedom which we thereby won from all custom and conventionalism, and fettering influences of man on man" (1141). Invoking the groundless value of currency to prop up Channing's untainted and uncommodified genius, Hawthorne again stands between two systems of value. And yet if the invocation of currency relies upon the instability of economic value to imply the transcendent nature of Channing's genius, Hawthorne is cleverly engaging in a relational valuation of his own: even when removed from the "public highway," philosophy and art are commodified by the very existence of a public that lurks on the other side of the gateposts. In other words, Channing's intellect succumbs to the economic logic of the marketplace for the very reason that it has no status as capital. The scene thus anticipates Hawthorne's depiction of the many strangers, "these hob-goblins of flesh and blood," who hover just outside the property, hoping to catch a glimpse of Emerson. As Hawthorne describes the effect of Emerson's writing on others, "the invariable character of persons who crowd so closely about an original thinker, as to draw in his unuttered breath, . . . [is that they] become imbued with a false originality" (1147). The world outside the gateposts of the old manse is one of spectacle, of celebrity, of "false originality," while the world inside contains a foundational kind of value that, with Hawthorne as our guide, has already been made unreal by the marketplace.

In the final paragraphs of "The Old Manse," Hawthorne reveals that he will soon be leaving behind the "free air" of Channing, Thoreau, and Emerson to enter the world on the other side: "Providence took me by the hand, and . . . has led me, as the newspapers announce while I am writing, from the Old Manse into a Custom-House!" (1148). When read in light of this disclosure, the earlier moments from the sketch in which Hawthorne contrasts the manse property with the inauthenticities of publicity and commercial culture appear as a fortification of Hawthorne's own integrity in anticipation of his entry into the public realm. As he appears before the public both in his new job and in the newspapers that announce his appointment (as well as in the pages of the book his readers hold in their hands), the author of "The Old Manse" affirms his own awareness that he is joining a fictional world. "So far as I am a man of really individual attributes," Hawthorne writes, "I veil my face; nor am I, nor have ever been, one of those supremely hospitable people, who serve up their own hearts delicately fried, with brain-sauce, as a tidbit for their beloved pub-lic" (1147). As in *The Story Teller*, Hawthorne adopts an authorial posture that attempts to reconcile his role as a purveyor of fiction to the public with a romantic ideal that equates publicity with the destruction of the true individual. If celebrities like Emerson and his cohort circulate in the pub-lic eye, Hawthorne's awareness of the public's commodifying gaze—his liminal place between two unreal worlds—affords the author of "The Old Manse" an untouchable and portable integrity.

In this way, "The Old Manse" helps us understand how Hawthorne's artistic predicament differed (in his portrayal) from the other romantic thinkers he invokes in the sketch. Hawthorne not only contrasts the Old

Manse with the world of literary consumers; he opposes himself to those romantic dreamers who never venture out beyond the gateposts. As a writer of fiction, and as a middle-class father and husband with a family to support, Hawthorne continually appeared in the marketplace—whether working in custom houses or peddling his writing before the public. Unlike Channing or Emerson, who are portrayed as thinkers entirely unconnected to the unrealities of economic exchange, the authorial persona of "The Old Manse" sits precisely at the line that divides these worlds. As in "The Artist of the Beautiful," where the romantic author resides between the pure artist (whose realities need no tangible form) and the misguided public (who entirely misunderstand the very premises of artistic creation), Hawthorne's intense preoccupation with the line between romantic truth and cultural spectacle emerges as a way of keeping his veiled face before the public. Even more profoundly, Hawthorne portrays Channing and the celebrity-obsessed public as two different kinds of dreamers—the one never leaving the groundless realm of pure philosophy, the other not able to recognize the illusionary nature of the marketplace. For Hawthorne, then, genuine humanity seems to reside at the nexus of pure intellect and the gaze that threatens to commodify it.

Following Hawthorne's very public dismissal from the custom house, in the wake of the Whig victory in the 1848 presidential election, he wrote another autobiographical sketch, one that charted his return back through the gateposts of romanticism. The "Custom-House" introduction to *The Scarlet Letter*, like "The Old Manse," loudly assails the inauthenticity of public life. Invoking the political scandal that followed his firing, Hawthorne answers the intrusion of journalism with the romancer's view that sees antebellum culture as an empty spectacle. As in his earlier letters to Sophia, where those who reside outside the lovers' shared ontological realm "do not know a shadow from reality," Hawthorne's calculated reaction to his dismissal is to reimagine the terms of selfhood by shedding the false skin of the public "Hawthorne": "Meanwhile, the press had taken up my affair, and kept me, for a week or two, careering through the public prints, in my decapitated state, like Irving's Headless Horseman; ghastly and grim, and longing to be buried, as a politically dead man ought. So much for my figurative self. The real human being, all this time, with his head safely on his shoulders, had brought himself to the comfortable conclusion, that everything was for the best; and, making an investment in ink, paper, and steel-pens, had opened his long-disused writing desk, and was again a literary man."[10]

By opposing the "real" Hawthorne to the headless image circulating in texts, and then charting the author's return to his writing desk, Hawthorne portrays the romance that follows as his public answer to the superficiality of journalism and politics. And yet his status as a "literary man" treats writing as a fundamentally economic undertaking: "making an investment in ink, paper, and steel-pens," Hawthorne depicts his return to "his long-disused writing desk" as a career change. In doing so, the romancer acknowledges the pervasiveness of the marketplace's logic, thereby reasserting the integrity of the unrepresented (and unrepresentable) "inmost Me" who exists outside of print.[11] More than simply an embodiment of genuine humanity, the romance is presented as a saleable fiction that protects the romantic subject—who must, by definition, remain out of the public's view. As in "The Old Manse," where Hawthorne invokes the celebrity of Emerson to imagine for himself a different relationship to the public gaze, here his account of an inaccessible, unrepresentable humanity is predicated on its location in a world of fictions.

Echoing his earlier notebook entries, the Hawthorne of "The Custom-House" takes great pains to highlight how his understanding of public life differs from those who attend only to its surfaces. In the final paragraphs of "The Custom-House," the romancer conspicuously retreats from view, describing himself in the third person as "a gentleman who writes from beyond the grave." Using the exact same phrase from the earlier letter to Sophia, in which he writes that Brook Farm "already looks like a dream behind me," the Hawthorne of 1850 describes "the life of the Custom-House" as "a dream behind me" (44). While much of "The Custom-House" is devoted to careful descriptions of those whom Hawthorne worked with, all of the figures he has already depicted are, by the closing paragraphs, "but shadows in my view"—as if the very act of describing them, of making them real to the reader, marks their unreality to the romantic imagination. Thus the ultimate subject of "The Custom-House" is the romantic "view" that sees the real world of its titular setting as unreal: "Soon my old native town will loom upon me through the haze of memory, a mist brooding over and around it; as if it were no portion of the real earth, but an overgrown village in cloud-land, with only imaginary inhabitants to people its wooden houses, and walk its homely lanes, and the unpicturesque prolixity of its main street. Henceforth, it ceases to be a reality of my life. I am a citizen of somewhere else" (44). Here he performs his departure from the political world by seeing that world as an unreality—or, rather, by telling his audience that he sees it as such. As with his account of his figurative self careering through the public, it is the actual Salem's very ability to be represented in language that renders it unreal. In other words, his rhetorical rebirth as "a citizen of somewhere else" is announced by the rejection of mimesis as a representational ideal, a move that Michael Davitt Bell famously calls the romance's "sacrifice of relation." And yet, as in the apple-dealer sketch, it seems not that Hawthorne is sacrificing such "relation" but that he is exploiting its fictionality to claim for himself an interiority beyond the reach of language.

In fact, let me pause here to register my dissatisfaction with this use of the term "mimesis," a phrase that is often invoked by critics as the antithesis of "romance." Richard Walsh, in his recent (and extremely clearheaded) discussion of the relationship between fictionality and mimesis, rejects any attempt to define fictionality by the criteria of referentiality, arguing instead that fictionality is "the product of a narrative's frame of presentation."[12] Fictional narrative, then, is defined precisely by its distinctiveness from nonfictional narrative—and the name we have traditionally given to the former is "mimesis." In other words, "mimesis" is not the referential use of language (as many critics assume or imply it is) but the self-consciously fictional imitation of this use of language.[13] Relying on the work of Paul Ricoeur, Walsh corrects the view that defines mimesis by the referential truth it claims to contain; rather, mimesis communicates the way that narrative creates meaning. In order to make this relevant to a theory of fiction, Walsh ultimately claims that fiction is "the exercise of our narrative understanding, as distinct from its application."[14] In fiction, we experience how particulars are configured and given meaning while understanding these particulars as disconnected from any actuality.

In many ways, Walsh's account of the distinction between fictional and nonfictional narrativity sounds like Hawthorne's own. The authorial use of narrative framing in The Story Teller, for example, recasts the line between fiction and nonfiction—between the storyteller's invented tales and the newspaper account of Higginbotham's murder—as a product of social consensus. In fact, works such as "The Custom-House" (like "The Old Apple-Dealer" and the love letters cited in the introduction) rely on this slipperiness to invert the meanings of reality and unreality. If such a reversal is itself a fiction, a rhetorical flaunting of the romancer's authority over the problematic terms by which his culture defines truth, such a realization should remind us that the very act of theorizing about reality for Hawthorne was most meaningful not for its philosophical acuity but for the way it sought to destabilize the reality that is the domain of the masses. For Hawthorne, "reality" never exists outside of scare quotes (even when they are invisible) because it is always invoked as an implicit challenge to the consensual meaning reality contains outside of the romantic view of things. Another way of saying this is that Hawthorne never merely invents romantic reality; he is always reinventing the reality that others believe in. Walsh's careful definition of mimesis, by reminding us that all fictional narration implies an argument about the relationship between storytelling and reality, implicitly refuses to privilege the romance's account of its own understanding of reality as more genuine than the reportorial idioms of journalistic or realist writing. Though Walsh's essay does not specifically address romantic writing, his definition of mimesis allows us to place the romance beside what we call "realism" as simply another story about the relationship between language and reality. Finally, what seems like Hawthorne's self-conscious rejection of mimesis in works such as "The Custom-House" and "The Old Apple-Dealer" is understood in such a paradigm as simply another type of mimesis—that is, as one among many ways of talking about the relationship between storytelling and reality. The significance of theorizing the romance as *a type of mimesis* (as opposed to a rejection or abandonment of mimesis) is that it deprivileges the long-standing assumption that Hawthorne's writing is divorced from the real, and replaces such an assumption with a view of romantic storytelling as the product of a culturally marked attitude vis-à-vis the question of reality.

Thus it is by continually bringing in contemporaneous technologies of representation that Hawthorne defines romantic storytelling by its singular awareness of the textual production of the real. Consider "Main Street" (1849), a sketch written in the months leading up to the publication of *The Scarlet Letter,* in which Hawthorne literalizes the project of taking his reader behind the curtain to peek at the machinery of storytelling. In the sketch, a Salem showman exhibits "a shifting panorama . . . somewhat in the nature of a puppet show" depicting the history of his town's main thoroughfare to a roomful of paying customers (*Tales,* 1023). "Main Street," which comprises both the showman's descriptions of his exhibit's shifting scenes and his intermittent arguments with the audience, anticipates the narrative complexities of the romance in its dialogic approach to storytelling: by juxtaposing the panorama-like display with the sketch's own narrative machinery, Hawthorne relies on a popular mode of representation to bring into relief the romancer's distance from traditional cultural practice. While the panorama of "Main Street" differs from the traditional moving panoramas that were something of a sensation in the late 1840s (these panoramas were each made up of a number of large sewn-together painted canvases depicting geographical and/or historical scenes that gradually unfurled before an audience), Hawthorne's story clearly speaks to the popular attitudes and assumptions that fueled the antebellum panorama phenomenon.

At least one audience member finds the show unrealistic: "The whole affair is a manifest catch-penny. . . . The trees look more like weeds in a garden, than a primitive forest; the Squaw Sachem and Wappacowet are stiff in their pasteboard joints; and the squirrels, the deer, and the wolf, move with all the grace of a child's wooden monkey, sliding up and down a stick" (1025). To the critic's remonstrances, Hawthorne's showman confesses that "human art has its limits," reminding him that "we must now and then ask a little aid from the spectator's imagination" (1025). He asks the audience member to change his seat, promising that "the proper light and shadow will transform the spectacle into quite another thing." But the critic refuses to budge, claiming adamantly "that it is my business to see things just as they are" (1029). Here the story's attention to the tricks of lighting and perspective that produce the illusion of reality antici- pate the famous preface to *The House of the Seven Gables.* But if such a parallel might imply that the showman serves as a fictive stand-in for the romancer—and if Hawthorne's readers typically read the sketch this way—this reading overlooks the important rhetorical distance between the showman's machinery and Hawthorne's own narrative.[15] The audience in the story is frustrated by the exhibition's clumsy craftsmanship, which subverts the illusion of reality the patrons seem to value. Hawthorne's pro- duction, however, willingly lets us peek at the panorama's machinery. In so reminding us that the panorama's reality effect is a product of narrative deception, the sketch draws attention to the transparency of its own nar- ration, for the showman speaks both to his audience and to Hawthorne's reader (with no quotation marks offsetting his words), imparting the impression of unmediated communication. In a narrative maneuver that anticipates the contrast between Holgrave's claims for the daguerreo- type and the invocation of the technology in the *Seven Gables* preface, Hawthorne uses the showman's dilemma to highlight the inadequacies of the panorama as an art form.[16] While the showman is able to verbalize the shortcomings of representation to his audience, the panorama (like the daguerreotype) is incapable of theorizing about representation while churning out the pictures its audience demands.

The problem with the showman's work, it seems, is not that it presents a contrived or politically irresponsible account of local history but that its mode of storytelling makes its creator beholden to the marketplace's arbitrary distinctions between truth and fiction. At the most basic level, the showman fails to understand the Barnum-age logic that audiences want their illusions to be well crafted, pointing out the crank that he will use to turn his "contrived" exhibition, even reminding the audience of "the casu- alties to which such a complicated piece of mechanism is liable" (1023).[17]

Eventually, the unhappy patron points to the stiff joints of the cardboard Indians, and he later remarks upon "a pasteboard figure, such as a child would cut out of a card, with a pair of very dull scissors" (1029). While the showman confesses from the beginning that his quasi-panorama is simply a contrived representation that comes largely from his own imagination, the audience essentially wants to be lied to—for even after the outspoken critic finally accepts the panorama as a work of imagination, he announces, "I am just beginning to get interested in the matter. Come! turn your crank, and grind out a few more of these fooleries" (1043).

What neither the crowd nor the showman can comprehend is what the audience of "Mr. Higginbotham's Catastrophe" also fails to realize, and what only the author understands—that the line between fact and fiction is a marketplace illusion. By having his fictive showman exhibit a cross between a puppet show and a panorama (as opposed to a traditional panorama), Hawthorne implies that the exhibit fails not because it is unrealistic but because it does not conform to the arbitrary standards of an antebellum culture of display in which panoramas successfully peddled the promise of verisimilitude. The showman's clumsy machinery, a hybrid of panoramic authenticity and puppet-show fiction, first fails to appease the audience's demand for the former by keeping its artifice in full view, then fails as entertainment when, in the story's final paragraphs, our showman informs his audience that "the scene will not move. A wire is broken" (1050). As the audience of "Main Street" couches its own appetite for narrative as a disinterested desire for information (it is, as the unhappy patron says, their business "to see things just as they are"), Hawthorne exposes the fraud of such a claim. Again echoing the notebook passages in which Hawthorne relied on the public consumption of spectacle to carve out his own idiosyncratic view of American culture, in "Main Street" the author alone looks down on both the showman, who is allowed just enough agency to serve the public's appetites, and the crowd, who exerts its power over everyone except the romantic author.

After the panorama's conspicuous fiction-making machinery breaks down, the fiction-making machinery of Hawthorne's writing is still humming along, right up until the story's final words. When this occurs, Hawthorne's writing emerges as the better-crafted production—one in which no wire is visible and no artifice is revealed. Paradoxically, this artistic triumph requires the text's exposure of effective storytelling as the product of careful narrative posturing, so that Hawthorne's integrity in the marketplace is protected (à la *The Story Teller*) by acknowledging that representations must always answer the demands of their audience. "As an artist substitute," Jeffrey Richards writes of the sketch, "the showman masks the presence of the author who is the one really turning the crank in silence."[18] But if the author is silent, his silence is conspicuous; Hawthorne's writing presents itself as if built upon invisible machinery, an invisibility made visible through a contrast with the panorama's obvious, and ultimately unreliable, mechanisms. His own authorial presence, located somewhere above the world of mere commerce, is defined against that of the showman, who has been made subservient to the marketplace. Hawthorne's manufactured narrative, as we now know it to be, ends with the words of the critical audience member, who calls off the entire exchange: with an outstretched palm, he tells the showman, "I said that your exhibition would prove a humbug, and so it has turned out. So hand over my quarter" (1050). Once the transaction is abandoned, the act of writing abruptly ceases. But if the showman falls into this silence, a victim of the market's arbitrary contracts, the author of "Main Street" seems to reside somewhere else entirely.

Importantly, the audience of "Main Street" approaches the panoramic puppet show with a set of assumptions shaped by the moving panorama's status in the late 1840s as a mode of popular representation that was profitable both for the entertainment value of sitting before an enormous moving picture and for the verisimilitude it claimed as a form of virtual travel. Booklets that accompanied productions such as Walter McPherson Bayne's *Gigantic Panorama of a Voyage to Europe* sought to capitalize on the thrilling effect of sitting before such large pictures (Bayne's panorama booklet, in an exaggeration typical of the format, billed the exhibit as "nearly twice the size of any panorama ever exhibited") while also advertising the pictures' "faithful similarity" to the various places represented.[19] Furthermore, many panoramists gave names such as the "moving mirror" to their exhibits to further highlight their accuracy and realism.[20] And panorama pamphlets typically concluded with testimonials that spoke to the fidelity and realism of its pictures. While most of these testimonials were taken from newspaper reviews, others came from military figures or steamboat captains who were familiar with the places represented. In an intriguing authentication of William Burr's *Pictorial Voyage to Canada, American Frontier, and the Saguenay,* the Ojibwe author George Copway reports, "I have traveled in a birchen canoe over all the region represented on your canvas, know almost every rock and tree, and I am much pleased in being able to give my testimony to the accuracy of your delineations, and am astonished to see how Art can transfer nature."[21] Other testimonials also focused on the artistry of the paintings as the key to the panorama's reality effect: "So perfectly is nature represented in this gigantic painting," the *Baltimore Patriot* wrote of *Hudson's Great National Painting of the*

Ohio and the Mississippi, "that as the canvas steadily revolves past the field of vision, it is difficult to realize that the spectator does not himself move, and in his progress, see a beautiful panorama of nature, instead of a work of art, before him; so happy is the illusion."[22]

The discourse that sought to authenticate the panorama's singular capacity to artistically capture the experience of reality for the paying customer quietly privileged a conception of reality as experience—as if the world were ready-made to be consumed by spectators such as those audiences that made the panoramas of the late 1840s so successful in America and Europe. As the *Baltimore Patriot* testimonial suggests, and as the descriptive booklets further reveal, the panorama presented distant lands in a form that echoed the tourist experience. The booklet accompanying *Lane's Panorama of the Hudson River* (an exhibit that stopped in Salem in September of 1848), for example, which presumably provided the text for the showman standing before the audience, tells its audience that "the visitor will here take the imaginary boat and ascend the stream, viewing the beautiful country on its borders."[23] Others, such as J. R. Smith's *Tour of Europe,* more explicitly sought to emulate the experience of travel, even describing one stop where "your trunks are opened and ransacked, *your private letters read,* your passports examined with all the scrupulous exactness of those jacks in office, who expect to get a red ribbon in their buttonhole and be promoted by catching John Smith Mazzini, Esq."[24] This entrepreneurial use of the panorama's motion (as opposed to pictures that merely sit still) allowed these showmen to rely upon the movement of the panorama in shaping a notion of authenticity that went beyond the visual accuracy of their paintings. In a formulation that anticipates the profound impact of the cinema on early twentieth-century thought, "reality" here is not stagnant but the exact opposite: it is moving. Copway's authentication replaces his own experience of riding in a canoe with the experience of sitting before a moving picture, so that the authenticity of these works is based upon the panorama's capacity as a mode of representation that quietly imposed upon reality the narrative movement of storytelling. In "Main Street," then, Hawthorne exposes the tricks of lighting and perspective on which the panorama's success as a mode of storytelling relied. But even more profoundly, the work takes as its deeper subject the contrived, carefully modulated process by which the individual subject is made into *the* (that is, the archetypal) mass consumer.

When read alongside Hawthorne's notebook sketches of antebellum audiences devouring a range of spectacles, the narrative strategy of "Main Street" suggests that just as Hawthorne was entering his major phase, he was experimenting with modes of storytelling that could oppose his own representational ideals with mass-oriented forms that merely contributed to the spectacle of antebellum life. Indeed, the narrative invocation of panoramic technology in "Main Street" anticipates *The House of the Seven Gables,* where Hawthorne crafts a dialogue between the machinery of romance and Holgrave's daguerreotype. In concluding my discussion of Hawthorne's career with a brief reading of *Seven Gables,* I hope to illustrate how the self-conscious fictionality of Hawthorne's romantic storytelling brings to the novel the same kind of authorial self-invention we see in his notebook entries and the other works cited above. As in these other examples, Hawthorne's authorial identity in the novel is predicated on his singular awareness of American culture as a spectacle—in the most literal sense of the word, for in Hawthorne's imagination modern culture is defined by the way in which it interpellates its subject as a spectator. As the older generation of Pyncheons come face to face with the chaos of modernization (opening up a penny shop, riding the railroad), and as the younger Holgrave and Phoebe are accommodated by the narrative into the middle-class respectability that emerged out of the market revolution (the "wild reformer" conforms himself "to laws, and the peaceful practice of society" [307]), the romancer makes his own entry into such social upheaval equipped with a rarefied understanding of contemporary society as a realm of carefully fabricated fictions. Like his storyteller from years earlier, these characters give up their past to join the unreality of the modern age—while the romancer remains above the fray.

Several moments in the novel read like the notebook entries cited above, where Hawthorne underscores the theatricality of American life as a way of protecting the romantic consciousness from the dehumanizing threat of mass culture. In the "Arched Window" chapter, for example, Clifford witnesses "a political procession, with hundreds of flaunting banners, and drums, fifes, clarions, and cymbals, reverberating between the rows of buildings" (165). Echoing the approach of "Main Street," Hawthorne depicts the pageant for us by situating the scene within a broader reflection on the question of individual perspective, as if the romancer is seeking out a more foundational view of American cultural change by trying to imagine and then elude the perspective of the mass subject: "In order to become majestic," the narrator tells us, "it should be viewed from some vantage-point, as it rolls its slow and long array through the centre of a wide plain, or the stateliest public square of a city; for then, by its remoteness, it melts all the petty personalities, of which it is made up, into one broad mass of existence—one great life—one collected body of mankind, with a vast homogeneous spirit animating it" (165). Connecting the political pageant with the traditional civic space of a city public square, Hawthorne's description contrasts a republican model of political participation, where the individual subject imagines itself as part of a republic made up of other individual subjects, with the far more dangerous threat of mass subjectivity: the narrator goes on to warn the reader that "if an impressible person, standing alone over the brink of one of those processions, should behold it, not in its atoms, but in its aggregate—as a mighty river of life, massive in its tide, and black with mystery," then the spectator "would hardly be restrained from plunging into the surging stream of human sympathies" (185). Of course, this is precisely what happens, as Hepzibah and Phoebe must seize Clifford to prevent him from throwing himself out of the arched window and plummeting into the "river of life . . . black with mystery" passing outside the house. In Hawthorne's rendering, to merge oneself into the passing spectacle of modern life is to commit a form of suicide; to see mere pageantry as something "calling to the kindred depth" inside the individual subject is to surrender one's humanity to the masses.[25]

In the chapter titled "The Flight of Two Owls," Hawthorne claims to resist the process by which its technologies hold sway over individual consciousness. While old Hepzibah Pyncheon flees from her ancestral home with her brother, she is unable to shake "the feeling of indistinctness and unreality [that] kept dimly hovering roundabout her." Once the two characters board a railcar, "drawn into the great current of human life," Hepzibah asks her brother whether they are not dreaming. Clifford responds, "A dream, Hepzibah! . . . On the contrary, I have never been awake before!" Here is how Hawthorne describes the world outside the railcar window: "Looking from the window, they could see the world racing past them. At one moment, they were rattling through a solitude;—the next, a village had grown up all around them;—a few breaths more, and it had vanished, as if swallowed up by an earth-quake. The spires of meeting-houses seemed set adrift from their foundations; the broad-based hills glided away. Everything was unfixed from its age-long rest, and moving at whirlwind speed in a direction opposite to their own" (256). As Clifford imagines himself in contact with the actual world for the first time, as Hepzibah wonders whether she is awake or asleep, the author hovers somewhere above the moving panorama that passes outside—as if the world his characters see were merely a mirage produced by technology. As in the parade scene, Hawthorne asserts the romance's foundational understanding of reality over the individual perspectives of both Hepzibah, whose "quality of . . . mind was too unmalleable to take new impressions" (258), and Clifford, whose long seclusion from humanity causes him to mistake the moving panorama outside his window for "life itself" (257).

Importantly, the scene as it appears in the novel borrowed heavily from a notebook passage in which Hawthorne recorded a trip aboard the Concord railroad taken in the spring of 1850. After describing the unused, weed-covered track that lies "desolate" outside his railcar window, he recorded the following: "Anon, you hear a low thunder running along these iron rules; it grows louder; an object is seen afar off, it approaches rapidly, and comes down upon you like fate, swift and inevitably. In a moment, it dashes along in front of the Station-house and comes to a pause; the locomotive hissing and fuming, in its eagerness to go on. How much life has come at once into this lonely place! Four or five long cars, each, perhaps, with fifty people in it; reading newspapers, reading pamphlet novels, chatting, sleeping; all this vision of passing life!" (487–88). Describing the departure of the train, Hawthorne opposes the spectacle of rail travel with the edifices of a church and farmhouse, which he connects to a stationary and rapidly receding past: "[A] solitude of hours again broods over the Station House, which, for an instant, has thus been put in communication with far-off cities, and then has only itself, with the old black, ruinous church, and the black old farm-house, both built years and years ago, before railroads were ever dreamed of" (487). He goes on to imagine the perspective of a "passenger, stepping from the solitary station-house into the train," who "finds himself in the midst of a new world, all in a moment" (488). Hawthorne's novelistic eye affords an escape from his individual experience as a passenger to one more attentive to the broader implications of rail travel, both as a way of connecting "far-off cities" and as a jarring intrusion responsible for the disruptive psychological conditions of modern life. In transposing the notebook entry into his novel, Hawthorne hovers above the panorama that passes outside the railcar window, as each of his characters must come to grips with what he portrays as the fragmenting, disruptive impact of industrialization. Within the individual consciousnesses of his characters, such modernization constitutes a whole new reality; in the foundational view of the romancer, this new "reality" is simply another trick of lighting and perspective.

Aboard the train, Clifford engages with a fellow traveler in a conversation about the various marvels of modern life: railroads, mesmerism, telegraphy. "It is an excellent thing," the traveler says of Morse's electromagnetic telegraph. "That is, of course, if the speculators in cotton and politics don't get possession of it" (264). When the traveler tells Clifford that the telegraph is "a great thing indeed . . . particularly as regards the detection of bank-robbers and murderers," Clifford is taken aback. "A bank-robber—and what you call a murderer, likewise—has his rights," he objects, arguing that "an almost spiritual medium, like the electric telegraph," should be used only for spiritual ends (264). Clifford, in seeing the telegraph as a spiritual medium, and his fellow traveler, in both worrying about the telegraph becoming a tool of financial speculation and embracing its potential as a means of surveillance and law enforcement, together embody the popular discourse surrounding the new technology. As my next chapter will suggest, while the telegraph was initially seen by many as a kind of "conjuring trick," by the mid-1840s many commentators hailed a new telegraphic age, one in which the disembodied and unmediated nature of telegraphic communication would allow for an informational ideal beyond the taint of commercial or political corruption—that is, as long as it could be kept out of the hands of speculators and stockjobbers.[26]

Using his characters to give voice to the range of meanings the telegraph held in the antebellum imagination, Hawthorne portrays telegraphy as a highly unstable symbol in the popular imagination. After all, the stranger's concern that the wrong kind of people might get their hands on the telegraph undercuts his own faith in the technology as an omniscient and infallible vehicle for detecting criminals; it was, after all, simply a way for humans to send messages to one another across great distances, and thus telegraphy might just as easily be seen as a way of consolidating and centralizing the public distribution of information (indeed, the Associated Press was founded in 1848 for just such a purpose).[27] As E. L. McCallum has argued, "The threat the telegraph poses [in the novel] . . . is that it materializes and augments the technology of public discourse—a technology often at odds with the truth."[28] But instead of descending into antebellum debates about the political or economic implications of Morse's invention, Hawthorne uses the character of Clifford to highlight how even the specter of telegraphic communication threatens to deform the psyche of the modern subject. After hearing his fellow passenger describe the telegraph as a tool of law and order, Clifford bemoans the way in which the technology infringes on the rights of the individual:

> For example, Sir, in a dark, low, cross-beamed, panelled room of an old house, let us suppose a dead man, sitting in an arm-chair, with a blood-stain on his shirt-bosom—and let us add to our hypothesis another man, issuing from the house, which he feels to be over-filled with the dead man's presence—and let us lastly imagine him fleeing, Heaven knows whither, at the speed of a hurricane, by railroad! Now, Sir,—if the fugi-

tive alight in some distant town, and find all the people babbling about the self-same dead man, whom he has fled so far to avoid the sight and thought of—will you not allow that his natural rights have been infringed? He has been deprived of his city of refuge, and, in my humble opinion, has suffered infinite wrong! (265)

In order to appreciate Clifford's objections, the reader must recall that he and his sister are fugitives—or, rather, in a narrative maneuver recalling the fictive "crime" of "Mr. Higginbotham's Catastrophe," they are fleeing a murder that has not taken place. Though, as the reader will come to understand, the judge has died of natural causes, Clifford and Hepzibah run from their home as if they are responsible for his death, as if the public perception of what has taken place will become the mass-mediated reality. Dominicus Pike, we remember, anticipates the newspaper accounts that will travel overseas in "Mr. Higginbotham's Catastrophe," vindicating his own fictional story by circulating it as information. In *Seven Gables,* it is now the telegraph transforming the modern world into a realm of storytelling from which the individual can find no "city of refuge"—so that the same information culture that makes the living Higginbotham into a murder victim turns the innocent Clifford into a fugitive.

As in his confused, near-leap from the arched window, Clifford's not-so-hypothetical third-person account of "another man . . . fleeing, Heaven knows whither, at the speed of a hurricane," suggests his own dislocation as an individual subject in the face of modern culture. With no sense of his own direction, without even an understanding of why he is fleeing, his agency seems compromised not merely by the machine that hurtles him through space and time but by the way he views *himself* through the eyes of a spectator. Reading his own story from the outside, Clifford becomes a cultural archetype—the fleeing criminal being outstripped by the telegraph—and is thus a victim of his own compromised sense of self. He is like Wakefield, the unseen character whose identity is co-opted by that story's narrator; having read a brief account of a man who leaves his wife only to return years later, the narrator reinvents the nameless man as "Wakefield." The deeper predicament of Clifford is that he is both narrator and subject, a divided self whose fragmented identity offsets the foundational perspective of the romancer; for, as Hawthorne seems to be implying, Clifford's problem is that he does not understand how his own consciousness is bound by the contingencies of modernization.

As Clifford is carried along by the railroad, deprived of both his own agency and the "city of refuge" that he considers his right, the romancer performs his own escape by returning to the judge's dead body as it sits in an otherwise empty house. While Hawthorne links the public space of the railroad with the mass information technology of telegraphy (he carefully tells us that the telegraph wires run along the railroad tracks), once the narrative returns to the Pyncheon home he invokes a technology associated with middle-class domesticity, the daguerreotype. Having recast the telegraph as another example of the unreality of modern life, Hawthorne moves to Holgrave's daguerreotype and in doing so claims for the romantic author a model of individual agency that he suggests is unavailable to any of his characters. Holding up his own self-conscious fiction-making against the theoretical impotence of Holgrave's camera, Hawthorne portrays the young daguerreotypist as incapable of exposing (and thus resisting) the fictionalizing forces of modernization.

In a chapter titled "Governor Pyncheon," Hawthorne foregrounds the disembodied, even supernatural dimensions of his narrator, taking his reader through the day Judge Pyncheon was to have experienced had he survived. As he begins the journey, the narrator seems to raise the judge from the dead: "Let him go thither, and loll at ease upon his money-bags! He has lounged long enough in the old chair" (270). From there we move from scene to scene, where our narrator reports on each of the judge's unexplained absences. Thus even though our narrator promises to reanimate the judge, he leaves the dead body behind and takes us to the realm of the living, a realm defined by the judge's absence at his scheduled events. It is not until the end of the chapter that Hawthorne's narrator decides "to make a little sport with the idea" (279) of ghosts by describing long-dead Pyncheons coming back to life and meeting together in the Pyncheon parlor. Ultimately, however, we are told that "the fantastic scene, just hinted at, must by no means be considered as forming an actual portion of our story" (281). The chapter ends with the narrator confessing that the promise of spiritualism was merely a means of proving temporary relief from "our too long and exclusive contemplation of that figure in the chair" (281). Here the conjuring of the dead is acknowledged by Hawthorne's narrator to be an absurd fiction, one driven by the desire for narrative action.[29]

Against the self-consciously romantic narrative of the "Governor Pyncheon" chapter, Hawthorne gives us Holgrave's daguerreotype of the dead judge, which is presented to young Phoebe to save her from the shock of seeing the corpse in person. At the moment Phoebe says of the picture, "This is death!" (302), the daguerreotype serves as a mode of depicting the fact of the judge's lifelessness—while Hawthorne's narration is presented as a means of satisfying the need for something to narrate. When read alongside Holgrave's daguerreotype of the dead judge's body (which is taken the following morning), the "Governor Pyncheon" chapter illustrates the difference between romantic storytelling and photography: our narrator fabricates an entire chapter out of the same body that Holgrave's camera represents as lifeless. "The judge is dead," Holgrave tells Phoebe, "and Clifford and Hepzibah have vanished. I know no more. All beyond is conjecture" (302). As Ronald Thomas reminds us, Holgrave is "confident that the . . . photographs he takes of the magistrate as he is dying will stand as a reliable 'pictorial record of Judge Pyncheon's death' and as 'a point of evidence' that will again clear Clifford of any suspicion in connection with these events." That is, "Holgrave's daguerreotypes consistently function in the text . . . as evidence, memorial, historical document. They tell the truth."[30]

In sharp contrast to Holgrave's preoccupation with fidelity, then, our narrator imposes the template of storytelling upon a unmoving, lifeless scene. Just as the fictive reader in "Old News" applies to decades-old newspapers his own desire for a story about the past, in "Governor Pyncheon" this need for narrative becomes justification enough for the appearance of ghosts. Unlike in the earlier sketch, where our narrator's stories pass as history, the entire action of the "Governor Pyncheon" chapter is undone by the narrator's acknowledgement that nothing has happened; Hawthorne's two-tiered narration contrasts the judge's body, which sits motionless, with his narrative, which is nothing more than the romantic narrator's omniscient narration. Ultimately, the narrator presents the story of "Governor Pyncheon" as a form of conjuring. And while our narrator tells us that "ghost-stories are hardly to be treated seriously, any longer," his own disembodied, omniscient narration seems ghostly. By denying the possibility of any supernatural presence at the very moment a narrative voice takes us through an empty house (who, after all, is speaking to us?), the narrator draws attention to the fictional nature of his own description.

Because the fact of the judge's death is meaningless to Holgrave until it is placed in the context of Hawthorne's fictional narrative, because his camera is powerless to do anything except report on what exists in an adjoining room, Holgrave's representation is devoid of any real authority within Hawthorne's story: he can carry his picture of reality from one room to another, but the picture has no meaning beyond its status as a representation without the romance's narrative to render it meaningful.[31] Of course, this story that surrounds it is a work of fiction—so that Hawthorne's authority is based on unapologetic invention, and Holgrave's powerlessness comes from the very fidelity that gives his daguerreotypic representation its value. In a sense, then, Hawthorne's ability to revalue (and thus devalue) Holgrave's picture allows him to perform his authority as the ultimate arbiter of meaning in his text by accomplishing what Alan Trachtenberg calls "a polarizing of modes of telling that becomes part of a diagrammatic structure of oppositions." In the very act of juxtaposing the camera and romantic storytelling, Hawthorne's dialogic approach exposes the theoretical flatness of Holgrave's pictures: "By itself . . . the camera has no theory of character, no independent ideology; it serves the discursive needs of its practitioners and clients."[32] Even more significantly, the authorial use of the daguerreotype allows Hawthorne (and only Hawthorne) to assume a role, neither practitioner nor client, that looks down on the partial, contingent truths of daguerreotypic meaning. As in "Main Street," where the audience's way of viewing the panorama renders the technology unable to acknowledge the complexity of the actual past, here the daguerreotype's function as a means of documentation vouchsafes its inability to grapple with the deeper truth that modern reality is simply an endless parade of representational surfaces.

As we have already seen, Hawthorne's desire to expose daguerreotypic authenticity as an unstable commodity went right to the very heart of how the emerging field of daguerreotypy sought to define itself. In a cheap pamphlet circulated in Boston in 1848 to advertise the daguerrean gallery of Lerow and Co., the hugely successful dime novelist Ned Buntline (born Edward Zane Carroll Judson) published a story called "Love at First Sight: or, The Daguerreotype." The story, which opens with Lerow himself in his Boston studio, follows a teenage girl who wishes to sit for a miniature likeness to give to her brother, who is going abroad. While much is made of the "exceedingly true and life-like" picture taken by Lerow, we learn that the poor girl has lost all of her money (including that which was to pay for the picture). The kind Lerow offers the picture for free if she will let him take another picture. Devastated by the loss of the money, the girl starts crying just as Lerow takes the second image, which we are told was so lifelike "it almost seemed to have the power of utterance."[33] Our narrator informs us that "the second was a more beautiful *picture* than the first, though in either the likeness was perfect" (7–8). Buntline's story goes on to introduce a friend of Lerow's, named Harry, who falls in love with the girl at the sight of her image. In tracking down the mysterious girl, Harry follows her to the clothing store where she works under dismal conditions. "Cold as it was," Harry recounts, the shopgirls "came thinly dressed, their worn and needle-pierced fingers, gloveless, and so numb that they could scarce pick up the coins which were so scornfully cast upon the counter as the paltry reward for their weary hours of toil by night and day" (11). Later, Harry hears the girl's landlord suggest that she prostitute herself in order to raise the money for her rent.

While the story predictably ends with the girl's marriage to Harry, I want to attend instead to Buntline's focus on his heroine's exploitation by the economic and social conditions of industrial Boston. Embedded within a story about the value of daguerreotypic images as a means of capturing reality, these invocations of capitalist exploitation allow Buntline to foreground for his reader the crucial fact that daguerreotypic artists (unlike textile manufacturers) *produce nothing* and thus exploit no one. Using the dismal conditions of his heroine to foreground the necessary conditions of production, Buntline's story upholds the daguerreotype industry's story about itself: artists such as Holgrave and Lerow merely capture a reality that already exists. But if portraits for the daguerreotypist (and for those who wrote advertising text for them) are as true as the sunlight itself, for Hawthorne they are all "delusions." His preface, by confessing the romancer's willingness to "manage his atmospherical medium" to produce the desired effect, essentially recasts the logic of Buntline's story as a showman's trick in order to elevate himself above the fictions of antebellum life.

Seeing the self-conscious rhetoric of romantic storytelling as an assertion of romantic agency allows us to read the ending of the novel as something other than an artistic or philosophical failure. When Holgrave reveals himself as a Maule, when he and Phoebe announce their intentions to marry, when the reader feels the jarring pull of the suspiciously neat, even sentimental closure, we feel also Hawthorne's authority as the ultimate author of the daguerreotypist's fate.[34] And we feel also that this "story" does not contain the most significant of Hawthorne's meanings. Rather, we experience the plot as the means by which the storyteller gives his audience what it demands, and we see the novel itself as the commodified text that locates its author somewhere outside the contingencies of the marketplace. If *The Story Teller* relied on the figure of Oberon to claim for Hawthorne a romantic ideal of authorship, in *Seven Gables* Hawthorne no longer needs the intermediary figure of the fictive storyteller; instead, the romance's portrayal of American society as an endless spectacle continuously claims for the romancer an ontological integrity unavailable to those who live amid its fictions. Having arrived at the end of the final chapter, then, we are like the reader of "Main Street" when the audience demands their money back: there is no more story to tell and so there is no more text. To want a better ending, we might say, is to be one of the mob.[35]

Seeking to contain and master an entire marketplace of representational practices, and treating such mastery as an assertion of human agency, Hawthorne equates romantic integrity with a particular way of seeing (through) American culture. Understandably, much recent scholarship has tended to read Hawthorne's preoccupation with the artifice and spectacle of American life as evidence of his ambitions as a social reformer.[36] Without debating Hawthorne's intentions, I would suggest that the way his fiction exposes and exploits the textual surfaces of mass culture was a method of protecting the integrity of individual consciousness from the delusions of mass subjectivity. One could make the argument that this is itself a social critique, a way of offering the reader a critical distance from the institutions and practices of American culture, just as we can see the authorial performances embedded in Hawthorne's fiction as self-consciously performative, relinquishing instead of embracing the quest for a self beyond the public gaze.[37] But to deny the romantic dimensions of Hawthorne's obsession with cultural surfaces is to make the shared logic of new historicism and romance a new kind of neutral territory, a foundational perspective that simply "sees through" the constructs of American life. For even as his fiction seems to echo back the ideals of late twentieth-century literary and cultural theory, it is perhaps more valuable for the way it suggests that seeing through the artifice of culture is also a means of inventing and defending a particular kind of self.

CHAPTER 4

"IN THIS WORLD OF LIES"

ZACHARY TAYLOR AND THE AMERICAN
TELEGRAPH IN MELVILLE'S NEW YORK

The Mexican War (tho' our troops have behaved right well) is nothing of itself.
—Herman Melville, in an 1846 letter to his brother, Gansevoort

HROUGHOUT the summer of 1847, a series of sketches titled "Authentic Anecdotes of Old Zack" appeared in the New York humor magazine *Yankee Doodle*. The object of their satire was General Zachary Taylor—or, more accurately, the New York editors responsible for mythologizing Taylor into "Old Rough and Ready" in the hopes of turning the hero of the ongoing U.S.-Mexican War into a viable Whig candidate in the 1848 presidential election. But the broader target of the "Authentic Anecdotes" was the ideal of authenticity being peddled by New York papers in their daily coverage of a war taking place more than two thousand miles away. As American readers were devouring the latest news from the front lines with the sort of jingoistic vigor captured in Richard Caton Woodville's famous painting "War News from Mexico," *Yankee Doodle* regularly satirized the unstable ideals of truth-telling that (the magazine argued) linked New York journalism with other aspects of New York culture: P. T. Barnum's American Museum, for example, or the Chinese junk that spent much of the summer of 1847 docked in the harbor (where, for a small fee, locals could tour the boat and visit the genuine Chinese sailors on board). Just as Barnum was regularly ridiculed in the magazine for exhibiting an apparently endless array of "authentic" curiosities—including the wooden leg of the Mexican general Antonio López de Santa Anna and a wax representation of the slaves involved in the Amistad revolt—local editors were lampooned for manufacturing stories about Taylor.

Most of this chapter will investigate the particular ideal of journalistic authenticity in circulation in New York during the war. My goal in doing so is to understand the cultural significance of the "Old Zack" pieces not just as political critique or social parody but as an authorial self-invention that relied on the contemporaneous myth of authentic information as a vehicle of mass American identity-making. As many scholars of nineteenth-century America know, the author of the "Authentic Anecdotes" was none other than Herman Melville, who moved between New York City and his family's home north of Albany during the years of the war.[1] At a time when American journalism was churning out broad and consequential myths about American expansion, Mexican inferiority, and racial heterogeneity as a threat to national cohesiveness, all under the aegis of a technology-based claim to infallible and instantaneous communication, Melville's parodic sketches exposed journalism as a carefully manufactured product that empowered such mythmaking. When we consider the status of journalistic authenticity during these years as both a commodity of a blatantly profit-minded information culture and a marker of American national identity, the "Old Zack" sketches offer a rich opportunity for understanding Melville's conception of reality, and the metaphysical ideals engendered by such a conception, as the by-product of a burgeoning mass culture.

As I reveal below, the emergent technology of electromagnetic telegraphy conspired with a thriving penny press industry to naturalize the invention of America during the war with Mexico as a racially pure nation that was at once perfectly united and constantly expanding. At the same time, this journalistic culture afforded authors such as Melville (and his colleagues at *Yankee Doodle*) an equally powerful method for inventing themselves. By recasting the delirium and sensation of the Mexican War as "nothing of itself," Melville attempted to locate himself somewhere outside the mass production of a nation at war. And while the "Old Zack" anecdotes themselves are of minor literary and political interest, they share with much of Melville's better-known work a preoccupation with the cultural practice of authentication. As countless critics have noted about works such as *Typee, Moby-Dick,* "Benito Cereno," and *The Confidence-Man,* Melville's narrative strategies oppose, almost to the point of obsession, his reader's appetite for totalizing, verifiable kinds of information. Tommo's narrative quest to interpret Typee culture, Captain Amasa Delano's insistent need to explain the confounding scene aboard the *San Dominick,* Ishmael's aborted attempts at interpreting Queequeg's mystifying rituals, the nameless narrator's unsuccessful attempts at penetrating Bartleby's maddening inscrutability—these and other examples suggest how often Melville dramatized and problematized the interpretive processes by which American eyes and minds attempted to make stories out of alien characters and foreign cultures.

By situating the "Authentic Anecdotes" in a complex and dynamic journalistic culture in which the communal logic of authenticity was a powerful marker of national and racial identity-making, I begin my discussion of Melville's career with a sustained analysis of the kind of textual consumption he so often seems to be writing against. Ultimately, I hope to reveal that Melville's fundamental assumption that the great artist always lives in a "world of lies"—what Edgar Dryden describes as his "vision of life as an empty masquerade"—was shaped by the information technologies and representational practices in circulation during these years in ways that can easily be overlooked.[2] While the majority of this chapter will address the political, racial, and social dynamics of telegraphic journalism from 1846 to 1847 in New York City, its final section (and the chapters that follow) will turn from journalistic authenticity as a signifier of nation-making on a mass scale to the deconstruction of authenticity as a constitutive element of Melvillean romanticism. In a sense, Melville gradually came to universalize what was an historically specific view of antebellum cultural life: while the "Old Zack" sketches, like *Typee*, attack the political and economic nature of information culture in a particular cultural setting, in many of the major works of the 1850s—*Moby-Dick, Pierre*, "Benito Cereno," and *The Confidence-Man*—the belief that the true artist lived amid a "world of lies" functioned as a defining assumption of Melvillean metaphysics.

O N June 4, 1846, the front page of James Gordon Bennett's *New York Herald* was dominated by a map depicting the "recent movements and present position of the American forces on the Rio Grande" (see figure 2). As war with Mexico appeared increasingly likely in the early months of 1846, the latest news about the impending conflict began replacing advertisements on the front pages of New York papers: by the ninth of May, when the *Herald* announced "War at Last!" readers had already come to expect front-page headlines informing them of the most recent developments in Mexico. Daily reports carrying "authentic particulars" from Mexico kept city readers updated on the day-to-day events of a conflict taking place thousands of miles away. By the fifteenth of May, the *Herald* was running front-page maps affording readers a geographic context for the stories that they were devouring daily. Thus the June 4 map claiming to chart the most recent troop movements was, in many ways,

FIGURE 2. FRONT PAGE OF THE NEW YORK HERALD, JUNE 4, 1846. (COURTESY AMERICAN ANTIQUARIAN SOCIETY)

typical of the New York press's eagerness to bring before readers information that was timely and authentic in a form that was attention-grabbing
and easily digestible.

But if papers such as Bennett's regularly boasted that their news had
taken "only thirteen days" to travel from Mexico to their newspaper
offices, how could a map promise to delineate the "present" situation of
soldiers who were fighting at a historical distance of nearly two weeks?
And why would the New York reader buy into the *Herald*'s claim of a
journalistic authenticity marked not only by factual accuracy but by the
promise of a simultaneity that was physically impossible? Certainly, New
York newspaper readers were eager to imagine themselves as experienc-
ing the events in Mexico in real time—a demand that editors stoked with
the use of present-progressive headlines such as "Santa Anna Advancing on Saltillo!" This popular conceptualization of what has much more
recently been called a "media event," however, simply did not exist only
a few years before the outbreak of the war with Mexico.[3] Only after the
emergence of Samuel Morse's electromagnetic telegraph in the early
1840s did newspaper readers have to grapple with "a new class of ideas,
a new species of consciousness."[4] With the instantaneous, disembodied,
and scientifically objective technology of telegraphy, readers suddenly
were able to imagine themselves as living within a present moment being
shared by people as far away as Texas.[5]

In a compelling confluence of political and technological circumstances, the early rumblings of the Mexican War coincided precisely with
the first significant expansion and use of the telegraph.[6] While a February 14, 1846, article in the *Herald* about the new technology saw in the
telegraph a *promise* of the imminent "annihilation of time and space" (a
popular phrase for describing the almost indescribable implications of
Morse's invention), by April of the same year news from Mexico already
began appearing beneath an illustration of telegraph poles carrying wires
into the distance, as if the reader were being linked with the world at the
other end of the wire (see figure 3). And on May 7, only hours before
New York would learn that war had finally broken out, the first headlines
appeared in the paper beneath the heading, "By the Magnetic Telegraph."
The telegraph had secured its journalistic place at the very moment the
city learned that the United States was at war.

Morse's telegraph afforded an ideal means of self-definition for a
country that imagined itself as both expanding (the Mexican War, after
all, was about America's right to foreign territory) and perfectly connected. As newspaper correspondents reported on the latest battles and
troop movements, editors kept their readers updated on the latest cities to

HIGHLY IMPORTANT
FROM
TEXAS AND MEXICO.

MANIFESTO OF PAREDES.

THE CRISIS IN AFFAIRS.

Advance of the American Army.

THE AMERICAN AND MEXICAN TROOPS ON THE EVE OF A BATTLE.

The Return of the Hon. John Slidell.

THE WAR FEELING IN MEXICO.

The Destruction of Point Isabel by the Mexicans and their Retreat before General Taylor.

The advices which reached us yesterday afternoon from Texas and Mexico, are of the highest importance.

The intelligence received is of the return of the Hon. Mr. Slidell to the United States—the advance

FIGURE 3. TELEGRAPH IMAGE, THE *NEW YORK HERALD*, APRIL 17, 1846, PAGE 2. (COURTESY AMERICAN ANTIQUARIAN SOCIETY)

be linked with telegraph wires—so that the telegraph's expansion echoed the nation's. Furthermore, the telegraph as a symbol of national cohesion allowed American commentators to oppose America's "unity" and "patriotism" with the disunity and racial heterogeneity of the Mexicans. An 1845 piece in the *United States Magazine and Democratic Review*, in arguing for the annexation of large portions of Mexico, sought to define annexation as the "natural" result of the lack of Mexican nationalism: "California will, probably, next fall away from the loose adhesion which, in such a country as Mexico, holds a remote province in a slight equivocal kind of dependence on the metropolis."

In America, however, technologies such as the railroad and telegraph promised to keep the new (i.e., potential) western states linked with its own metropolitan capital: "These considerations give assurance that the day cannot be distant which shall witness the conveyance of the representatives from Oregon and California to Washington within less time than a few years ago was devoted to a similar journey by those from Ohio; while the magnetic telegraph will enable the editors of the 'San Francisco Union,' the 'Astoria Evening Post,' or the 'Nootka Morning News' to set up in type the first half of the President's Inaugural, before the echoes of the latter half shall have died away beneath the lofty porch of the Capitol, as spoken from his lips."[7] In 1847, after war had already broken out, the magazine advanced its project of nation-building by describing the difference between Mexico and the United States in racial terms. While John L. O'Sullivan's democratic beliefs saw American power as emanating from its people, so, too, did he place the blame for Mexican disunity with a populace of "5,000,000 ignorant and indolent half-civilized Indians [and] 1,500,000 free negroes and mulattoes" who have "not interested themselves in the matter" of national affairs. As the magazine continued to define the "American people" as both unified and enlightened, the 1847 piece ultimately concluded, "The political state of Mexico is so far dissolved, that it has no head which can represent or bind it."[8]

As easy as it might be to interpret the telegraph as a means of imagining the "binding" of the country into one unified body, telegraph wires covered only a tiny portion of the distance that separated New York from the Mexican frontlines. By February of 1846, for example, telegraph lines had been completed between Washington and Baltimore, and between Philadelphia and Newark, New Jersey. In other words, while the telegraph promised to bind the country with its "infallible" wires, in the mid-1840s the technology itself was still most meaningful as a promise, as a symbol of national connectedness, unity, and expansion. New York newspaper editors relied on its prominence in the national imagination (which spiked soon after Morse exhibited his invention publicly in 1844) to peddle an authenticity founded upon the telegraph's combination of scientific authority and a supernatural-seeming reliability and speed. The telegraph promised to make communication perfect and instantaneous; the fact that the Mexican War news printed in New York had traveled by steamboat to New Orleans, then by railroad to Washington (and again from Baltimore, at least until the line was completed between the capital and New York) was far less salable than the idea of a pure, unmediated link to the war itself.

Indeed, in a fascinating example of New York papers tempting their readers to imagine such a link, a large front-page sketch depicting a "view of the celebrated castle of San Juan D'Ulloa" included not only a light-house, tower, and citadel but also *telegraph wires*—as if the *Herald*'s own telegraphic icon cited above (in which the foregrounded wires place the soon-to-be-outdated communicative modes of horseback and the railroad in the background) promised an unbroken connection from New York to Mexico. And by June 15, 1847, Bennett had replaced the telegraphic image cited above with one that was even more explicit about the increasing irrelevance of horses and steamships (see figure 4). As a short piece on page 3 described the new image, "The idea is that the lightning line has superceded every means of conveying news from point to point; and our artist has, therefore, strewn the road under the wires with broken locomotives, the bones of horses, &c., &c., &c. Steam and horse cannot go ahead of lightning." In reality, of course, the latest news from Mexico would continue to travel via both of these modes of conveyance, for the duration of the war and beyond.

In a sense, the telegraph allowed commentators and readers to imagine the nation as an ongoing narrative that could be written into the future and across the continent.[9] Only weeks after Taylor's victory at Buena Vista, as dreams of American expansion were growing even more feverish, the *Herald* reported that the Polk administration was contemplating "the establishment of a line of communication over the Mexican territory."[10] The newspaper, which published a map delineating the various areas included in the plan, reported that Polk sought to make the entire stretch between Washington and the Pacific coast navigable by boats, with railroads making up the difference. Within weeks of this report, Amos Kendall, then the president of the Magnetic Telegraph Company, sent a petition to the Senate requesting that commissions be appointed to designate the place that telegraph wires would cross the Hudson River. Reminding the Senate of the importance of the telegraph to the nation's destiny, the petition read, "the line of telegraph from Washington to the shore of the North

TO THE
LATEST MOMENT.

TELEGRAPHIC

HIGHLY INTERESTING INTELLIGENCE

FROM THE

SEAT OF WAR.

Advance of General Scott upon the City of Mexico.

THE RESIGNATION OF SANTA ANNA.

NEWS FROM GEN. TAYLOR.

The Exciting Rumors from Puebla.

Arrival of part of Colonel Doniphan's Regiment at Saltillo.

&c. &c. &c.

The New Orleans *Picayune* Extra, issued at noon on the 7th inst., announces the arrival of the steamship New Orleans, from Vera Cruz, whence she sailed 1st inst. She touched at Brazos on the 4th.

Gen. Scott had left Jalapa at the head of six thousand troops. Gen. Twiggs and his division entered Puebla on the 29th.

It was not positively known, but supposed, that Gen. Scott would advance on the capital with his present force.

Authentic news has been received that Santa Anna had resigned the Presidency on the 28th, but it was not known whether Congress had accepted the resignation or not. He took the step, in consequence of opposition to his views of the defense of the capital.

FIGURE 4. TELEGRAPH IMAGE, THE *NEW YORK HERALD,* JUNE 15, 1847, PAGE 3.
(COURTESY AMERICAN ANTIQUARIAN SOCIETY)

River, opposite New York, is destined to be the main line from which branches will diverge to the South and West along the Atlantic coast, and through the valley of the Mississippi; extending ultimately to the city of Mexico!"[11]

In fact, even before the onset of the war, those who argued for the importance of the telegraph regularly invoked nationalistic themes in theorizing about the future significance of the technology. And yet it often seems that its greatest significance was the authority it afforded these writers for their own stories about American superiority. In one of the more remarkable examples of national imagining, an 1844 piece in the *Albany Argus* appeared under the heading, "The Magnetic Telegraph—Its Contemplated Extension—Its National Importance."[12] Like the headline itself, in which dashes seem to stand in for telegraph wires, the article finds in the symbolism of telegraphy a narrative logic that quietly writes America's future. The writer of the piece begins by praising the contemplated extension of the telegraph from New York to Boston as "a stride in the march of intelligence of no ordinary importance" (3). But it soon becomes obvious that the telegraph promises something far more valuable to the national imagination than mere intelligence:

> It is one of those triumphs of the arts of Peace that knit our people in closer relations of union and brotherhood. The Magnetic Telegraph annihilates distance. So complete is this annihilation that the newspapers at Baltimore have made arrangements to report the proceedings of congress by Telegraph, so as to have the intelligence from the capital (40 miles distant) as soon as the Washington papers. A like effect will happen when the line is established between New-York and Boston. . . . Will not the Telegraph literally render our people one family?—for when it is fully extended throughout the Union, our brethren in Louisiana will receive intelligence from their brethen in New-York and Maine, almost as quick as if they were seated around the same board—within the sound of each other's voices. Perhaps it is not figurative to say that hundreds of miles will seem no more than previously as many hundred feet. (3)

The writer's repeated claims that the telegraph is far more than a symbol (it will "literally" render the country into a family; it is "perhaps . . . not figurative" to imagine distance as redefined) suggest the complexity of the technology's status in the months following Morse's successful installation: no longer just a promise, the telegraph was now an accomplishment—but one that was still most meaningful as a symbol (a fact the author of the *Argus* piece clearly recognizes). If the meaning of the telegraph at this moment resided in the fact that people could communicate outside of the physical transportation of bodies, once this occurred the country could reimagine the body as national symbol: either the country could exist as a population of virtual bodies around a virtual table, as in the above excerpt, or, once the country unified itself in the face of war with Mexico, as one body taking on a disunited enemy—one with "no head that can represent or bind it."[13]

The same article from the *Albany Argus* illustrates the importance of the telegraph as a symbol of imagined national cohesion to what O'Sullivan would soon label "manifest destiny." In following the logic of the article, one senses that the expansionist paradigm of the 1840s required (or at least utilized) the promise of telegraphic connectedness in order to conceive of a country that was both expanding and unified. While we have already seen how the *Argus* writer moves from the question of sharing intelligence to the production of a nation of conferencing bodies, what is perhaps even more noteworthy is how the piece concludes. In imagining the telegraph's capacity to render the nation as one unified subject, the writer merges the expansion of America's borders with the completion of the national body, as if the America of 1844 were an infant needing to grow into a complete version of itself: "It is impossible to enter into a tithe of the results which will flow from the adoption of this wonderful agent. Good must come of it, that is certain. While the Patriot and the American who looks forward to the time when our great confederacy shall stretch over the Mississippi and Oregon Territories, embracing perhaps sixty states, some of which are separated by thousands of miles, will regard this new and mighty agency in interchanging thoughts, sentiments and feelings, as one of the indissoluble links of firm and enduring union, and of making us all feel we are still one nation—with one language—one Capitol—and more than all, with one heart" (3).

The long final sentence, itself seeking to embrace the totality of the writer's vision, quietly naturalizes the progression from the conception of America as a "confederacy" of individual states exchanging thoughts and feelings between them to the closing image of the nation as a body sharing one heart. Another article from the *Argus*, published three months earlier, claimed that the telegraph "seems destined to draw the states of our Union, in links so close, that the twenty-six states will seem as one state."[14] In a sense, the telegraph as a means of unification, as a symbol by which the American imagination could not only connect distant regions from one another but also envision a particular future that was somehow a natural outgrowth of the present, functioned in the 1840s much like the free verse of Whitman's *Leaves of Grass* would a decade later: as a means of rhetorically connecting the totality of America into a unified vision. Whitman's "I" provided a body for the poet's naturalizing of America into the symbol of a "form, union, plan"—as if the poet's capacity to find a "form" to contain the nation were itself proof of the nation's destiny. In the 1840s the telegraph afforded the popular imagination its own means of embodying the nation, an act of nation-forming that authenticated the highly politicized sense of a national "destiny."

Because the electromagnetic telegraph could be understood in the objective terms of science, American commentators attributed to Morse's invention an authority that was not only objective but infallible. Thus the telegraph effaced the human presence on which telegraphic communication relied, even as the country used the technology to imagine the nation as sharing a single virtual body. A fascinating piece from the *Baltimore Patriot* that appeared late in 1844 reported on a game of checkers played between telegraph operators. Here is how the writer of the article described what occurred following an error by one of the participants: "At one point of the game, Willis forgot to place his man upon the number mentioned, which created a little confusion. The mistake, however, was promptly corrected by the telegraph. It said, 'you have neglected to place your man where you have mentioned. He is now on No. 27 of the board.' This was the fact, and not only exhibited the accuracy of the telegraph, but instantly called to memory the mistake. . . . Thus it will be seen that . . . not a single mistake occurred on account of the telegraph."[15] The newspaper account chooses this moment of human error not only to highlight the infallibility of the telegraph but also to imply its ability to correct human fallibility. It is, inexplicably, "the telegraph" that reports the error and corrects the problem. The meaning of the telegraph in the story is its inhuman reliability, but it is a meaning that allows the writer to move far beyond the technology's actual role as a means of communication between human operators.

It is a small step, then, from the above account of the telegraph correcting human error to the following vision of the telegraph as the corrective to human fallibility and corruption:

> The most important and thoroughly revolutionary result of the telegraph will be upon the daily press. This will inevitably lose its character as the rapid and indispensable carrier of commercial, political, and other intelligence. For this purpose the newspapers will become emphatically useless. Anticipated at every point by the lightning wings of the Telegraph, they can only deal in local "items" or abstract speculations. Their power to create sensations, even in election campaigns, will be greatly lessened—as

the infallible Telegraph will contradict their falsehoods as fast as they can publish them . . . and in short lay bare the actual state of the field *at* every point *to* every point at once; so that fraud and deception will be next to impossible and altogether useless.[16]

Here the "infallible Telegraph" is imagined as the antidote to the political and economic manipulations of newspaper editors. Imagining a nation in which "newspapers will become emphatically useless," the writer of this piece elides the human presence on which telegraphic communication relied in order to prop up a vision of America wherein people are connected (without newspapers!) to authentic news, and thus to one another.[17] The problems posed by the reality of actual human bodies—fraud, political maneuvering, financial speculation—are quietly replaced by a vision of a country in which internal difference no longer exists.

As this unifying logic of the telegraph allowed commentators to contrast American cohesiveness with the disunity of Mexico, another conversation was also taking place, one that used Morse's invention to verbalize America's autonomy from European influence. In a series of articles published in 1847, under the title "The American Electric Telegraph," the *New York Observer* (whose editor was Morse's brother, Sidney) clarified the difference between the British and American telegraph, even attacking one British author for implying that Morse's invention was "adopted" from the British version.[18] Similarly, in a pamphlet that included the reports on Morse's telegraph submitted to Congress, Alfred Vail claimed that "for priority as well as originality, America has the preeminence, not only at the time of invention, but up to the present period; nothing having yet been brought forward that fulfills so completely the conditions of what is satisfied by the term telegraph, as that plan invented by Professor Morse."[19] While asserting the superiority of Morse's invention, the writer simultaneously asserts the preeminence of America. And even more subtly, Morse's telegraph (as opposed to the British version) allows the writer to imagine "America" as signifier that is distinct from Europe.

The repeated attempts at defining the "American telegraph" against European versions of the technology obviously reflected the larger national project (typified by the Young America agenda of O'Sullivan's *Democratic Review*) of locating an Americanness that was separate from British influence.[20] Not surprisingly, the rhetorical use of the telegraph to carry out such a project was deeply connected to the country's geographical imagination and to the imperialistic paradigm that fueled this way of thinking. When James Polk took office in 1845, the United States was engaged in a bitter dispute with England over the Oregon Territories.

Thus the piece from the *Albany Argus*, in which the writer "looks forward to the time when our great confederacy shall stretch over the Mississippi and Oregon Territories," invokes the telegraph as a means of authenticating America's natural right to the disputed territory. An 1844 article that appeared in the *Baltimore American* only days after Morse successfully exhibited his invention argued that "the day of iron bars must now yield to that of copper wires."[21] More specifically, the writer highlighted the importance of the invention to the goals of American expansion: "What difficulty does extent of territory present to permanency of government, but the delay and inconvenience of transmitting intelligence from one portion of it to another . . . ? Suppose the line of wires to extend to Oregon, and that a squadron lay off the mouth of the Columbia which it was desired to order home, or to send to Honolulu." Invoking the example of Oregon allows the writer not only to justify America's claim to a disputed land (as if the telegraph proves the country's capacity to properly govern the distant territory); it also places Oregon within a larger narrative of American expansion, in which we move westward from Oregon to the Sandwich Islands. Ultimately, the story of expansion is one without an apparent ending: "Instances might be multiplied without end of the availability of the Magnetic Telegraph of Professor Morse." The promise of telegraphy, it seems, is as open-ended as the promise of manifest destiny.

Before the end of 1846, after the war with Mexico had begun, Polk's administration resolved its dispute with England, and much of the Oregon Territories officially became American land. But even before the "Oregon Crisis" was officially resolved, American writers and editors had already turned to Mexico as the object of choice for their attempt at national storytelling. As I have already suggested, many popular invocations of Mexico in American papers portrayed the country as a diverse population of racially ambiguous people that failed to live up to the criteria of nationhood. This failure of Mexico as a national concept provided a counterpoint for the American body politic, which was authenticated in part by a telegraphic metaphor that guaranteed its own unity and connectedness. At the same time that American commentators questioned the viability of Mexico as a nation, the coverage of the war defined the conflict in explicitly racialized terms. For example, cartoons appeared in New York papers depicting the "typical Mexican soldier," with conspicuously dark skin, and often betraying a "characteristic" Mexican idleness. As Shelley Streeby argues, depictions of the war by writers such as George Lippard sought to "identify 'America' with a particular racially defined community in order to justify U.S. empire-building."[22]

The parallels between this ongoing act of national imagining and the technology-based ideal of informational authenticity in circulation at the time suggests that the concept of authenticity played a singular and vital role in the process of national identity-making. As New York editors published authentic dispatches (both American and Mexican) from the front lines, they formulated a story about America in which the country was defined by an honest and straightforward linguistic style, while Mexico was repeatedly defined by the characteristic equivocating and deception of its generals. Even more significantly, the juxtaposition of these "characteristic" idioms occurred as a New York newspaper culture was itself peddling an emergent journalistic ideal of linguistic efficiency and telegraphic objectivity. In fact, at the moment when technological and economic circumstances were shaping a new kind of journalistic idiom in New York and elsewhere, American journalists were using the very markers of this new idiom to carry out a project of popular hagiography that exemplifies the era's merging of jingoism and information: the production of Zachary Taylor as an authentic American hero. As American journalism was rapidly becoming defined by the terse, no-nonsense language of telegraphic dispatches, the "Zachary Taylor" that was circulating in New York papers portrayed such a linguistic ideal as quintessentially American.

From 1846 to 1848, New York editors regularly published anecdotes about the general in which he was portrayed as a straight-talking, clear-thinking folk hero.[23] One typical story that appeared in the *Herald* on July 10, 1846, depicts a "gentleman soldier" who complains to Taylor about the poor sleeping conditions. After telling the soldier he will switch sleeping arrangements for the night, the general tells him to lie down anywhere (as Taylor himself presumably does). The gentleman soldier replies, "no wonder they call you 'Rough and Ready.'" Far more compelling than such anecdotes is the way in which papers argued back and forth with one another about the authenticity of these accounts. While it was extremely common for papers to debate the accuracy of rumors regarding the latest news from Mexico (in March of 1847, for example, several New York papers sought to defuse rumors of Taylor's death), it was almost as common for these same papers to debate the accuracy of particular quotations attributed to Taylor. Addressing a well-known story in which the general is said to have responded to a question about military strategy, on the eve of a major battle, with the request, "A little more grape, Captain Bragg," the *Herald* uses the rejection of this story's authenticity to assert an even more heroic (and hyperauthentic) version of Taylor:

We were informed a day or two since, by a gentleman, who knows, that the Old General never made use of the expression at the head of this article, nor any of those which have been laid at his door. He is represented as remarkably plain and unassuming, and not in the slightest degree disposed to indulge in slang or vulgarity. The only slang that is told of him, which has a mixture of truth in it, is that related of him when he received Gen. Scott's letter taking from him his brave volunteers, who accomplished such wonderfully brilliant achievements under his direction. He really did act as represented on that occasion. He did actually put mustard in his coffee and sugar his meat, when he read it, and it was some minutes before he recovered his wonted composure, which, however, soon followed, and then his brow was clear as ever. "A little more grape, Captain Bragg," is very good, but not very true.[24]

Of course, such statements sought to establish a paper's authority as the arbiter of fact by correcting or rejecting competing accounts of the general's bravery and wit. If the *Herald,* for example, could correct a false rumor published by a competing paper, they could establish the authority of their own sources over those of rival papers. But these pieces also implied a parallel between the journalistic ideal of unadorned fact and Taylor's own status as the characteristic American, one who was marked by his "plain and unassuming" style. Each paper's desire to deflate overly romanticized accounts of Taylor provided a rhetorical means of asserting *their own* commitment to a reliable, unadorned mode of communication.

As the *New York Atlas* wrote in presenting another Taylor anecdote, "Truth is truth, and should be told. The old man does now and then use a hard word, contrary to scripture license."[25] So while editors never claimed that their Taylor anecdotes were received by telegraph, these stories shared with telegraphic discourse a privileging of unadorned language and an almost obsessive focus on authenticity. In fact, this preoccupation with the "genuine" Taylor shaped a discourse in which authenticity was defined almost entirely against the conception of journalistic writing as an economic production. Thus the *Atlas* could ascribe the circulation of inauthentic Taylor anecdotes to the financial motives of New York editors, even as the paper regularly published stories about "Old Rough and Ready." For example, the July 18, 1847, issue of the *Atlas* contained both a front-page account of Taylor worried about an American soldier whom he considered too good-looking for the war (given the proclivities of Mexican women) and the following attack on rival New York papers: "All sorts of people are writing all sorts of paragraphs, stating that General Taylor is doing all sorts of things. Old Zack does nothing that is not sensible. Therefore, when you see a paragraph ascribing to him any foolish act or expression, rest assured that it is a weak invention of a penny-a-liner—a Washington correspondent—who, unable to arrive at facts, indulges in fancies, in order to be amusing."[26] Rejecting the "inventions" of these writers, the *Atlas* attributes the manufacturing of Taylor anecdotes to the economic motives of journalists who reside not in Mexico but in Washington—nearly two thousand miles from the seat of war. And yet the appearance of this attack in the same issue that ran one of these anecdotes suggests the rhetorical act of exposing invented stories was itself a means of authentication; the *Atlas* here attacks artifice as a strategy for propping up its own stories as authentic. The "real" Taylor, defined by his own lack of rhetorical flourish or polish, exists somewhere outside of the "fancies" of market-driven penny-a-liners. Reality, then, is the opposite of rhetoric, artifice, hype.

Another article that appeared in the same July 18 issue of the *Atlas* corroborates such an understanding of the problem of reality amid the commingling of information and entertainment in 1840s New York. Sometime earlier in the summer of 1847, a Chinese junk had appeared in the harbor, becoming something of a minor sensation in the city. For the price of a quarter, visitors could board the boat and gaze at (and even attempt to communicate with) the "authentic Chinese" sailors on board. On July 18, the *Atlas* reported the appearance of the boat, while also suggesting that some believed the notorious Barnum to be involved in what must surely have been a hoax. In the following week's issue, the *Atlas* again addressed the question of the boat's authenticity: "Had the vessel been built here, under the direction of that arch necromancer Barnum, who takes the eyes out of your head without your knowing it, she would have been so advertised that everybody would have gone to see her. Captain Kellet evidently knows nothing of the puff system that Barnum so well understands. It would be an insult to the latter to suppose that he would let anything rest exclusively on its own merits."[27] Referring to Barnum as "necromancer," the *Atlas* implies that the showman achieves the market's equivalent of bringing the dead to life—that is, he creates capital out of things with no intrinsic value.[28] Furthermore, the writer moves from addressing the role of advertising in Barnum's "necromancy" to the conclusion that the junk must be authentic, precisely because it has not been widely advertised and has not been as well attended as it could have been. The writer's definition of authenticity thus reaffirms the previous issue's sense of "reality" as the realm that lies beyond the market's corruption of writing and beyond the criteria of the marketplace. If newspaper "puffing" produces fraudulent truths as a mode of drumming up business, then genuine truth must exist beyond the taint of such manipulations. Finally, and paradoxically, it is the lack of any apparent rhetorical flourish that serves as the marker of reality.

This was certainly the case in the ongoing journalistic attention to Taylor's letters and dispatches, which were often cited for their honest and straightforward style. A famous letter written to Henry Clay on the death of Clay's son, for example, was described by the *Atlas* as "a record of his kindliness of heart, that clothes him with a new grace, and renders him as a man . . . worthy our respect and love."[29] While the letter serves to humanize the general in the popular imagination, his dispatches allowed papers to theorize about the capacity of written language to convey the realities of war. "Glorious are Taylor's despatches," wrote the *Atlas*. "No vain glory characterizes them."[30] Most other commentators agreed with this sense of Taylor's writing as the perfect embodiment of a characteristic style that somehow epitomized the lack of subjective, emotional, or political agenda. In other words, Taylor's own style looked a lot like the emerging ideal of American journalism, one shaped by the telegraph's promise of objective, impersonal communication.

As in the debates over the Taylor anecdotes, the circulation of the general's official dispatches led to an ongoing argument about their authenticity. Given the desire of most New York editors to establish Taylor as a Whig, it is not difficult to comprehend the political nature of the papers' interest in authenticating their own version of the general. From the earliest days of the war, newspapers around the country obsessively sought evidence of the general's political leanings. In July of 1847, for example, the *Tribune* attacked a letter supposedly written from Taylor to the *Cincinnati Signal,* in which the general held off on answering questions about his politics until after the war. Addressing the letter, the *Tribune* writes, "There is nothing like Gen. Taylor in this silly letter. The whole world will pronounce it a counterfeit at once; because the whole world knows the style of the hero of Buena Vista."[31] Not content to merely attack the letter as a fraud, the paper compares the counterfeit with another "genuine letter from the old thunderer from the N. O. *Bulletin.*" Unsurprisingly, the *Tribune* finds that the letter "breathes the genuine sentiments of an out-and-out Whig writing to a brother Whig." In conclusion, the paper asks, "Is there anything in it like the twaddle of the 'Signal' forgery? Nothing." Such attacks remind us that the question of authenticity was a commodity not only for selling papers but also for advancing the partisan objectives of these papers.

Another *Tribune* article from July of 1847, reprinted from the *Hagerstown (Md.) Torchlight,* took up the question of whether Taylor actually wrote his own dispatches. In seeking to settle the debate, the writer of the article articulates what many commentators considered the unmistakable style of Taylor's writing: "In conversation with Gen. Gibson, of the U.S. Army . . . our friend asked the question if Major Bliss did not write the dispatches. This old General's eye sparkled with indignation, and he replied that he had served with Gen. Taylor upon 13 court martials, and that he (Gen. Taylor) had been selected by each court to draw up its report, because of his superior ability in composition—that all were willing to accede to him the faculty of expressing in the clearest, strongest, and most forcible manner, the views of the Court, and hence he was uniformly selected for this purpose."[32] The "indignation" of General Gibson's response suggests the national importance of Taylor's dispatches, not for the glimpse they provided into the war itself but for the way in which the general's characteristic style conveyed an equally characteristic national identity. Indeed, this same piece reveals that Taylor's dispatches have become so crucial to the construction of American identity that their "fame has spread over Europe and our country." Finally, the article's mythologizing of Taylor's writing turns to the actual sheets of paper on which the general handwrites his dispatches: "Instead of leaving, as is customary, a margin at the top and side of the sheet," the reader is told, "General Taylor commences at the extreme limit and fills the sheet so completely, that, as our informant observed, it is impossible to crowd in, anywhere, even a little i."

The clear, strong, and forcible manner of Taylor's writing was often presented as a contrast to the equivocating writing of the enemy. Following the news of Taylor's victory at Buena Vista in March of 1847, the *Tribune* published the Mexican general Antonio López de Santa Anna's official account of the battle, which was reprinted from a Mexican newspaper, along with a commentary taken from the *Washington Union*. In a lengthy preface to the actual excerpted text, the *Union* prepared its reader to see in Santa Anna's dispatch both proof that the news of Taylor's victory was accurate and evidence of the Mexican general's unwillingness to give the facts in a straightforward style: "We publish Santa Anna's account of the battle, from which it will be seen that he has suffered a defeat, though he covers up his retreat with a flourish of words." Even more significantly, the prefatory comments use the Mexican general's obfuscations as evidence for a broader story about Mexican inferiority:

As these details are from a Mexican journal we of course have to receive them as such, and give them just so much credence as each individual may suppose them to be worth, making a proper allowance for the known disposition of the people to exaggerate everything, from the noble conflict of two courageous armies to the allurements of the cockpit. When the contents of the said paper were promulgated first, there was such horror commingled with the recital that one would have supposed that Alexander the Great was again at the head of the Macedonians, carrying triumph and devastation wherever his army appeared, and there was such an air of grandeur thrown around the stratagems of the dignified and conquering Mexican chieftain, that we were carried back to the days of Roman warriors.[33]

The "commingling" of drama with fact in Santa Anna's account, the "air of grandeur" in which the actual details of the battle are presented, is interpreted here as a testimony of the "known disposition" of the Mexican people. As the *Union* editors pull the facts out of the Mexican account, thereby authenticating their own account of Buena Vista, they continue to contrast Santa Anna's unreliability with the fact-based, objective-sounding style that was coming to define American journalism: "The enemy, outnumbering our army about four to one . . . is reduced to inventing subterfuges to account for an unpardonable want of success, amounting, in a word, to defeat. This is humiliating indeed."

When the *Union* finally gets around to publishing the actual document, the paper again adopts this fact-based style, announcing, "Here is the precise document—let it speak its own shame for the present." Of course, the newspaper's long preface had already sought to speak for the document, thus betraying the profound ideological work of its own journalistic voice. To give facts, to separate information from rhetoric, to assert one's relationship to the details of battle as disinterested and authentic—these were the very markers of the American identity manufactured and peddled by American newspapers during the war. And in the writing style of Zachary Taylor editors found the ideal subject by which the emerging idiom of modern journalism, one that recast "reality" as a story of facts that could be transmitted across continents, could corporealize the nation in the body of white masculinity.[34]

The above account of Taylor's status as exemplary American, of course, should in no way suggest that the country's national identity was in any sense unified or even stable.[35] Rather, the rhetorical use of Taylor by northeastern newspapers reminds us again of the ways in which a critical attention to what Timothy Brennan calls the "national longing for form" in fact destabilizes our sense of the nation as a coherent entity.[36] Indeed, the attempts of papers such as the *Atlas* to correct the public "misapprehension" of Taylor as prone to using slang or vulgar language suggests a northern Whiggish anxiety over the presumptive nominee as a folksy, inurbane character in the tradition of the ultimate Democrat, Andrew Jackson. In a fascinating piece that appeared in the *Atlas* early in the autumn of

1847, the paper attacks the "half-dozen portraits of Gen. Taylor, each of which is certified, by officers of the army, to be an excellent likeness; but every one of which is as much all the others as possible." In this article, the *Atlas* again takes the opportunity to correct the "low" depiction of Taylor as an unpolished rough who was responsible for "the parentage of several expressions of gallant blasphemy." Adopting a conspicuously "gallant" tone of its own, the paper assures its readers that it has spoken with several "gentlemen" who contradicted such assertions.

But even more compellingly, in describing the popular portraits of the general circulating around the country, the paper writes the following: "Go where we will, a large mulatto-colored head, with the eye of a pig, the mouth of a satyr, and bristling hair, stares us in the face. This, forsooth, is an imaginative portrait of Gen. Taylor! . . . It is very evident that not one of the artists have [*sic*] ever seen the general, and it is equally evident to us, that, if they had, they could not take his likeness."[37] It is necessary, to understand this moment, to know that the writer of the piece has already informed his audience that he, too, has never seen the general in person. It would seem, then, that the *Atlas* writer is defining the authentic Taylor merely by rejecting the representations of him that circulate in the public sphere. Furthermore, what is being rejected is in part the racial ambiguity of these portraits. The authentic Taylor embodies a racial "purity"—a whiteness—that is nothing but a rhetorical product. Having never seen the real Taylor, the writer of the piece manufactures a genuine one who is white simply because his portraits suggest otherwise. If the juxtaposition of Taylor's dispatches with those of his enemies implied a project of nation-making marked by racial undertones, this account of Taylor's image goes even further in betraying the instability of the authentic "Taylor" as an embodiment of a racialized national character.

Significantly, Taylor was not the only white male American during this era whose authenticity signified as a marker of national identity. Now long forgotten, Corydon Donnavan was an American newspaperman who was kidnapped in Mexico and sold to a publisher of a Mexican newspaper "to set up villainous Mexican type." Upon Donnavan's escape and return to the United States, he published an account of his adventures and traveled with a panorama depicting Mexican battlegrounds, scenery, botany, and "geographical resources." Donnavan's account refers to the inhabitants of Mexico as "strange and incomprehensible animals," and the panorama is presented as rendering places with "unpronounceable names" in a manner that could be digested easily by the American spectator. In the passages from Donnavan's *Adventures in Mexico* that describe the moment of his being sold, he relies on the vocabularies of American journalistic practice to foreground the savagery of his Mexican captors:

Here was a scene for philosophical reflection. We had often accused our brother editors of being "bought and sold." In the heat of party warfare we had been somewhat lavish in the use of such reproachful and disgusting epithets as "British Whigs" and "Bank-bought federalists." We had stigmatized our own countrymen as being sold into the servile slavery of party; and had reprobated the idea of "*white slavery*" in the most earnest manner. But this was only the most enthusiastic romancing incident to youth, led away by the tyranny of party discipline, in the excitement of heated political contest. We had now come to experience some of the realities of a *purchased editor,* and humiliating as was the "bargain and intrigue" to our native sense of justice, we found ourselves transferred into unlimited bondage.[38]

The concept of partisan American journalism is portrayed by Donnavan as the product of youth, a description that locates party-run newspapers squarely in the past—which is precisely how mid-1840s editors sought to cast politically interested journalism. Donnavan's account goes on to describe the printing office where he was put to work, a setting that "was a perfect museum of curiosities to an American printer" (68), before characterizing the Mexican newspaper where he worked as distinctly un-American: "The Mexicans are by no means a literary people, and they have few newspapers. 'El Republicano' is a super-royal sheet. . . . It is sustained by contributions from individuals and the government, and contains very little intelligence besides official announcements" (69).

Later in his narrative, Donnavan informs his reader that Mexican newspapers "do not contain the same variety, nor are they conducted with the ability of ours." Furthermore, *El Republicano* "is supported chiefly by the high functionaries and large proprietors, and its principal aim seems to be to uphold the existing state of things" (87). Having already defined American newspapers as unpartisan (through the invocation and rejection of the idea of "bought" editors), Donnavan uses the contrast of two journalistic cultures to perpetuate a common myth about the Mexican people as innately antidemocratic. As a correspondent for the *Tribune* wrote in the days leading up to the war, "The character of the Spaniard is most hostile to the principle [of Democracy], and in my opinion, reconciliation is most impracticable."[39] Against the rhetorical ideal of the representative American as racially pure and committed to authentic, uncorrupted information (epitomized by Taylor but clearly reflected in this account of Donnavan), the representative Mexican is defined by both racial heterogeneity and linguistic and narrative duplicity.

From our own twenty-first-century perspective, it is not difficult to see that this national obsession with authentic information in the 1840s was fundamentally connected to the commercializing of news during these years. The slipperiness of information as a category can be seen, for example, in the many warnings against the use of the telegraph for financial speculation (especially in the years leading up to the 1848 founding of the Associated Press). As the *New York Atlas* wrote early in 1847, "If the wires can be kept intact, and free from speculators, the telegraph will prove a valuable annihilator of time and space."[40] Whenever telegraph wires had been cut (a common occurrence), suspicion almost always was laid at the feet of nameless speculators. And yet the papers that ran the latest stories about Taylor, dismissing the "inauthentic" documents or anecdotes of rival papers, had a great deal in common with the speculators who were said to manipulate the distribution of information for their own financial gain.[41] Authenticity, in other words, was a particular way of appealing to the public for their patronage, one that relied upon the rejection of unauthorized modes of information peddling to establish its own authority. In a short 1846 article titled "Fraud on the Press and on the Public," Horace Greeley's *New York Tribune* attacked Bennett's *Herald* for hiring a pilot boat to intercept a mailbag (containing a letter from Polk and a dispatch for the secretary of state) from the *Liberty*, a ship that had recently docked in New York Harbor. "This was a scandalous fraud on the newspaper press and the public," the *Tribune* argued, "and it ought to excite universal indignation."[42] Describing Bennett's maneuver as a "fraud," Greeley's paper invokes the language of inauthenticity—implying that authenticity is a matter not of factual accuracy but of an emerging journalistic protocol. Just as significantly, Bennett's ruthless scheming would seem to contradict his own paper's repeated assault on stockjobbing and other methods of financial speculation, especially those involving the public exchange of information.

Except, of course, that there was no contradiction at all: as long as editors such as Bennett were using information to inform the public, such manipulations were not only acceptable but downright patriotic. In March of 1846, Greeley's *Tribune* published the latest news received via a "Special and Extraordinary Express from Halifax," which they shared with two other New York papers and which the *Tribune* claimed brought European news (from the steamships arriving at Halifax) to New York at least twelve hours earlier than any other method. In justifying their arrangement with the Halifax railroad—a practice that would seem to have been no different than Bennett's employment of a pilot boat—the *Tribune* argued the following: "The necessity of such an express arose from the fact that the LIRR Co. had sold their right of way for express trains for that week to the Herald, and we were compelled either to let that paper receive and hold back the news for speculators, as was their habit, some five or seven hours, (a whole business day in New York) or go to the enormous expense of some $3000 to receive the news by way of Halifax."[43] A few weeks later, in a story on New York as an emerging financial and information center, the *Tribune* pointed to the newspaper press as the source of the city's ability to keep apprised of all the information circulating in Boston. Referring back to the Halifax express, the paper claimed that "on all occasions, when the interests of the City of New-York or of the nation seemed to require it, we have arranged extraordinary Expresses in order to lay before subscribers of the Daily Tribune the earliest possible authentic information." Painting Bennett as a manipulator of information on the side of the speculators, Greeley uses his own commitment to timely and "authentic information" to assert the patriotic nature of his own journalistic practice.

My point is not simply that New York newspaper editors were using a disingenuous promise of authentic information to build their circulation. Rather, I want to highlight the paradox of a nascent information industry founded on the principles of profit-making: while a conversation was taking shape about "information" as both an economic and political commodity, newspaper editors turned to the telegraph as a symbol that allowed them to imagine an informational purity beyond the taint of the marketplace. Indeed, in many of the earliest accounts of the new technology, writers spoke of the telegraph not as a means for two human beings to communicate with one another but as the source of perfectly reliable and objective information—as if "information" existed somewhere, in an uncorrupted form, outside of the political and financial duplicity that marked 1840s journalistic culture. And thus if these commentators claimed for the telegraph an inviolable connection with truth, such a claim merely served to reify the process by which the merging of information and commerce had transformed "reality" according to its own logic. The world at the other end of the telegraph wire already existed as a true story, one that newspapers could readily capture and circulate to the masses.

And so, as we now turn to the work of Melville, an author who repeatedly portrays the production of informational narratives as a method of political and cultural mythmaking, and the appetite for authenticity as both dangerous and misguided, we can consider his own "Art of Telling the Truth" as a by-product of the information-obsessed world in which he lived. At a time when the question of what constituted authentic information was a salient topic of popular debate, even a defining characteristic of mass cultural participation, Melville invoked his culture's superficial practices of authentication as the rhetorical antithesis of romantic truth-telling. That is, Melville's literary practices allowed him to keep the criteria of an emerging mass culture at a distance but also very much in view.

HE excerpt that serves as this chapter's epigraph, in which Melville claims that the Mexican War "is nothing of itself," suggests that the author experienced the war as an event whose meaning resided more in its status as a national spectacle than as a political conflict. What follows is a longer description of the war hysteria from the same letter: "People here are all in a state of delirium about the Mexican War. A military arder [*sic*] pervades all ranks—Militia Colonels wax red in their coat facings—and 'prentice boys are running off to the wars by scores.—Nothing is talked of but the 'Halls of Montezumas' [a]nd to hear folks talk about those purely figurative apartments one would suppose that they were another Versailles where our democratic rabble meant to 'make a night of it' ere long."[44] Melville's perspective vis-à-vis the "democratic rabble" places the author squarely outside of the "delirium" that marks the war in the popular imagination. Furthermore, the description of the Halls of Montezuma as "those purely figurative apartments," an imagined place laughably unheroic in comparison with the French Revolution, helps us understand his claim that the war "is nothing of itself." Focusing on the war as an imagined spectacle, as something that exists only in the popular imagination, the author positions himself as the one who sees through his society's sham sensations. Writing in the weeks following the outbreak of war, Melville writes to his brother in London (who, unknown to Herman, had actually died weeks earlier) of a war that was a spectacle—that was, in fact, nothing but a spectacle.

Crucially, one should not misread Melville's critique of the national obsession with a place and a struggle that was "purely figurative" as a righteous stance against the imperialist implications of the war. The letter, after all, is careful to acknowledge that American troops have "behaved right well." Indeed, the distinction between these two readings of Melville—as the critic who lampoons his nation's dramatizing of a distinctly undramatic war and as the enlightened writer who comprehends the war as an immoral conflict betraying America's imperialist nature—warns against reading the author's deconstructive worldview as evidence of his political and ethical sensitivity to cultural imperialism. After all, his letter to Gansevoort places the actual behavior of American troops in parentheses, reserving the main narrative of his writing for the hoopla and artifice surrounding the war. Adopting a stance toward the "democratic rabble" that allowed him to expose the journalistic methods by which the spectacle was being manufactured, Melville uses the Mexican War as a vehicle for his own self-invention as the enlightened arbiter of what constitutes genuine reality.

In much the same way, Melville's most sustained invocation of the war appears more interested in mocking the popular "delirium" over the war than in attacking it on moral grounds. The "Old Zack" sketches, which were written in July of 1847 and appeared serially from that month through September in *Yankee Doodle,* evidence little of the artistic or philosophical ambition that characterizes the rest of Melville's corpus. Nevertheless, they help us gauge the cultural valence of Melville's long-standing preoccupation with the popular appetite for contrived representations of distant realities. In the brief lifespan of *Yankee Doodle,* the magazine regularly lampooned the public's appetite for sham authenticities like the displays of Barnum's American Museum, the Chinese junk that drew visitors in the summer of 1847, and Morse's electromagnetic telegraph.[45] The magazine, which modeled itself after the far more successful British journal *Punch,* ran a cartoon in which an apparently Irish immigrant stares out her window at a telegraph wire, wondering why she hasn't "seed [*sic*] a single letter or anything else pass." Another cartoon shows a pipe-smoking man (again apparently Irish) at a telegraph office, asking to send his "wee bundle by telegraph til Baltimore." And a poem titled "The Last Newsboy" (and accompanied by an etching of a weeping newsboy holding a copy of *Yankee Doodle*) ironically bemoans the death of the newspaper that will inevitably result from Morse's invention. As the newsboy asks,

> . . . ven every blessed soul
> Can see yer brains, as if a hole
> Vas drilled inter yer skull;
> Who'll be so jolly green to pay
> Sixpence for half yer got to say,
> Ven he has read the hull?[46]

The Irish- and German-inflected dialect in such pieces suggest that the magazine relied on the status of the telegraph as a symbol of (racist, nativist) nation-making to place recent immigrants outside the margins of the white "America" imagined during the war with Mexico. Reading the "Old Zack" sketches against the backdrop of these other pieces reminds us that Melville's critique of the popular appetite for unstable ideals of authenticity—in the sketches and in his more successful and better-known work—carried with it an entire series of assumptions about cultural hierarchies: claiming to understand the true nature of reality in the age of telegraphy, Barnum, and the penny press was very much a marker of national and racial privilege. My later discussion of "Benito Cereno" will argue that Melville's intellectual and ethical relationship to the problem of slavery was shaped by antebellum conceptions of whiteness in ways that critics tend to overlook. What I wish to point out here, however, is that the *Yankee Doodle* pieces cited above suggest that the myth of authenticity already existed in antebellum discourse about telegraphy *as a myth,* one the editors could use to lampoon the simple-mindedness of recent immigrants while exposing (as they often did) the transparent political and economic motives of New York newspaper editors.[47] In other words, Melville's sense of authenticity as an invention of print capitalism was a view that he borrowed from his culture, one that signified a particular relationship to mass journalism and thus claimed access to the privileged truth that reality is a construct.

As I have already shown, Zachary Taylor had emerged by the summer of 1847 as the subject of widespread national mythologizing, a phenomenon that was fundamentally connected to a discourse of informational authenticity. And so, in underscoring the authenticity of the anecdotes, Melville's mock-editorial voice informs his reader that *Yankee Doodle* "has sent on a correspondent to the seat of war for the express purpose of getting together and transmitting to us all reliable *on dits* connected with old Zack" (*Piazza Tales,* 212). Old Zack, we are soon told, receives the correspondent with such admiration and generosity that "our aforesaid correspondent is now permanently domiciled as one of the General's family." To further make the point of this correspondent's unquestioned link to the authentic Zack, Melville continues: "Suffice it to say, that after venting his ire upon the anecdote-making editors of the North the old hero expressed his unbounded satisfaction at the prospect of henceforth having his most trifling actions and sayings faithfully chronicled by a man of purity." Finally, eager "to prevent for the future the circulation of any but authentic anecdotes concerning him," Old Zack is reported to give the correspondent a written certificate, "asserting our columns to be the only true source where an anxious public can procure a correct insight into [Taylor's] private life and little personal peculiarities." The certificate, quoted in the body of the introductory sketch, occupies "a conspicuous place in our office, where it may be seen from 9 A.M. till 3½ P.M. every day, Sundays excepted" (213).

Melville's parodies carry to the level of absurdity popular journalism's claim to an authentic relationship with the world it seeks to represent. Indeed, the "Authentic Anecdotes" argue that journalism is very much a game, one in which the writer seeks to posit a specific political agenda while rather transparently donning the guise of reportage. Furthermore, Zack's written certificate invokes the debates among American editors over which of Taylor's authentic letters and signatures were real and which were fabrications. The certificate, which sits "in a brass frame cast from a captured Mexican forty-two brass shot," reveals how the reportorial writer must always refer to some ground outside of his writing to found his claims for "real value" (much like the writer who describes the actual sheets on which Taylor handwrites his dispatches), even though that ground is no less a part of his narrative's fictional landscape. One thinks, for example, of the newspaper commentator who devises his own picture of the "real" Taylor based only upon the sketches he has seen—all of which are somehow inadequate. In short, Melville's introductory sketch flaunts how completely the journalistic writer may construct the appearance of truth-telling without ever leaving the fabric of representation itself—thereby dramatizing how journalistic writing fabricates "authentic" pictures of the material world.

The mock certificate also allows the author to forge a link, one that appears throughout his major phase, between reportage and an American entertainment culture rooted in the transparent fiction of authenticity. By turning the certificate itself into an exhibit, Melville underscores how writing creates the very facades of authenticity that fuel antebellum display culture. In the very first anecdote, Melville explicitly connects journalistic authenticity to the figure that was synonymous with the museum culture of antebellum New York: P. T. Barnum. After describing Old Zack's encounter with a shell with a burning fuse at Buena Vista (so as to reveal the general's "surprising self-collectedness and imperturbability in times of the greatest peril" [214]), Melville tells us that Barnum happened to appear in the offices of *Yankee Doodle* as the editors were reading of Old Zack's exploits. Barnum, we are told, quickly writes to an acquaintance to look for the actual shell, while also giving "orders for a shell of the proper dimensions to be cast at one of the foundries up town." "We feel confident," Melville writes, "in stating that the latter will not be exhibited for the genuine article, unless the genuine article fails to come in hand" (215). The juxtaposition of Melville's own manufactured anecdotes beside Barnum's manufactured "genuine article" relies upon the reader's recognition that writing easily manufactures truth—creating reality by casting it in the proper dimensions.

Melville's mock-journalistic tone undercuts the possibility of any narrative stance to merely represent a fixed actuality without transforming that actuality into something quite different. Throughout the sketches,

Melville employs a conspicuously objective narrator: at one moment he describes the "Cincinnatus-like simplicity and unaffectedness" (215) of Old Zack; at another he says of Old Zack's nose, "The nostrilian organ, or probiscus, is straight, but neither inclining to the Roman, or Grecian, or, indeed, the Doric or Composite order of nasal architecture" (220). The laughably conspicuous "objectivity" is anything but objective, of course, but its salient contrast with Old Zack's "simplicity and unaffectedness" allows Melville to dramatize how the teller inherently infects his narrative subject. Of course, this is precisely what had occurred in the journalistic coverage of the war: American newspapers had located in Taylor the ideal subject by which they could impose upon an external subject the very ideals—straightforwardness, integrity, objectivity—that were rapidly coming to define an American journalism that was, paradoxically, increasingly commercialized. Claiming a transcendent perspective on this culture, Melville satirizes the authenticating process to recast journalism as a mode of manufacturing both the nation and the category of reality.

As part of this process, Melville's narrator mocks the popular obsession with the general's idiosyncratic use of language. Such a moment relied on the reader's awareness of the regular appearance in New York papers of letters written (or perhaps not written) by Taylor, and the careful attention editors would pay to every word in attempting to evaluate each letter as genuine or humbug. In telling the anecdote of the lit shell, for example, our narrator includes a footnote regarding Old Zack's unschooled way of speaking: "In all cases we give the old man's very words. If they show a want of early attendance at the Grammar School, it must be borne in mind that old Zack never took a college diploma—was cradled in the backwood camp—and rather glories in the simplicity and unostentation of his speech. 'Describe me, Sir,' he said to our correspondent,—'describe me, sir, as I am—no polysyllables—no stuff—it's time they should know me in my true light'" (214). The quotation concluding the above excerpt reflects the entire piece in a number of important ways. Melville's "Zack" consistently slips back and forth from his "real" unschooled mode of talking—of the lit shell, he says, "them 'are chaps don't bust always" (214)—to a well-spoken mode capable of theorizing about authenticity while speaking in the language of the narrator—such as above, when he implores the correspondent to "describe me, Sir, as I am [with] no polysyllables." Melville's "Zack" is thus both authentic and, in his awareness of authenticity, comically savvy. His constant slips from unschooled dialect to the prosy language meant to be understood as that of the correspondent dramatizes the impossibility of narrating while maintaining an authentic object of narration. "Old Zack" is quite obviously (and somewhat laughably) created as he is being described—not unlike the "genuine" shell Barnum's people fabricate for his museum. If narrative writing entails merely another mode of manufacturing, as Melville's piece suggests, authenticity is one of its chief products.

The shell anecdote, with its obvious concern with Old Zack's "authentic" way of speaking, follows immediately in the wake of the mock certificate. The certificate's language, with its references to "the highly respectable correspondent" from *Yankee Doodle* and the "base and malignant publications" circulating inauthentic anecdotes, contrasts sharply with the "simplicity and unostentation" of the genuine Zack's mode of speaking. This contrast between the narrator's verbosity and Zack's dialect again allows the reader to trace the certificate to the narrative stance of the mock correspondent and not to the "genuine" subject of the narrative. In other words, parody allows Melville to render absurd the division between writer and subject, to comically undercut the idea of an authentic subject unshaped by the language used to describe him. Melville thus opposes the practice of authentication with his own sense of reality as a narrative product peddled in the textual marketplace.

When read in the context of Melville's later fiction, this view of the Mexican War as all "delirium," as "nothing in itself," suggests that the author's metaphysics owed a substantial debt to the slippery ideals of authenticity that defined antebellum mass culture. In Captain Ahab's famous diatribe against the world of pasteboard masks, in the attack on life's endless panorama of masquerades in *The Confidence-Man,* in the "blunt-thinking" Amasa Delano's eager consumption of the racial role-playing and artifice aboard the *San Dominick,* Melville advances his own philosophical project by portraying the truths of others in the language of humbuggery. As Edgar Dryden writes of *Pierre,* for example, Melville's novel addresses "the writer's relationship to the pseudo-reality which is society and to the conventions and formulas which structure it." Indeed, Dryden's reading of Melville's major fiction brilliantly captures the way Melville's imagination depended on the question of reality as the ultimate yardstick of artistic achievement. Dryden argues, for example, that Pierre's "self-conscious role-playing . . . exposed him to the truth that all life is a masquerade and the world a house of fictions, a labyrinthine enclosure with mirrors instead of windows."[48]

Now almost four decades after such an insight, new historical modes of reading allow us to consider Melville's ongoing preoccupation with inauthenticity as a culture-bound articulation of romantic selfhood. In *Moby-Dick,* for example, the superficial criteria of antebellum commercialism allows for the romancer's idiosyncratic story of a mythical whale who must, like all true things, remain "unpainted to the last"—who continually eludes the corruptive reach of a marketplace that commodifies the very process of representation.[49] Indeed, the mock certificate of the "Old Zack" sketches anticipates "The Affidavit" chapter of *Moby-Dick* in that each moment, by pretending to document the veracity or feasibility of a story acknowledged to be fictitious, eviscerates the kind of superficial authenticating practices of both penny press editors and the notorious Barnum. Furthermore, in "The Affidavit" (as in the "Old Zack" pieces) Melville links the empty postures of authentication to the narrative momentum of his story. "So far as what there might be of a narrative in this book," Melville writes, "the foregoing chapter, in its earlier part, is as important a one as will be found in this volume" (203). In "The Town-Ho's Story," too, the misguided logic of authentication offsets Melville's deeper truths: "I entreat you," Don Sebastian asks Ishmael upon the conclusion of the narrative, "tell me if to the best of your own convictions, this your story is in substance really true? . . . Did you get it from an unquestionable source?" (258). Though Melville is far from the first writer of fiction to employ the gestures of documentation to create a novelistic reality effect, his ongoing reliance on such a practice seems to invoke the superficial authenticating practices of an imagined reading public to claim an authorial autonomy over the terms by which his work is defined.[50] He adopts the empty postures of truth-telling not simply to add to his reader's enjoyment or edification but to foreground the distance between an imagined reader's misguided practices and the truths that lurk beneath textual surfaces.

If, as Dryden suggests, such "self-conscious gestures" in *Moby-Dick* "distinguish his creative venture from the unconscious acts of god-making and society-making which characterize the 'world of lies,'" it is in *Pierre* where the individual artist's ability to see through cultural surfaces emerges most clearly as the self-defining, and self-destroying, achievement of romantic existence. Like his creator, Pierre Glendinning lives in an inauthentic world, one where publishers demand "false, inverted attempts at systematizing eternally unsystematizable elements."[51] In response to such a dilemma, Melville's protagonist "pierce[s]" the "speculative lies" with "the one sensational truth in him" (141). Fittingly, it is at the very moment when Pierre destroys the portrait of his father—the moment when he recognizes "the painted self" of the portrait as a "visible memorial for every passing beggar's dust to gather on" (197)—that he imagines himself as unbound to family history and immune to the unwashed masses (whose "passing . . . dust" threatens the integrity of true art). Here and elsewhere in Melville's fiction, the threat of mass consumption appears in the romantic mind in the language of inauthentic representations. As in Raymond Williams's famous assertion, "There are in fact no masses; there are only ways of seeing people as masses,"[52] Pierre's attention to the inauthenticity of mere copies emerges as a way for Melville to see the "democratic rabble" as a collective being, a way of seeing that simultaneously articulates the (equally mythic) romantic self. And so it is that, after destroying the "unsolid duplicate" of his father's image, along with family letters and "all sorts of miscellaneous memorials in paper," Pierre announces, "Henceforth, cast-out Pierre hath no paternity, and no past; and since the Future is one blank to all; therefore twice-disinherited Pierre stands untrammeledly in his ever-present self!—free to do his own self-will and present fancy to whatever end!" (199). Like Emerson, Pierre imagines himself free from the burdens of inheritance; but just as significantly, this emancipation is announced by rejecting a portrait as an unreal copy available for mass consumption.

As readers of *Pierre* will recall, another portrait appears near the novel's climax. In chapter 26, Pierre, Isabel, and Lucy visit a New York gallery on whose "thickly hung walls" is displayed a "most hybrid collection of impostures" of European masterworks (350). Hanging "at a good elevation in one of the upper tiers" (351), far above the crowd of spectators and the fraudulent knockoffs, is "a real Italian gem of art" (350), a portrait of an attractive young man with an ambiguous smile. Melville describes how two of his characters respond to the portrait: "To Isabel, in the eye and on the brow, were certain shadowy traces of her own unmistakable likeness; while to Pierre, this face was in part as the resurrection of the one he had burnt at the Inn" (351). That is to say, while Isabel sees the portrait as an authentic rendering of an actual person who could only be her father, Pierre sees it as a skillful copy of a copy. This question of the true nature of the painting is crucial to the novel's narrative, for Pierre now begins to doubt whether Isabel is indeed his long-lost sister. Earlier, the portrait of his father seemed to Pierre unquestionable evidence of Isabel's identity as his sister ("the portrait's painted *self* seemed the real father of Isabel" [197]); now, however, the appearance of the new portrait throws Pierre into disequilibrium: "How did he *know* that Isabel was his sister? Nothing that he saw in her face could he remember as having seen in his father's. The chair-portrait, *that* was the entire sum and substance of all possible, rakable, downright presumptive evidence, which peculiarly appealed to his own separate self. Yet here was another portrait of a complete stranger—a European; a portrait imported from across the seas, and to be sold at public auction, which was just as strong an evidence as the other. Then, the original of this second portrait was as much the father of Isabel as the original of the chair-portrait."

Pierre attempts to resolve the apparent indeterminacy of Isabel's true identity by considering whether the new portrait is something other than a realistic depiction of an actual person: "perhaps there was no original at all to this second portrait; it might have been a pure fancy piece" (353). This leads Pierre to more self-reflection, during which he realizes that, as one "who professionally deals in mysticisms and mysteries," he possesses "the apparent anomaly of a mind, which by becoming really profound in itself, grew skeptical of all tendered profundities; whereas, the contrary is generally supposed." As the skeptical artist who sees through the unrealities peddled and consumed as truths, Pierre decides that perhaps the "wonderful story" of Isabel's European birth and journey across the ocean "might have been, someway, and for some cause, forged for her, in her childhood, and craftily impressed upon her youthful mind . . . till it had become this immense staring marvel." After all, he reasons, "tested by any thing real, practical, and reasonable, . . . what less probable than that fancied crossing of the sea in her childhood" (354).

As this rather convoluted thought process suggests, the example of Pierre is meaningful not only for the character's association of the destruction of "unsolid" representations with "untrammeled" selfhood but also because Pierre's descent into nihilism and self-destruction dramatizes the metaphysical darkness built into Melville's own conception of the artist. Like the author of the "Old Zack" sketches, Pierre sees inauthenticity everywhere; but, like the author of *The Confidence-Man,* he is unable to simply leave the question of authenticity behind: he must question every fact he knows, finally deciding that everything he thought he knew is a lie. Thus what feels like philosophical triumph in destroying the representations prized by others quickly becomes something much darker, as the romantic seer recognizes artifice everywhere: "Yet now, forsooth, because Pierre began to see through the first superficiality of the world, he fondly weens he has come to the unlayered substance. But, far as any geologist has yet gone down into the world, it is found to consist of nothing but surface stratified on surface. To its axis, the world being nothing but superintended superfices. By vast pains we mine into the pyramid; by horrible gropings we come to the central room; with joy we espy the sarcophagus; but we lift the lid—and no body is there!—appallingly vacant as vast is the soul of a man!" (285).

Once the awareness of inauthenticity is held up as the constitutive insight of romantic being, the self undergoes an ontological collapse. Like the world of lies that surrounds him, then, the individual (whose identity is predicated on such a view) is "nothing of itself." Melville's only apparent choice is to depict Pierre's demise in a world now recognized by both author and protagonist as nothing but a staged spectacle—Pierre "unentangledly" meets his fate at "the very proscenium of the town," an open space "built round with the stateliest public erections" (359)—so that the climax of the novel is precisely the kind of lie demanded by an inauthentic world: "All's o'er," Melville concludes, "and ye know him not!" (362). With no apparent refuge from the world of lies, the artist can protect his own intellectual sovereignty only by exposing and condemning the empty surfaces of American social life—including his own fictions.

That Melville saw the act of exposing the superficial logic of authentication as both a form of self-realization and a potentially nihilistic pursuit should come as little surprise. As I suggested in my introduction, and as critics have long recognized, his surviving correspondence from the late 1840s reveals that the author of *Typee* and *Omoo* was continually frustrated by a publishing industry that imposed on his work (what he considered) the unstable categories of truth and humbug. Writing fiction was thus a way of negating not only the marketplace's sense of him as the "man who lived among cannibals" but also the superficial reading practices that undergirded such a view. At the very least, reading the "Old Zack" anecdotes in their original cultural context, and alongside a work like *Pierre,* suggests that Melville's obsessive attention to the inauthenticity of American life was always something more complex than simply an attempt at reforming popular reading practices. Melville, much like Hawthorne, seems most comfortable looking at his culture when he can invoke and reject alternative ways of witnessing and representing the world he sees. My next two chapters will argue that the narrative strategies of *Typee* and "Benito Cereno," more than just vehicles of political critique, exploited the instability of particular ideals of authenticity to carry out dynamic acts of authorial self-imagining. Chapter 5 will illustrate how the model of informational writing Melville employs in *Typee* seeks to elude the cultural logic of telegraphic connectedness; chapter 6 will consider how the model of romantic truth-telling on display in "Benito Cereno" elevates the romantic artist over the mass-oriented abolitionism of Harriet Beecher Stowe and the surface-oriented epistemology of that archetypal mass American subject, Amasa Delano. In each of these readings, my goal is to reveal that, as in the "Old Zack" sketches, these works reflect Melville's particular subject position as a white male American author continually evading the authorial and communal identities foisted upon him by the mass marketplace. If these discussions of two of Melville's most progressive works seem to blur the line between the author's moral beliefs and his ongoing self-invention as an autonomous artist, I would suggest that this is because the line between belief and identity is never as stable as we would like it to be.

CHAPTER 5

THE ISLAND TELEGRAPH

INFORMATION CULTURE AND THE
MELVILLEAN SELF IN *TYPEE*

———

W H E N Herman Melville returned home in October of 1844 from four years at sea, he came back to a different reality than he had left behind. In May of 1844, Samuel Morse displayed his "American telegraph" before Congress and the American people, an event that suddenly made it possible for the country to imagine a mode of communication that was both instantaneous and disembodied. By the early months of 1846, as the telegraph was rapidly becoming a fixture on the top of news columns in New York papers, Melville had written and published his first book, *Typee.* The book, which was based on the author's experience on a Marquesan island after he and a shipmate had jumped overboard, has long been read as a relativistic critique of Western culture. Given the popular obsession with Morse's newly established invention at the time Melville was writing *Typee,* it comes as little surprise that among the various aspects of American culture he transposed to the island was the telegraph.

What is more surprising, in light of the technology's prominence in public discourse at the time Melville was writing, is that the text's symbolic use of the telegraph has received little critical attention—even as scholars have long recognized the book's preoccupation with the political dimensions of information exchange. Over the course of this chapter, I want to trace Melville's use of telegraphic symbolism in *Typee* to reveal how his embrace of narrative indeterminacy as both a political and artistic ideal spoke to the information culture from which *Typee* borrowed one of its most compelling, and least interrogated, metaphors. As I have already shown, American journalists and commentators began praising Morse's invention in the second half of 1844 with an unprecedented enthusiasm and an almost unrestrained imagination. Thus Melville's invocation of the telegraph as a crucial narrative symbol invites us to explore his first book's preoccupation with the problem of information exchange in light of the rapid emergence of the technology-fueled myth of informational omniscience and reliability. In juxtaposing the philosophical assumptions of Pierre Glendinning alongside the cultural preoccupations of Melville's "Old Zack" sketches, I have suggested that the author's conception of artistic truth-telling was shaped by the status of authenticity as a powerful, and highly unstable, ideal of American mass culture. In this chapter I take a sustained look at Melville's first book in order to examine how it reflects the same preoccupation with the slippery nature of information that connects Melville to the America of Barnum and the telegraph.

So many excellent postcolonial readings of *Typee* are founded on the question of how Tommo, Melville's autobiographical narrator, problematizes his quest for authentic information about the Typee. If the most obvious example of such questing is the narrative suspense that circulates in the book regarding whether or not the Typee are cannibals, it seems that almost every chapter contains some narrative mystery: Have Tommo and his companion, Toby, wandered into the valley of the friendly Happar or the dreaded Typee? Whatever happens to Toby when he departs for the coastline to get medical supplies for his ailing friend? What is the "strange meaning" of the religious feasts and rituals that Tommo witnesses during his time with the Typee? While some questions are clearly answered, and while others are clearly not, there are some that we simply cannot be sure about. As Geoffrey Sanborn reminds us, two readers of *Typee* might conclude the book with two entirely different opinions about whether or not Tommo has indeed found evidence of cannibalism on the island.[1]

In my own reading, Melville's concern with information in *Typee*—Tommo's individual search for authentic information, the intracultural transmission of information among the Typee, the role of information exchange as a vehicle of intercultural oppression—is meaningful not as evidence of the book's colonialist or anticolonialist thinking but for the way in which this conspicuous attention to the cultural meaning of information resonated in the earliest days of telegraphy. Situating the text in the discourse surrounding the question of information exchange in 1844–46 reveals that Melville's reliance on the contemporaneous status of the telegraph signified his own autonomy from the production of national identity on a mass scale. The subject matter of *Typee* afforded a singularly valuable means for such a self-invention: by carving out a critical distance from what we might call "information culture"—that is, from the role of information exchange within both Typee and American societies—Melville verbalizes Tommo's independence from the collective logic of cultural identity by claiming a position for his textual persona between two cultures of information.

Critics such as John Samson have highlighted for us how Melville constantly fought in his work against the strictly informational type of writing his writers expected of him.[2] But the assumption of this line of inquiry has been that Melville's refusal to neatly narrate facts was the product of an ethical conscientiousness that separated him from the myopic racism of the information-hungry masses. The discussion that follows approaches Melville's "Art of Telling the Truth" in *Typee* not as the morally well-intentioned antidote to the shallowness of the American reader but as a by-product of the reality-obsessed information culture in which Melville lived and wrote; for his own preoccupation with (what he considers) inauthentic accounts of Typee culture emerged alongside an informational discourse in which the production and consumption of "authentic" facts signified as a nationalizing characteristic. In *Typee* Melville at once exposes information as a political and economic fiction and depicts the cultural reality of the Typee as a realm of performance and masquerade, carving out for Melville alone an apparently transcultural identity by deconstructing what mass culture considers the real.

To understand Melville's use of telegraphic symbolism in *Typee,* one must recognize that the telegraph is, in Melville's reworking of it, a conspicuously slippery symbol. In fact, it is its very slipperiness that defines the telegraphic metaphor in *Typee* against the technology's symbolic meaning in the popular imagination. As I have already revealed, though the telegraph was seen as something of a conjuring trick in the days before it established itself as a viable technology, American commentators in the months and years following the successful installation of Morse's technology were nearly unanimous in their sense of a new telegraphic age. As a symbol of national connectedness, informational timeliness and reliability, omniscience and objectivity, the telegraph was a popular phenomenon whose symbolic meaning allowed commentators to rhetorically efface the myriad contingencies that threatened national cohesiveness and consensus. In the very act of making the telegraph a symbol, after all, antebellum commentators visualized and verbalized the nation as a unified signifier. At the same time, the cartoons and parodies that ran in *Yankee Doodle* (including Melville's "Old Zack" sketches) imagined a space outside of this mythic realm of the authentic nation; and so it was there that Irish and German immigrants appeared, laughably unsavvy about the implications of the new technology.

In much the same way, Melville's use of the telegraph in *Typee* exposes it for what it was—a symbol—relying on its instability to redefine the ideal of telegraphic connectedness as a culturally specific myth, one that empowered far-reaching and consequential acts of cultural storytelling. Far from an escape from the assumptions of his own information culture, though, Melville's rhetorical transposition of the telegraph projected onto the Typee the Western view that sees specific modes of transmitting and circulating information as defining cultural practices. The value of assessing the text's use of telegraphic symbolism, then, is that the very prominence of the telegraph in *Typee* suggests that Melville's salient preoccupation with information exchange was an imposition of a culturally specific story about the "nature" of reality onto what he claimed was a social and cultural setting that had been largely uncorrupted by Western life. In *Typee,* I am arguing, Melville portrays his own view of information as a textual, political, and economic fiction, his own understanding of culture as a surface-oriented realm of spectacle and performance, as a transcultural insight.

MELVILLE'S first use of the telegraphic metaphor occurs soon after Tommo and Toby discover that they have indeed wandered into the valley of the Typee. At this relatively early point in the narrative, Tommo witnesses the "telegraph" from the perspective of a white, Western outsider. Even more significantly, his use of the telegraphic metaphor subtly relies on the technology's status in the Western world as a guarantor of an unprecedented kind of authenticity:

> Deterred by the frightful stories related of its inhabitants, ships never enter this bay, while their hostile relations with the tribes in the adjoining valleys prevent the Typees from visiting that section of the island where vessels occasionally lie. At long intervals, however, some intrepid captain will touch on the skirts of the bay, with two or three armed boats' crews, and accompanied by an interpreter. The natives who live near the sea descry the strangers long before they reach their waters, and aware of the purpose for which they come, proclaim loudly the news of their approach. By a species of vocal telegraph the intelligence reaches the inmost recesses of the vale in an inconceivably short space of time, drawing nearly its whole population down to the beach laden with every variety of fruit.[3]

When read in light of the technology's triumphant rise to prominence in 1844, the inconceivability of the metaphorical telegraph's efficiency expressed here appears as an echo of the contemporaneous view that Morse's technology was a near miracle. But Melville's careful description of the inaccessibility of the harbor is perhaps more meaningful: as a symbolic link to the uncorrupted, authentic Typee culture, the telegraph functions in Melville's text much as it was then functioning in the popular imagination. Indeed, in the very next paragraph, Melville writes, "I have no doubt that we were the first white men who ever penetrated thus far back into their territories, or at least the first who had ever descended from the head of the vale" (74). By projecting the logic of telegraphy onto the island, Tommo defines the value of the narrative that will follow according to the criteria of American information culture. The reader, Tommo promises, will be connected to an authentic reality that has been heretofore unreachable.

Even before the chapter ends, however, Melville begins to disrupt his own promise of telegraphic omniscience. Upon receiving Tommo and Toby, the Typee attempt to get information from their visitors: "They then plied us with a thousand questions, of which we could understand nothing more than they had reference to the recent movements of the French, against whom they seemed to cherish the most fierce hatred. So eager were they to obtain information on this point, that they still continued to propound their queries long after we had shown that we were utterly unable to answer them. . . . In the end they looked at us despairingly, as if we were the receptacles of invaluable information; but how to come at it they knew not" (75). Though this chapter begins with Tommo and Toby's own quest for invaluable information—"Typee or Happar? A frightful death at the hands of the fiercest of cannibals, or a kindly reception from a gentler race of savages?" (66)—by the end they are confronted with an information culture that is entirely alien to them, one in which they embody an unknown but profound value. If we read the telegraphic metaphor when it first appears as evidence of the text's subtle promise of unprecedented authenticity, the chapter's clash of two cultures of information suggests that the American imagination that sees the Typee through the lens of telegraphic thinking will have to ultimately recalibrate its very understanding of information exchange.

And indeed, in the second appearance of the vocal telegraph, Melville transforms his symbol from a guarantor of authenticity to a vehicle for cultural domination. Near the beginning of the fourteenth chapter of his narrative, Tommo, already suffering from a mysterious illness, is "plunged in melancholy reverie" after realizing that he was "cut off . . . from all intercourse with the civilized world . . . [and] knowing too, that so long as I remained in my present condition, it would be impossible for me to leave the valley" (104). Soon, however, Tommo and the reader learn that boats have appeared in the bay. Here is how Melville shares the information with us:

> The word "botee! botee!" was vociferated in all directions; and shouts were heard in the distance, at first feebly and faintly; but growing louder and nearer at each successive repetition, until they were caught up by a fellow in a cocoa-nut tree a few yards off, who sounding them in turn, they were reiterated from a neighboring grove, and so died away gradually from point to point, as the intelligence penetrated into the farthest recesses of the valley. This was the vocal telegraph of the islanders; by means of which condensed items of information could be carried in a very few minutes from the sea to their remotest habitation, a distance of at least eight or nine miles. On the present occasion it was in active operation; one piece of information following another with inconceivable rapidity. (105)

Melville's juxtaposition here of a conspicuously Western, even urbane narrative voice with the notably exotic setting (the two discourses merge into formulations such as, "they were caught up by a fellow in a cocoa-nut tree") is typical of the book's interest in highlighting the distance between Western ways of seeing and the inscrutable lives of the islanders. And the telegraph serves an analogous function: its scientific authority is replaced with the quaintness of the islanders' vocal telegraph. Tommo calling it a "telegraph" is meaningful, of course, because it ironically underscores the island's status as undeveloped, uncivilized. While a typical mid-1840s description of the electromagnetic telegraph portrayed the technology as a way of connecting, and thus defining, "the civilized world," Melville's invocation of telegraphy would seem to echo his novel's larger concern with the irrelevance of Western progress to the world of the Typee.

And yet I would argue that Melville is up to something far more complex here—for the vocal telegraph is at the very center of the novel's narrative and epistemological complexity. After all, Tommo tells us (in consecutive paragraphs, no less) first that he is "cut off from all intercourse" with the outside world and then that his inward spot on the island is connected by "telegraph" to the coast (where European and American boats regularly appear). This "telegraph," rapid and reliable as it might be for the islanders, thus is recast as a technology by which the Typee appear to extend their cultural and physical dominion over our narrator. Indeed, later in the same chapter Tommo and his American companion, Toby, lose contact with one another. Because Tommo is Melville's narrator, the reader, too, is left to wonder why Toby fails to return with those islanders he accompanied to greet a group of recently anchored boats. Of course, the only link between the inland Typee and the happenings of the shore is the "telegraph" that sends information inland through human conduits—and therefore it is the "telegraph" that fails to keep our narrator connected to those events that lead to Toby's final departure from the island and his disappearance from Melville's narrative.

At the very moment when Melville was writing *Typee,* the telegraph allowed American commentators and readers to conceive of "America" as a collective and cohesive body. Such an act of national imagining, I have argued, saw in the technology's promise of disembodied communication the divorce of information from the individual bodies that constituted the nation, thus envisioning a realm of informational purity beyond the reach of commercial or political duplicity. In referring to an "infallible telegraph" capable of correcting both human error and corruption, these writers used the technology to efface the social, political, and economic agendas that were rapidly defining the information culture of antebellum America. In other words, as American culture was increasingly shaped by the merging of information and market capitalism, an alternative, mythic "America" was taking shape—one that was defined against the very idea of information as commodity. Significantly, Melville's metaphor of the "vocal telegraph" reintroduced to telegraphic symbolism precisely what the contemporary popular imagination sought to efface: the presence of actual human bodies in the act of information exchange. As important, it is at the very moment when telegraphy becomes recorporealized by Melville that the technology emerges as a vehicle for cultural oppression: Melville's Western narrator becomes foreign when he invokes the telegraphic metaphor. To think in the terms of connectivity, Melville implies, is not (as antebellum commentators argued) to unite humans in some mythical realm of perfect connectedness; it is to carve out a particular kind of cultural identity.

This use of the telegraph as metaphor recasts one of antebellum America's most powerful myths—the idea that information could be exchanged in a realm untainted by human fallibility—as a by-product of the Western impulse to draw racial and national boundaries. And so Melville's oft-cited interest in foregrounding Tommo's particular difficulties penetrating the mysteries of Typee culture can be understood not only in light of what Mary Louise Pratt calls the "imperial eyes" through which the Western travel writer sees her nonwestern subject but also in the context of the telegraphic promise of disembodied, omniscient information exchange. By invoking this telegraphic promise only to reveal it as a culturally specific ideal, and by continually acknowledging narrative omniscience as an impossible promise, *Typee* quietly claims a global, bird's-eye view on the meaning of information within and between cultures—at the very moment when Melville's own information culture was being defined by the ideals his work invokes and rejects.

The key to this invocation and rejection of the journalistic ideals of the emerging telegraphic age is the careful use of narrative indeterminacy in the face of the readerly quest for omniscience. When the islanders return from the beach without Toby, our narrator is "filled with a thousand alarms" (107). After earnestly asking the natives about his friend, Tommo finally is told that Toby departed with the ships that had anchored in the harbor, promising to return after three days. As readers of the novel will recall, Toby never returns, and Tommo is unable to close this narrative thread: "no tidings of Toby ever reached me; he had gone never to return" (109). It is, of course, a meaningful indeterminacy. Other critics have taken up the subject of cannibalism in the novel, and so it is not my goal here to interpret the cultural implications of Melville's manipulation of "the sign of the cannibal."[4] Instead, I wish to connect the symbolic meaning of cannibalism in the book with Melville's invocation of the telegraph as symbol. As Morse's invention, with its compelling promise of communal connectedness, was claiming a place in the American popular imagination, Melville employs telegraphy as a symbol defined by its conspicuous slipperiness: while the island "telegraph" initially promises a rapid and reliable link to the coast, it soon comes to represent the impenetrability of Typee society to Tommo's eyes. Ultimately, the metaphorical telegraph recasts technologies of communication as nothing more than symbols.

And yet to say "nothing more" is not quite right—for the telegraph as symbol carried with it (in *Typee* and, only months later, in the U.S.-Mexican War) profound and violent cultural implications. While Tommo claims to be haunted by the specter of cannibalism (that oft-invoked marker of the most depraved form of savagery), he is ultimately a victim of his own unconscious manner of erecting racial and cultural boundaries: Typee or Happar? Cannibal or noncannibal? And if the telegraph, with its implicit promise of omniscient and inviolable information, is not the source of Tommo's malaise, it is undoubtedly one of his mind's readiest and most potent symbols. Fittingly, Melville formulated his telegraphic metaphor at a moment at which the telegraph, having not transmitted more than a few pieces of information of any consequence at all, had already brought with it a "new species of consciousness." In the years leading up to the installation of the telegraph as a viable journalistic and economic tool, then, the technology was meaningful in the very way in which

Melville's fiction uses it: as a symbol within the Western imagination. By merging telegraphy and the threat of cannibalism, Melville (in a move that adumbrates the racialized production of Mexican identity in American papers only months later) foregrounds the Western logic of telegraphic connectedness as a force that empowers cultural mythmaking. Tommo is most preoccupied with the danger of cannibalism when he understands reality through the logic of telegraphy: to believe that the other end of the telegraph wire contains a neat resolution to his drama is to impose a narrative shape onto the world; and to impose narrativity is always to impose a certain type of story, one built from the materials of one's cultural milieu. Thus Tommo imposes upon the Typee his culture's most soul-shuddering myth, the myth by which savagery and civilization are alike defined.

Melville asks his audience to recognize their own complicity in such mythmaking by inviting the reader to apply the logic of telegraphic connectedness to his story and then subverting such an expectation. At the conclusion of the first edition of *Typee*, Melville's narrator and the reader are left together to wait for a telegraphic message that never comes. Having depicted Tommo, earlier in the narrative, at the receiving end of a "vocal telegraph" he is incapable of interpreting, Melville concluded *Typee* by informing his audience, "The mystery which hung over the fate of my friend and companion has never been cleared up. I still remain ignorant whether he succeeded in leaving the valley, or perished at the hands of the islanders" (253). This insistence on keeping the unconcluded narrative of Toby's disappearance before the audience deepens the meaning of the telegraphic metaphor: his linking of the metaphor to this example of narrative unknowability unified the reader and Tommo into a collective perspective defined by their inability to complete the story of Toby's disappearance and thus subverted the popular conception of the telegraph in the mid-1840s as an omniscient and infallible means of unifying the nation. While Melville's "vocal telegraph" united the Western reader and narrator into a shared perspective regarding this "mystery," it is a profoundly unprivileged perspective that they share, one that is best defined as the very antithesis of the popular claims that the telegraph would allow Americans to sit around a virtual table in a realm of informational omniscience. Melville here redefines the telegraph from an informational technology to an epistemological one: Tommo and the Western reader are defined entirely by a narrative perspective that comprehends the Typee as outsiders. And so the authorial decision to end with an unresolved narrative thread at once confronted the reader of the first edition with a conspicuous distance between the closure of Melville's novel and the unconcluded story of Toby's disappearance, and used this rhetorical distance to expose telegraphic symbolism as both source and symptom of Western taxonomizing.

As those familiar with the fate of *Typee* will recall, Melville's English and American readers participated in solving the mystery regarding Toby's disappearance.[5] When the book was first published, some readers were highly suspicious of the truth of Melville's account and demanded authenticating evidence that the author had actually lived abroad. The public debates over the authenticity of *Typee* culminated in the emergence of Richard Tobias Greene (a.k.a. "Toby"), a housepainter living in Buffalo, New York, who publicly attested to the veracity of Melville's narrative.[6] As a result, the second American edition of *Typee* concluded with "The Story of Toby," which, in laying out what happened to Toby after he said good-bye to Tommo, neatly resolved for the reader one of the central indeterminacies of Melville's narrative. The public's hunger for authentication of Melville's account thus reshaped the narrative ambiguity of his first edition into the totalizing narrative of the second, essentially reconnecting the first edition's broken telegraph wire.

Even more interesting than the demands of Melville's evidence-seeking readers, I would argue, is the way in which these demands defused the political agenda of the first edition. In the second American edition, "The Story of Toby" took the place of the original appendix, a brief account of European imperialism in the Pacific. The reader of the first edition was left with the obvious suggestion that Toby could have been killed and cannibalized by the Typee people. From there, the first edition moved to the appendix, which opened with Melville's arrival at Tahiti, on "the very day that the iniquitous designs of the French were consummated by inducing the subordinate chiefs, during the absence of their queen, to ratify an artfully drawn treaty, by which she was virtually deposed" (254). In the original appendix, Melville subtly connected the artful writing utilized by the French with the equally deceptive rhetoric through which their imperialist activities were reported in American newspapers. In comparing the harsh journalistic treatment of England's exploits in the Sandwich Islands to the more sympathetic depictions of the French in Tahiti, Melville argued that "with all the woe and desolation which resulted" from France's "piratical seizure of Tahiti," it "created not half so great a sensation, at least in America, as was caused by the proceedings of the English at the Sandwich Islands" (254). Defending the English against charges that they sought to annex the islands, Melville writes: "During a residence of four months at Honolulu, the metropolis of the group, the author was in the confidence of an Englishman who was much employed by [Lord George Paulet]; and great was the author's astonishment on his arrival at Boston, in the autumn of 1844, to read the distorted accounts and fabrications which had produced in the United States so violent an outbreak of indignation against the English. He deems it, therefore, a mere act of justice towards a gallant officer briefly to state the leading circumstances connected with the event in question" (254). The original *Typee* thus concluded with a reminder to the readers of their own inability to know what happened to Toby, and then with a brief account of European activities in the Pacific that Melville tells us have been distorted and fabricated by missionary and newspaper writers. While Melville's account is decidedly pro-England, the deeper argument of the appendix was that imperialism had become a battle over who controlled the representation of such exploits published in newspapers and travel books back home. As with the island telegraph, information exchange more broadly is recast in *Typee* (or was recast, in the first edition) as both a source and function of intercultural domination.

That the popular reader's demand for authentication of *Typee* resulted in the resolution of the first edition's indeterminacy regarding Toby's disappearance suggests the profound connection between the public's need to authenticate Melville's story and its appetite for narrative closure. The mystery that ended the first edition was an important rhetorical device for Melville, one that was at the heart of his book's notorious attack on missionary writing. The first edition exposed both the rhetorical means by which missionary writers had created their misleading accounts of Typee culture and the unsightly realities that such rhetoric sought to keep veiled. By transforming their own experiences of foreign cultures into the omniscient, objective-sounding rhetoric of ethnographic description, these authors were claiming to describe for their Western audiences what such cultures looked like with and without a missionary presence.[7] As John Carlos Rowe writes, "Melville's anthropological gesture in *Typee* destabilizes our very processes of understanding 'other' people." Against what Rowe calls "the prevailing ethnographic models of its time," Melville's narrator accepts, even foregrounds his own inability to render Typee culture so perfectly.[8] By juxtaposing, for example, Tommo's repeated confessions of ignorance regarding Typee religion beside missionary accounts claiming to understand (and thus condemn) this aspect of Typee culture, Melville's concessions to indeterminacy combat the rhetoric on which the political agenda of missionary writing relied. And so the author's decision to end with the unresolved mystery of Toby's disappearance reasserted Melville's rejection of the assumptions and expectations of popular reading.

But did Melville seek to complicate the American and British reader's sense of what it means for Western eyes to gaze upon foreign people, as Rowe suggests, out of a principled stance that perfectly echoes our own critical and ethical priorities? Or does such a reading of the author's narrative idiosyncrasies betray our own critical eagerness to understand the ways in which a text problematizes the act of narrating primarily as a marker of an author's moral self-awareness? After all, Melville clearly understood that his first book (as well as its sequel, *Omoo*) owed its success largely to the access it afforded its audience to a distant, exotic culture. As Stephen Railton says of the author's first two books, "Melville wrote both of these books from the outside in: he was clearly less interested in expressing himself than in establishing a career as a writer."[9] Even if Melville repeatedly foregrounds the attempt to narrativize a society that he portrays as inscrutable, such a strategy was essentially an alternative manner of presenting the Typee to Western eyes, one that seems to have answered the contemporaneous demand for transparency, omniscience, and closure. Though Melville's book (especially the American first edition) rejects the totalizing narratives published by those writers more obviously driven by political agendas, such moments shaped an idiom in which he could still place the Typee before his audience, even as he kept popular readerly expectations at arm's length. Indeed, Melville's rhetorical use of telegraphy and journalism in *Typee* suggests that his idiosyncratic art of telling the truth portrayed reality as something that can only be defined by invoking the unreal world of information exchange. More than simply a prophetic adumbration of postmodern thinking, *Typee* echoes the priorities of the antebellum media age by peddling authenticity, albeit one defined by the acknowledgment that information is a kind of capital.

Critics such as David Spurr have revealed for us how works like *Typee* exhibit the "fundamental characteristics of Western thinking" by placing foreign cultures on display as "the dream of [the capitalist West's] own opposite."[10] In lieu of merely reiterating such a reading by attending to Melville's belief in the "simplicity" and "purity" of the uncivilized world, I want to point out how Melville's theories of foreign travel ultimately uphold the broader logic of antebellum information culture, even as a text like *Typee* rejects the premises of narrative omniscience and transparency. Consider the following moment from one of Melville's travel lectures in the late 1850s, in which he tells his audience that "the modern progress in some of these islands is seen in the publication there of newspapers; but on close inspection I have often found them to be conducted by Americans, English, or French. I have recently met with a Honolulu paper, the Honolulu 'Advertiser,' which is a mark of the prosperity of the Sandwich Islands, being almost a counterpart of the London 'Times' with its advertisements, arrivals, and departures of vessels, and so on—and that, too, where not long since the inhabitants were cannibals."[11] As in *Typee,* the above moment invokes the presence of the newspaper as evidence of the colonial "progress" made in the Sandwich Islands. But even as he links the commercial nature of the Honolulu paper with Western journalism, and then to the economic exploitation of the islands, Melville's description of the newspaper appears to simultaneously critique colonial notions of "progress" and uphold journalism as a marker of civilization. For Melville's implication seems to be that if these newspapers were native-run, they would indeed be a welcome sign of progress (without quotation marks); the problem, he implies, is that these papers are run by foreigners.

I would argue that such a claim echoes the paradoxical narrative approach of *Typee,* in which Melville deconstructs the truth-telling of previous Western writers while upholding the broader question of information exchange as a defining marker of cultural identity. In seeing the Hawaiian newspaper as inauthentic, after all, he quietly privileges the ideal of a localized (yet still Western) newspaper culture over the urban-based and increasingly global journalism of the 1840s and 1850s. In a sense, he wants the Sandwich Islands to look not like mid-nineteenth-century London or New York, but like a late eighteenth-century New England town before the advent of mass journalism. The lecture goes on to mention a report in a recent newspaper suggesting that Americans and other foreigners have proposed abolishing the Hawaiian language in Hawaiian schools and expelling all those students who speak it. Here is how he registers his opposition: "I threw down the paper on reading this, exclaiming, 'Are they to give up all that binds them together as a nation or race—their language? Then are they indeed blotted out as a people'" (420). Though concerned with the broader process of imperialism, Melville depicts himself in the act of reading the proposal and throwing down his American newspaper, placing the author somewhere between American and Hawaiian print cultures—a rhetorical space that cannot be considered simply anti-imperialist or postcolonial. Rather, in equating Hawaiian autonomy with an ideal of nineteenth-century Western journalism, Melville uses the example of the Sandwich Islands to offset the commercial artifice of modern journalistic culture.

Melville's travel lectures provide a useful context for comprehending the narrative strategies of *Typee* because they remind us that Melville's ideological critique of the political exploitation of his subjects was not also a rejection of writing as a way of placing the Typee on display. Justin Edwards and Douglas Ivison (each of whom relies on the theoretical arguments of Mary Louise Pratt, David Spurr, and Edward Said) have unveiled the myriad ways in which Melville's "anti-imperial critique is ultimately imbricated with imperial hegemony."[12] And Wai Chee Dimock has highlighted how in Melville's narrative each islander "exists only as a key to a communal phenomenon" and each of the author's descriptions "leads to a generalized view of the Typees as a whole."[13] Such work makes it possible, in talking about a book such as *Typee,* to consider the work's narrative approach as a particular manner of exploitation, one in which Melville's way of seeing (and often not seeing) the truth of his subject allowed the author to contrast the mass exploitation of the Pacific (which his work rejected) with the individual exploitation of the Typee as an object of Melville's own epistemological and artistic drama. As he would tell his audience in his lecture on "Travel," one virtue of encountering foreign cultures is to discover the singularity of one's own mind: for "every individual sees differently according to his idiosyncrasies" (in *Piazza Tales,* 423). In this way, exposing the neat narrativizing of an alien culture as disingenuous or otherwise problematic was a two-tiered representational strategy, allowing Melville to place an exotic subject before his reader while also placing on display the idiosyncratic mind of the author-artist—a rhetorical reading that complicates the scholarly view that celebrates Melville's understanding of the constructed and performative aspects of culture.[14]

Again and again in *Typee,* Melville depicts an alien culture while replacing perfect transparency with a foregrounding of that which is too alien for Western eyes, making the impossible idea of narrative transparency a constant presence in his work. Describing the Typee's Feast of Calabashes, for example, Melville's Tommo "questioned Kory-Kory and others of the natives, as to the meaning of the strange things that were going on; all of their explanations were conveyed in such a mass of outlandish gibberish and gesticulation that I gave up the attempt in despair" (168). In the beginning of the very next chapter, "still baffled in my attempts to learn the origin of the Feast of Calabashes," Tommo turns from seeking to make meaning of the festival to complicating other visitors' accounts of the same rituals: "As a religious solemnity . . . it had not at all corresponded with the horrible descriptions of Polynesian worship which we have received in some published narratives, and especially in those accounts of the evangelized islands with which the missionaries have favored us. Did not the sacred character of these persons render the purity of their intentions unquestionable, I should certainly be led to suppose that they had exaggerated the evils of Paganism, in order to enhance the merit of their own disinterested labors" (169). Melville's ironic stance regarding the missionary narrator's disinterestedness anticipates the mock correspondent of the Old Zack anecdotes. But even more interestingly,

Melville's specific analysis of these published accounts adumbrates the *Yankee Doodle* sketches' concern with the means by which all reporters necessarily construct a fictional persona in making their narrative adhere to the postures of reportage.

In referring to missionary accounts of Polynesian religion, Tommo continues: "In certain work incidentally treating of the 'Washington, or Northern Marquesas Islands,' I have seen the frequent immolation of human victims upon the altars of their gods, positively and repeatedly charged upon the inhabitants. . . . These accounts are likewise calculated to leave upon the reader's mind an impression that human victims are daily cooked and served up upon the altars; that heathenish cruelties of every description are continually practised; and that these ignorant Pagans are in a state of the extremest wretchedness in consequence of the grossness of their superstitions" (169–70). Melville's readerly stance in the first of the above lines ("I have seen") critiques not simply what is depicted but the way in which writing attempts to operate in such texts—that is, the missionary writer seeks to make his narrative perfectly transparent, to replace the act of reading with the act of seeing. Melville begins with this realist ideal and quickly replaces it with the more fitting description of such text as a text, one that is "calculated to leave upon the reader's mind" not a specific picture of Marquesan culture but a sense of the reality of Marquesan life as a product of Western storytelling. Melville immediately reveals that behind such a linguistic portrait—behind any written narrative—looms the writer. In this case, we are told, "all this information is given by a man who, according to his own statement, was only at one of the islands and remained there but two weeks, sleeping every night on board his ship, and taking little kid-glove excursions ashore in the daytime attended by an armed party" (170). In stark contrast to such a writer, Tommo's mode of descriptive storytelling acknowledges his own epistemological limits, rejecting realist portraiture in the interest of locating a higher mode of truth-telling.

While describing those missionary authors who do make it ashore, Melville turns both to the language of supply and demand and to the conventions of a Barnumesque museum culture. Finally, these seem to be the only facts underlying such published narratives:

> The fact is, that there is a vast deal of unintentional humbuggery in some of the accounts we have from scientific men concerning the religious institutions of Polynesia. These learned tourists generally obtain the greater part of their information from the retired old South-Sea rovers, who have domesticated themselves among the barbarous tribes of the

Pacific. Jack, who has long been accustomed to the long-bow, and to spin tough yarns on a ship's forecastle, invariably officiates as showman of the island on which he has settled, and having mastered a few dozen words of the language, is supposed to know all about the people who speak it. A natural desire to make himself of consequence in the eyes of the strangers, prompts him to lay claim to a much greater knowledge of such matters than he actually possesses. In reply to incessant queries, he communicates not only all he knows but a good deal more, and if there be any information deficient still he is at no loss to supply it. The avidity with which his anecdotes are noted down tickles his vanity, and his powers of invention increase with the credulity of his auditors. He knows just the sort of information wanted, and furnishes it to any extent. (170)

The South Sea rover operating as "showman" suggests that Typee culture is already a production—shaped, in part, by our own culturally specific manner of witnessing and narrativizing foreign cultures. Melville's title, with its "peep" at Polynesian culture, makes it clear to the reader, before we even arrive on the island, that we can only approach such cultures in a mode of seeing dramatically shaped by how we view foreign lands at home—for as Justin Edwards has suggested, Melville's travel book is very much a "peep-show." The language of Barnum-like showmanship in the above passage is especially meaningful in the wake of the earlier passage in which Melville-as-reader first "sees" through a missionary narrative before zooming out to reveal the fictional world contrived by linguistic and narrative manipulation. The description of such a contrived world as "humbuggery" invokes Barnum to imply that all staged depictions of culture, however carefully displayed, are contrived for a particular audience.

Writing about such scenes, Paul Lyons describes how "Melville denounces the 'humbuggery' spread by 'learned tourists' in the Pacific before him . . . , or between those who have wandered much in the realms of texts and those who have had direct experience of the thing described."[15] Using the work of Jonathan Culler, who seeks to collapse the conventional distinction between tourist and traveler, Lyons reads Melville's desire to contrast his own account of the Typee from "less authentic productions" as a "staple feature of such Euro-American writing, whose degree of authenticity as adventure has always been a financial necessity, and whose admissions of befuddlement in interpreting adventures are often perversely taken as a measure of their general trustworthiness." Thus Melville's repeated confessions of his inability to penetrate the taboos of Typee culture constitute, in Lyons's convincing reading, "a central self-authenticating trope." To be sure, such a reading helps us understand Melville's rhetorical use of competing textual accounts of the Typee as a product of the Western fetishization of cultural authenticity. And yet Melville's invocation of antebellum museum culture, like the telegraphic metaphor, should remind us that the sense of reality as a show does not appear in Melville's imagination solely as a function of his place in a Euro-American tradition of travel discourse. For as his invocations of both Barnumesque showmanship and telegraphy suggest, the narrative stance of *Typee* relied also on the status of reality in 1840s New York as an increasingly marketable commodity. How different the text's use of Western vocabularies such as "showman" and "telegraph" look when we consider that even his deconstruction of these phenomena are the product of the author's cultural embeddedness: instead of marking Melville's awareness of the false authenticities of all cultures, these moments remind us that such an understanding of reality as a production was a view borrowed from the world in which he lived.

As Melville juxtaposes his own experiences of Typee rituals and practices with (the often corrupted) published accounts of these phenomena, his very sense of the authentic Typee requires the foil of informational writing—a kind of writing that is always inadequate, and often in the service of political and economic exploitation. Consider the following passage, which highlights for the reader the important distance between missionary rhetoric disguising itself as description and the secret reality of slavery in the Sandwich Islands. Here Melville defines his own understanding of reality against the goals of mere storytelling:

> Look at Honolulu, the metropolis of the Sandwich Islands!—A community of disinterested merchants, and devoted self-exiled heralds of the Cross, located on the very spot that twenty years ago was defiled by the presence of idolatry. What a subject for an eloquent Bible-meeting orator! Nor has such an opportunity for display of missionary rhetoric been allowed to pass by unimproved!—But when these philanthropists send us such glowing accounts of one half of their labors, why does their modesty restrain them from publishing the other half of the good they have wrought?—Not until I visited Honolulu was I aware of the fact that the small remnant of the natives had been civilized into draught horses, and evangelized into beasts of burden. But so it is. (196)

Melville's narration takes the template of missionary rhetoric ("civilized," "evangelized") and forces it upon the violence of slavery that such rhetoric tries to keep hidden.[16] Through the use of a narrative mode interested at once in the reality of Western colonialism and the textual accounts of such a reality, Melville reveals how the rhetoric of impartial description answers the needs of its writers' colonial objectives. In a sense, the first version of *Typee* presented the reader with two narrative realms, each representing a particular phase of colonial imposition: the land of the Typee, where missionary writing had only recently begun its corruptive work; and the Sandwich Islands, where such rhetorical duplicity had culminated in both slavery and an embedded colonial presence. Melville's own claim to authenticity thus relied on the broad backdrop of colonial contact to remind his readers of the unprecedented access he was affording them—and thus also implied the integrity of his own literary idiom. If he wished to reveal the hidden truth of slavery in the Sandwich Islands, he also used the authority of this cultural access to claim this untouched region for his own story about the nature of reality.

As part of such a rhetorical project, Melville links competing modes of writing with the goals of Western imperialism and colonialism, thereby implying the purity of his own writing as a way of capturing Typee culture. The parallel Melville draws between the Sandwich Islands and the island of the Typee is echoed by the parallel between the newspaper and travel writing, two modes of storytelling Melville portrays as marred by political and economic corruption. In opening the chapter in *Typee* that is most scathingly critical of missionary work, Melville briefly refers to the Sandwich Islands, where "the republican missionaries of Oahu cause to be gazetted in the Court Journal" the most regal and gracious descriptions of the king of the islands (188). Against the "gazetted" version of the honorable king, Melville employs racial caricature, arguing that "His 'gracious majesty' is a fat, lazy negro-looking blockhead, with as little character as power" (189). In the context of the first edition's various exposures of missionary fabrications regarding Typee culture, Melville's use of the newspaper in the more "civilized" Sandwich Islands suggests that the move from the travel writer's misleading depictions of Typee culture to the newspaper's more obviously corruptive mode of discourse is merely a matter of time; travel writing, Melville implies, marks the first step of a narrative imperialism that relies upon the reader's demand for informational authenticity to violently rewrite the world.

Of course, the quieter implication of such a passage is that his own work, providing his reader access to the real face of imperialism, is defined by its distance from both travel writing and journalism. By exposing the press as an instrument of Western exploitation, Melville foregrounds his own access to a reality unexploited by the combined forces of journalism and colonization—one that Melville claims to both access and protect by framing all acts of storytelling as politically corrupt. Outside of what we might call the colonial temporality set up by the juxtaposition of Typee with the Sandwich Islands, then, is an authorial persona undeceived by the misleading stories of the newspaper and travel writer, existing, it seems, outside of the unreal world of information exchange. And so Melville is telling a clear story about the march of the West into the Pacific as he disavows storytelling, and even the very idea of information, as tools of imperialism. In a sense, he has beaten the force of colonization to this inland spot and thus seeks to establish a literary relationship to his heretofore untouched—that is, authentic—subject. But he cannot do so without bringing in the Sandwich Islands and the colonial predicament by which the islands are defined. Searching for an idiom that could present the Typee to the Western reader outside of the story of colonization, Melville promises an authenticity markedly different from that which was embodied in missionary stories of cultural contact but which nonetheless relied on the presence of colonialism elsewhere to define itself.

Hence the deeper meaning of the telegraphic metaphor in *Typee:* its very presence reminds us that the author's refusal to privilege storytelling as a method of organizing and interpreting the Typee was a way of being an outsider to both American and Typee cultures. In *Typee* Melville's critique of newspaper writing combines with the metaphor of the "vocal telegraph" to expose the myths of narrative omniscience and transparency as important tools of political manipulation.[17] Information exchange is a constant subject of *Typee,* in the various moments in which Tommo attempts to make sense of native communication, or in the example of the "vocal telegraph." To see all cultures—either that of the Western writer, who hastily manufactures textual pictures of distant lands for the reader, or that of the Typee, who (like the slave revolters in "Benito Cereno") place the bones of the dead on display for Western eyes—as performances, as Melville does, is to claim to occupy a rhetorical realm beyond the mythmaking of any culture.

As I have already shown, the early use of the telegraph as a guarantor of authenticity evolves into the more complex view that sees the island telegraph as a tool of cultural oppression. In other words, the telegraph morphs from a sign of the enlightenment Tommo promises his reader to a signifier that unveils this very faith in informational enlightenment as a culturally contingent myth. But long after Toby has departed from the scene, Melville again uses the telegraphic metaphor—this time not to foreground the impenetrableness of Typee culture but to communicate Tommo's partial acculturation. In chapter 28 he describes the anticipation of his hosts as they await the return of a recently departed fishing party:

During their absence the whole population of the place were in a ferment, and nothing was talked about but "pehee, pehee" (fish, fish). Towards the time when they were expected to return the vocal telegraph was put into operation—the inhabitants, who were scattered throughout the length of the valley, leaped upon rocks and into trees, shouting with delight at the thoughts of the anticipated treat. As soon as the approach of the party was announced, there was a general rush of the men towards the beach; some of them remaining, however, about the Ti, in order to get matters in readiness for the reception of the fish, which were brought to the Taboo groves in immense packages of leaves, each one of them being suspended from a pole carried on the shoulders of two men. (206–7)

Perhaps the first thing to notice about this passage is its contrast with some of the more talked-about moments in *Typee*, at which Tommo foregrounds his own inability to make sense of the mystifying practices that confront his narrative eye. Here Melville's narrator understands everything about how their society works, translating "pehee" without so much as a stutter and carefully outlining the role of each member. Just as significantly, here the telegraph functions in the narration precisely as it functions for the Typee itself: as an instrument for the rapid and efficient exchange of intelligence. While the chapter with the book's first invocation of the island telegraph ended with Tommo and his captor/hosts scrutinizing one another for information, this chapter ends with our narrator partaking in Typee culture: "When at Rome do as the Romans do, I held to be so good a proverb, that being in Typee I made a point of doing as the Typees did. Thus I ate poee-poee as they did" (209). Not bothering to put "poee-poee" inside quotation marks, Tommo's acceptance of Typee custom occurs at the very moment when their telegraph is presented as the efficient, even picturesque tool of harmless, even benevolent cultural practice.

In the chapters that follow, though, Tommo's life quickly becomes "one of absolute wretchedness" as he is daily "persecuted by the solicitations of some of the natives to subject myself to the odious operation of tattooing" (231). As he begins "bitterly to feel the state of captivity in which I was held," he plots his escape. Tommo is like Melville in that he is only comfortable when he can imagine himself at the margins of any one culture—Western or otherwise. Though we can certainly read the significance of tattooing in light of Tommo's unwillingness to give up the "whiteness" he maintains throughout his narrative, much of Melville's career can be defined by this conspicuous refusal to be "tattooed" by any culture.[18] After all, the implication that his true self requires the loud rejection of cultural standards of popularity is everywhere in Melville's correspondence—in his refusal of an invitation to be daguerreotyped for a magazine ("The fact is, almost everybody is having his 'mug' engraved nowadays . . . so that this test of distinction is getting to be reversed");[19] in his begging Hawthorne not to publish a review of *Moby-Dick* (for his fellow author "understood the pervading thought that impelled the book," and so a public review would "rob" Melville of his "miserly delight");[20] in his striking confession that "it is my earnest desire to write those sort of books which are said to 'fail.'"[21] In politely refusing the offer to sit for a daguerreotype, for example, Melville suggests that "this test of distinction is getting to be reversed," thereby using the marketplace's own logic to imply his private autonomy from the gaze of the reading public. His almost gleeful unwillingness to sit for a daguerreotype (and his unapologetic inability to even spell the word) should remind us that it was not only the practices of Typee culture by which he felt persecuted. Because the telegraph signifies in *Typee* as a rhetorical counterpoint to the text's invention of the Melvillean self, it should not surprise us that at the very moment the telegraph begins functioning in *Typee* the way it was functioning in 1845 America (that is, once Tommo sees the telegraph from the perspective of a cultural *insider*), it is a sign that Tommo is growing susceptible to the collective logic of culture itself, and so it is time for him to move on.

It is this ironic relationship to the technologies and practices of any one culture that is a defining characteristic of the Melvillean self. In his correspondence from the 1840s and 1850s, Melville's rhetorical flight from the terms of antebellum culture seems more than a posture, more than the public persona of a writer who, as Charles Fiedelson once wrote, "from first to last . . . presents himself as an artist, and a conscious artist."[22] Asking Hawthorne not to publish a review of *Moby-Dick,* for example, Melville refers to the praise that Hawthorne shared with him outside of public view, implying that its value is far greater than anything that could ever appear in the realm of mere puffery: "Truth is ever incoherent, and when the big hearts strike together, the concussion is a little stunning. Farewell. Don't write a word about the book. That would be robbing me of my miserly delight. I am heartily sorry I ever wrote anything about you—it was paltry" (213). Much like Hawthorne writing to Sophia, Melville here defines the intense authenticity of his shared contact with his friend against the paltriness of the print culture where he published "Hawthorne and His Mosses." Indeed, Melville seems aware, in his reference to his "miserly delight," of his own need to imagine a literary marketplace that fails to understand the genuine value of his books and Hawthorne's appreciation for them.[23]

But even as he rejects the superficial practices of the literary market-place, his sense of himself as an artist is indebted to the contingencies of antebellum culture in ways he seems unable to acknowledge. Later in the same frenzied letter begging Hawthorne not to write publicly about *Moby-Dick*, Melville confesses: "I have written a wicked book, and feel spotless as the lamb." Desperately seeking some language for conveying the intense bond he feels with Hawthorne, he writes, "I feel that the Godhead is broken up like the bread at the Supper, and that we are the pieces. Hence this infinite fraternity of feeling" (212). After rejecting Hawthorne's offer to write a review—indeed after having already signed his name—Melville is still unable to put down his pen: "I can't stop yet. If the world was entirely made up of Magians, I'll tell you what I should do. I should have a paper-mill established at one end of the house, and so have an endless riband of foolscap rolling in upon my desk; and upon that endless riband I should write a thousand—a million—billion thoughts, all under the form of a letter to you. The divine magnet is on you, and my magnet responds. Which is the biggest? A foolish question—they are *One*" (213). Earlier in the same letter, Melville had asked Hawthorne, "Lord, when shall we be done changing?" (213), and this closing image continues the theme by imagining a technology by which he could communicate in real time with his beloved Hawthorne—without mediation, without the artifice of publication and publicity.

Of course, Melville's imagined technology resembles nothing if not Morse's own electromagnetic telegraph: the responding magnets, the ribands of paper, even the "Magians" (evoking the technology's supernatural implications). In a letter obsessed with the implied threat posed by mass culture to Hawthorne and Melville's private bond, the author invokes telegraphic symbolism to underscore the intense and unmediated nature of their connection. This strange image, finally, suggests that as Melville imagined himself in perpetual flight from a "world of lies," such an escape was really a rewiring of antebellum culture's own machinery to serve the needs of the romancer's self-invention. In much the same way, I would suggest, the presence of the island telegraph in *Typee* reminds us that Melville's refusal to simply impart information to his audience was always something more complex than a philosophical or moral insight; rather, it was a way of looking at reality that connects the American author to the culture he never really left behind.

CHAPTER 6

"BENITO CERENO" AND THE
BLUNT-THINKING AMERICAN

O VER the past three decades, Melville's "Benito Cereno" has increasingly been celebrated as a "prophetic" and morally enlightened work, one that anticipates the insights and priorities of late twentieth- and early twenty-first-century criticism.[1] Consider, for example, the introductory essay to a recent special issue of *American Literature* on "Aesthetics and the End(s) of Cultural Studies," in which Christopher Castiglia and Russ Castronovo argue convincingly that "aesthetics disrupt the individual subject and provide the groundwork for an alternative, post-identity collectivism." In making such a claim, Castiglia and Castronovo invoke the lessons of Melville's novella: claiming that "Melville well understood both the danger and the potential of aesthetic encounters across histories, cultures, and institutions," they use "Benito Cereno" to embrace a twenty-first-century study of aesthetics that can "facilitate collective becoming, and, with it, collective social interests."[2] Seeing in "Benito Cereno" the possibilities of a postracial and postnational mode of "post-identity collectivism," Castiglia and Castronovo's invocation of the text captures the appeal it holds to the twenty-first-century critical mind: brilliantly preoccupied with the white racist imagination's complicity in the spectacle of slavery, "Benito Cereno" exemplifies the sort of narrative and epistemological self-consciousness valued by postcolonial and new historical models of reading.

But even as the novella helps us understand how the white literary imagination might resist and critique prevailing models of racial (and racist) consciousness, such an approach runs the risk of losing sight of "Benito Cereno" as both a romantic and a racialized text—a literary production that emerged out of its author's subject position as a white American author whose hostility to popular models of spectatorship and reading cannot simply be celebrated as a model of national or global citizenship. As my previous chapters have suggested, to read Melville as an avatar of collective identity-making is to smooth over the contradictions of his writing, both public and private. If it is no doubt true that as an "exploration of the white racist mind" "Benito Cereno" presents a moral complexity and self-awareness that continues to be rare among white-authored depictions of slavery, it is also true that it is the work of an author whose fiercest hostility was reserved for what he considered the dehumanizing menace of mass identity.[3]

Indeed, one of the most meaningful tensions of Melville's career was the pull between his self-styled "ruthless democracy" and his resentment of what he famously called "the tribe of general readers"—a tension so profound that both of these phrases come from the same 1851 letter to Nathaniel Hawthorne.[4] The letter's frenzied tone suggests that what he considered his radical democratic beliefs must also be understood as a way in which Melville attempted to distance himself from the threat of collective becoming:

I am told, my fellow-man, that there is an aristocracy of the brain. Some men have boldly advocated and asserted it. Schiller seems to have done so, though I don't know much about him. At any rate, it is true that there have been those who, while earnest in behalf of political equality, still accept the intellectual estates. And I can well perceive, I think, how a man of superior mind can, by its intense cultivation, bring himself, as it were, into a certain spontaneous aristocracy of feeling,—exceedingly nice and fastidious,—similar to that which, in an English Howard, conveys a torpedo-fish thrill at the slightest contact with a social plebeian. So, when you see or hear of my ruthless democracy on all sides, you may possibly feel a touch of a shrink, or something of that sort. It is but nature to be shy of a mortal who boldly declares that a thief in jail is as honorable a personage as Gen. George Washington. This is ludicrous. But Truth is the silliest thing under the sun. Try to get a living by the Truth—and go to the Soup Societies. . . . It seems an inconsistency to assert unconditional democracy in all things, and yet confess a dislike to all mankind—in the mass. But not so. But it's an endless sermon,—no more of it. (190–91)

Early in this passage, Melville suggests that it is Hawthorne who, due to an "intense cultivation," possesses an "aristocracy of feeling" that might lead him to feel "a touch of a shrink" in hearing of Melville's "ruthless democracy." Over the course of these sentences, though, Melville's *own* distaste for the masses emerges as a philosophical challenge to his *own* democratic views, as if he understands the need for the apparent contradiction to be resolved. And so when he invokes the paradox of his "unconditional democracy" and his "dislike" of the masses, he implies the value of the masses as a touchstone (like the plebes are for the English aristocrat) for the higher truth of his democratic views. Finally, his sense of such an argument as an "endless sermon" betrays his comprehension of the dialogic nature of his own identity: he can never get closer to communicating the "truth" of his belief than by continually invoking the masses as its opposite.

My readings of the "Old Zack" pieces and *Typee* have suggested that his ongoing attention to the inauthenticity of antebellum culture afforded him a language for the sort of self-invention attempted in the letter to Hawthorne: by devising storytelling strategies that foreground the social and narrative construction of reality, Melville negotiates a privileged and idiosyncratic relationship to truths beyond the reach of "the superficial skimmer of pages." In what follows, I argue that Melville's fragile identity as a democratic truth-seeker in a mass of misguided humanity found its most sustained literary expression in the complex narrative machinery of "Benito Cereno." For the democratic vision of "Benito Cereno," in which racial inferiority emerges as the product of the American captain Amasa Delano's racist mind, is, like his letter to Hawthorne, also a condemnation of the middlebrow American reader. Just as Melville's letter attempts to balance the author's egalitarian beliefs and his hostility to "all of mankind—in the mass," after all, so too does the narrative idiom of "Benito Cereno." And just as it is critically disingenuous to privilege the letter's claim to a ruthless democracy over its elitism, we should not simply embrace the story's narrative agenda as the pure expression of its author's progressive politics.

This chapter will read the novella as an articulation of romantic selfhood that relied on the status of slavery as the most hotly debated topic of mid-1850s America. As in so much of his work, the theoretical distance in "Benito Cereno" between Melville's narrative strategies and the authenticating practices of an imagined mass American readership—here embodied by Captain Delano, "the blunt thinking American"—locates for the romantic author an escape from the collective logic of representative "Americanness." In lieu of reading "Benito Cereno" as an attempt at saving "the experiment of American democracy," then, the following analysis of its place within mid-1850s abolitionist discourse portrays the text as a rhetorical high-wire act that sought for its author a space outside the archetypal thinking of mass culture.[5] While today we can (and should) celebrate the rhetorical space envisioned by such a project as a potential site for "collective becoming," when read in the context of Melville's ongoing flight from antebellum culture, this realm seems more the space of white romantic individualism. And so as we continue the important critical project of using "Benito Cereno" to create "a new kind of reader . . . [who] would view her necessarily dispersed and uncertain attempts to read the narrative not as a tapping into an already-agreed-upon truth, but as establishing an understanding that is always provisional and subject to change,"[6] we should also remember that, as his letter to Hawthorne suggests, Melville's literary artistry *required* the existence of popular misreading in order to find a language for Melvillean truth. For if today's reader sees the work as an attempt to convert the American reader to its own understanding of reality as something elusive to prevailing modes of description, we must also consider that the realization of such a goal would have meant the death of Melville as an artist.

I N the famous final paragraphs of "Benito Cereno," Amasa Delano is unable to comprehend the "shadow" cast upon his Spanish counterpart. From the perspective of the American captain, the narrative mystery of the slave revolt has been resolved, and the events of the rebellion have been undone: "'You are saved,' cried Captain Delano, more and more astonished and pained; 'You are saved; what has cast such a shadow upon you?'"[7] Rather than attending to the Spaniard's famous response to Delano's inquiry, let us linger for a moment on Delano's astonishment. Such a reaction betrays the American's unacknowledged commitment to narrative as a way of ordering and understanding the events he has experienced and witnessed. Consider the following passage from the text, one of many moments at which the American attempts to ascertain the authenticity of a story placed before him: "He recalled the Spaniard's manner while telling his story. There was a gloomy hesitancy and subterfuge about it. It was just the manner of one making up his tale for evil purposes, as he goes. But if that story was not true, what was the truth? That the ship had unlawfully come into the Spaniard's possession? But in many of its details . . . Don Benito's story had been corroborated not only by the wailing ejaculations of the indiscriminate multitude, white and black, but likewise—what seemed impossible to be counterfeit—by the very expression and play of every human feature, which Captain Delano saw" (68–69). Our narrator's phrasing of "But if that story was not true, what was the truth?" suggests the process whereby the American imposes upon the category of "truth" the subtle logic of narrativity. Ultimately, it is Delano's commitment to authenticating Don Benito's story that renders him incapable of reflecting on the implications of that commitment.

Furthermore, Delano's need to simply assess the authenticity of the story before him appears as the warping influence of American culture. When he reminds the Spanish captain that "yon bright sun . . . and the blue sea, and the blue sky" have all forgotten the events of the rebellion, Cereno famously responds that this is "because they have no memory . . . because they are not human" (116). According to both Cereno and Melville, then, Delano's refusal to "moralize" upon a past that is "passed," his assumption that the reality of the ship is a story to be either exposed as a hoax or authenticated as genuine, reflects a deformed and compromised humanity: while Cereno's tragedy is the "shadow" cast over him by the moral and epistemological lessons of the slave revolt, Delano's is that he attends to reality as if it were simply a narrative mystery.

Instead of focusing on portraying Cereno's descent into grief and philosophical despair, Melville's text is far more interested in critiquing Delano's approach to reality and treating it as the key feature of a representative Americanness; like a patron of Barnum's museum, or a skeptical reader of *Typee,* Delano skates along surfaces, obsessively searching out evidence to back up the truth claims in front of him. When, in the final paragraphs, the American is content to leave the story of the slave revolt in the past, Melville implicitly critiques Delano's inability to comprehend his own logic as an epistemological contingency: the world for Delano simply exists in narrative form, and so when the story is resolved there is nothing more to reflect on. Here Melville juxtaposes the narrative puzzle that confronts Delano aboard the *San Dominick* with the "shadow" that exists beyond the narrative closure found by the American captain. Melville, of course, is tempting the reader to apply Delano's superficial logic to his text: the secret of the *San Dominick,* after all, *can* be explained by means of an alternative story to the one contrived by the slaves (with the enforced participation of the Spanish sailors)—that is, the "true" story of the slave rebellion. But to simply locate this more authentic narrative among the official court papers is to miss, with Delano, all the meaning that resides beyond the ken of the story-seeking mind. In recasting the reality of slavery as a performance that exploits the American's eagerness to devour the world in narrative form, "Benito Cereno" at once posits an argument about slavery as an institution grounded in racial role-playing and formulates a critique of the American reader, whose appetite for true stories about slavery is recast by Melville as a superficial practice that threatens to make us something less than human.

Although countless critics have addressed the narrative complexities of "Benito Cereno," I wish to briefly consider how Melville's story confronts the distance between the fabric of his narration and the inaccessible reality of what is taking place aboard Cereno's ship. While Melville's narrator inhabits a third-person stance closely allied with Delano's perspective, at times the prose of the narrator (by his own admission) moves too slowly, as in a film where the camera's inability to keep up with the scene creates the very illusion of fast-paced action.[8] Indeed, this seems to be Melville's very point—not merely that language is incapable of keeping up with the world it claims to represent, but that the very act of storytelling fabricates the illusion of an authentic world beyond itself that moves too quickly for words. By distancing his narrator, if only slightly, from Delano's perspective, Melville continuously foregrounds the narrative we read as a dramatization of the attempt to see reality as a story. At those moments that our narrator shares Delano's point of view, Melville tempts us into accepting the validity of the story we read. And yet validity here is defined merely by the concurrence between our narrator's and Delano's perspectives, so that narrative authenticity is recast as consensus. Outside of the very quest for such consensus is the authorial view that recognizes the contingencies of all acts of narration.

As Delano's boat approaches the *San Dominick,* for example, the reader apparently moves from the captain's initial impression to a more objective understanding of what lies before him:

> Upon gaining a less remote view, the ship, when made signally visible on the verge of the leaden-hued swells, with the shreds of fog here and there raggedly furring her, appeared like a white-washed monastery after a thunder-storm, seen perched upon some dun cliff among the Pyrenees. But it was no purely fanciful resemblance which now, for a moment, almost led Captain Delano to think that nothing less than a ship-load of monks was before him. Peering over the bulwarks were what really seemed, in the hazy distance, throngs of dark cowls; while, fitfully revealed through the open port-holes, other dark moving figures were dimly descried, as of Black Friars pacing the cloisters. (48)

Melville's vividly descriptive language in the above passage masks the ambiguity of what is even being described here. While the narration seems to move from Delano's association of the scene with a monastery to a more authoritative view, in fact we move only from the suggestion of such an impression to that impression becoming a reality. The easily missed but important phrase "what really seemed," with its paradoxical juxtaposition of subjectivity and objectivity (what does it mean to "really seem"?), performs for the reader the ease with which perception occupies the language of the authentically true: the narrator's story becomes "true" merely by confirming Delano's arbitrary sense of what is real. When, in the next paragraph, our narrator informs us that "upon a still nigher approach, this appearance was modified, and the true character of the vessel was plain," we seem again to move from the inauthentic to the authentic. The only difference, of course, is that while the first move remained true for only a matter of sentences, this latter picture of "plain" reality—that the boat is "a Spanish merchantman of the first class; carrying negro slaves, amongst other valuable freight, from one colonial port to another" (48)—survives until it is overturned in the final pages of the story.

Of course, the novella's critique of Delano's appetite for an authentic story about slavery occurred in the wake of Harriet Beecher Stowe's best-selling *Uncle Tom's Cabin*—that is, just as masses of American readers were brought into the slavery debate *as readers*. Amid this development, Melville devised a literary idiom that, in exploring the implications of hungering after a true textual picture of slavery, was defined largely by its contrast with the objectives and practices of mainstream abolitionist storytelling.[9] This aspect of "Benito Cereno," its refusal to privilege storytelling as a means of accessing the true face of slavery, is most thoroughly understood when we consider that, more than just a subject of moral disagreement, slavery in the mid-1850s was at the center of a public conversation about the relationship between reading and reality. In the wake of *Uncle Tom's Cabin*, abolitionist and proslavery writers argued back and forth about what life in the American South actually looked like. Many writers on both sides published "firsthand" narratives seeking a true picture of American slavery, while each movement attacked the authenticity of its opponent's partisan reports. To much of the country abolitionism equaled radicalism, and at the heart of this view was the belief that the abolitionists' published depictions of slavery greatly exaggerated the life of the typical slave. Neither side could win a battle of pure reportage, for each side of the slavery debate could (and often did) find anecdote to answer anecdote, or newspaper article to answer newspaper article. By the middle part of the decade, as the volleys continued to fly back and forth, Ralph Waldo Emerson found no end to the rhetorical circuit of accusation and denial: in his 1855 "Lecture on Slavery," he concluded that "the subject seems exhausted . . . endless negation is a flat affair."[10] As commentators debated which depictions of slavery were most truthful, Emerson distanced himself from the public by wading into the question of slavery while portraying it as an "exhausted" subject.[11] Emerson's description of the act of debating slavery as a mere "affair" provides a useful touchstone for approaching the complexity of Melville's own invocation of slavery in "Benito Cereno." With its notorious manipulation of narrative perspective, "Benito Cereno" could uproot the assumptions of both the Stowe and anti-Stowe camps, portraying the popular discourse about slavery as a "flat affair."

When "Benito Cereno" is read in the broader context of Melville's career, the debates over Stowe's novel seem to offer Melville a cultural ideal of authenticity against which he could verbalize his deeper understanding of reality. But even more significantly, the example of "Benito Cereno" illustrates the racialized nature of Melville's ongoing claim to a foundational "axis of reality"—not only the racial logic at work in the narrative itself but also the extent to which Melville's artistic ideals were a marker of white privilege. To make such an argument, I want to briefly illustrate how the popular debates regarding the authenticity of Stowe's best-selling novel relied on the idea of a textually representable reality to prescribe clearly racialized roles for the white author and the black eyewitness. By interrogating the racial logic of Stowe's *Key to Uncle Tom's Cabin* (in which she sought to defend the authenticity of her novel), I will suggest, as others have before me, that the realist ethos of 1850s white abolitionism reserved for the white author the privilege of arbitrating between fiction and reality, while relegating the black former slave to the role of eyewitness. My point in doing so is to unveil how the act of telling stories about slavery functioned as a racializing force at the moment Melville was writing "Benito Cereno"—a force that, in imposing its narrative logic onto reality, imposed its racial logic as well. While many excellent scholars have highlighted these racial dynamics of the abolitionist marketplace, my ultimate goal is to reveal that when Melville indicts the logic of storytelling as a source of racial and national mythmaking, he is rejecting the Stowean ideal of white progressive authorship in favor of his own romantic ideal, one that could not entirely shed the racial logic of mainstream abolitionism even as it rejected its claims of literary realism.

While the publication and subsequent popularity of *Uncle Tom's Cabin* in the early 1850s predictably led to charges of invention and misrepresentation, its success also initiated a public debate about the implications of using literature to carry out the goals of social reportage. In arguing back and forth about what slavery actually looked like, abolitionists and apologists considered what it meant to represent a real-world problem in a literary idiom grounded in artifice.[12] At the same time, as conversations about the conditions of life in the South became more heated, slave testimony became even more valuable to the abolitionist cause. In other words, as the slavery debates grew more theoretical in considering the relationship between storytelling and reality, abolitionists relied more than ever on firsthand accounts of genuine slaves to prove the claims made in Stowe's novel.

In her *Key to Uncle Tom's Cabin,* Stowe relied on newspaper stories, advertisements, and legal codes to answer her critics. But as much as the *Key* may be read as a documentation of her novel's depiction of slavery, it should also be approached as a defense of fiction as a tool of reportage and social protest.[13] In the sixth chapter of the *Key,* for example, Stowe examines the legal requirements for protecting slaves in an attempt to jus-tify her depiction of Legree's violent treatment of Tom. After opening with brief excerpts from legal codes in South Carolina and Louisiana, Stowe writes, "Let us give a little sketch, to show how much it does amount to."[14] The "sketch" Stowe includes is an account written by Angelina Grimké Weld (originally included in Theodore Weld's *Slavery as It Is*) of her family's plantation in South Carolina. Weld's "sketch" begins with the claim that "the treatment of *plantation* slaves cannot be fully known, except by the poor sufferers themselves, and their drivers and overseers" (90). The reason this is so, Weld explains, is that she, like all southern women, "never visited the *fields where the slaves were at work,* and knew almost nothing of their condition." Even the slaveholders, Weld reports, "must, to a considerable extent, take the condition of their slaves on *trust,* from the reports of their overseers." Finally, Weld concludes, "these slave-holders (the wealthier class) are, I believe, almost the only ones who visit the North with their families; and Northern opinions of slavery are based chiefly on their testimony" (91).

In one of the most intriguing moments in the *Key,* Stowe responds to Weld's account of the remoteness of the "reality" of southern slavery by composing a story: "Now, suppose, while the master is in Charleston, enjoying literary leisure . . ." (91). Soon Stowe inserts into her fictional narrative a character named "Master Legree," who "finds himself, one sunshiny, pleasant morning" in the middle of Stowe's tale. While moments such as these seek to defend sentimental storytelling as a viable antislav-ery tool, such writing relies on the black body remaining an object and thus carves out two distinct and distinctly racialized notions of abolition-ist selfhood: the white author, who mediates between fact and fiction to expose the emotional horrors of slavery, and the black eyewitness, whose value is determined by the meaning-making voice of white abolitionism.

In the *Key,* Stowe places herself between fact and fiction, arbitrating for the reader between the two.

Weld's claim that "the treatment of *plantation* slaves cannot be fully known, except by the poor sufferers themselves, and their drivers and overseers" holds the slave's account of slavery as the gold standard of such documentation.[15] In a passage typical of her use of such materials, Stowe takes a long excerpt from (what she calls) "Life of Frederick Douglass" to "show that the case of George Harris [from *Uncle Tom's Cabin*] is by no means so uncommon as might be supposed" (19). Stowe then imports a paragraph from the narrative of Josiah Henson to prove the authenticity of a scene from *Uncle Tom's Cabin* in which a slave auction leads to the breaking up of a family. As Stowe relies on slave writing to validate her claims about slavery, she tells her reader that she has discussed such scenes "with a very considerable number of liberated slaves . . . and, what was most affecting about it, the narrator often considered it so much a matter of course as to mention it incidentally, without any particular emotion" (19). Here the white editorial voice determines the value of slave expression, essentially recasting the slave's voice as meaningful in a way that the slave's own words fail to register.

In an even more telling bit of phrasing later in the same chapter, Stowe is explicit about the irrelevance of slave voice: "But we shall be told the slaves are all a lying race, and that these are lies which they tell us. There are some things, however, about these slaves, which cannot lie. Those deep lines of patient sorrow upon the face; that attitude of crouching and humble subjection; that sad, habitual expression of hope deferred, in the eye,—would tell their story, if the slave never spoke" (20). Stowe's progression from the anticipated concerns regarding slave reliability to her cataloguing of those physical features that prove the horrors of slavery—sounding much like an auctioneer trumping the qualities of a genuine slave—suggests that the slaves' value resides primarily in their status as objects. As Dwight McBride writes, in the abolitionist marketplace the black body was "more truthful than the word of white abolitionists."[16] Thus Stowe's white abolitionism could find value in such bodies even "if the slave never spoke." White authorship (which Stowe depicts as the humane unearthing of the emotional dimensions of slave suffering) relied on the public objectification of the black body. And even more significantly, Stowe implies that the slave's voice could never do more for the cause of abolitionism than the voiceless black body—for all that the passage allows the former slave testifier to do is "to tell their story," which the body as object does on its own. Slave "voice," then, threatened, somewhat paradoxically, to vouchsafe the slave's own objectification by transforming the slave's body into a narrative—by turning an object on public display into a "life" for sale in the abolitionist marketplace.

The racialized prescriptions outlined here were even more explicit in other defenses of Stowe's novel. In F. C. Adams's *Uncle Tom at Home: A Review of the Reviewers and Repudiators of Uncle Tom's Cabin by Mrs. Stowe,* the author moves through an entire cast of slave characters, asking them to testify to the realities of life in the South. Near the end of his defense, Adams attacks southern laws that allowed state governments to recapture slaves freed by their owners upon the owner's death. Adams, who spends much of the book addressing the proslavery southern author William Gilmore Simms, invites Simms to visit an actual slave woman and her family who have lived for three years in the "work-house" of the court, awaiting an order of sale: "You have said to the world that the book was a tissue of falsehood. We say to the world, there are truths of Mrs. Stowe's book, staring you in the face; and before you again raise a pen against them, go to that municipal slave pen . . . [and] you will find Eliza Price and her child. Her cell is seven-by-four feet, or nearly, and if you cannot get *into it,* call her to the door—sit down by her, ask why she was put in there instead of the jail? . . . Listen to the story of her wretched life. Imagine it just as full of poetry as if it came from white lips, for her soul is *white,* and her lips are nearly so."[17]

Adams's evidence sits in her cell, ready to refute apologist objections and skepticism. But while Adams gives Price a voice, it is one that is limited to the details of her life ("Let the story of her wretched life . . ."), so that the black voice prescribed by white abolitionism is prefabricated to conform to the narrative shape that vouchsafed its success as a commodity. Over the course of the passage, the author moves from an account of "Mrs. Stowe's book" to the story told by Price, which lacks the poetry of Stowe's writing. As in the *Key,* here Adams performs the importance of sentimental fiction to infuse the black body with a "poetry" that could only come from white lips. The function of the white author, then, is to mediate between the human evidence who sits voiceless in her prison of authenticity and a readership who demands the "poetry" of sentimental storytelling. In the phrase "as if it came from white lips," Adams accepts the distinction implied by Stowe's *Key* between the black body serving as evidence and the white author whose words vouchsafe the value of such a body. In Stowe-like fashion, Adams's use of Eliza Price betrays slave "voice" as the means by which the public body—that of the imprisoned Price, who sits in a cell on display for the white audience—becomes a narrative object, a story for white consumption.

The predicament of the slave eyewitness provides a useful context for comprehending Melville's own invocation of slavery. After all, the closing image of "Benito Cereno"—after the *San Dominick* is taken back from the slaves by Captain Delano's men, after the legal documents that attempt to piece together the facts of the rebellion, after the final conversation between Delano and Don Benito—is the severed, unspeaking head of the African slave Babo. Melville's final paragraph is less interested in giving a clear sequence of concluding events than in placing black silence at center stage as the curtain falls on the narrative: "Some months after [the conclusion of the trial], dragged to the gibbet at the tail of a mule, the black met his voiceless end. The body was burned to ashes; but for many days, the head, that hive of subtlety, fixed on a pole in the Plaza, met, unabashed, the gaze of the whites; and across the Plaza looked towards St. Bartholomew's church, in whose vaults slept then, as now, the recovered bones of Aranda; and across the Rimac bridge looked towards the monastery, on Mount Agonia without; where, three months after being dismissed by the court, Benito Cereno, borne on the bier, did, indeed, follow his leader" (116–17). Does Cereno die before or after Babo is executed, his body burned, and his head fixed upon a pole? Melville leaves the chronology vague, opting instead to focus on the "voiceless end" of "the black," on the very fact of black voicelessness in the story. Babo's voicelessness is further foregrounded by the closing line of the penultimate paragraph, in which our narrator informs us that "on the testimony of the sailors alone rested the legal identity of Babo" (116). Of course, critics have long recognized that when Melville introduces legal documentation in the final pages of "Benito Cereno," he does more than ask his reader to accept these documents as proof of what occurred aboard the *San Dominick*.[18] Highlighting how the identity of "Babo" is produced by the one-sided legal testimony, and then confronting the reader with the African's lack of voice among the text's various accounts of what happened aboard the ship, Melville exposes black identity as a product of white storytelling.

But Melville's use of Babo's untalking head as a closing image for his narrative relies upon the unspeaking slave as a symbol for another white-authored text—his own—even as the author's use of the legal documents foregrounds Babo's identity as a product of white narrative. This maneuver allows Melville to redefine the fact of Babo's voicelessness according to his own narrative logic: while Babo's silence initially represents the untold story of the slave rebellion from Babo's perspective, in Melville's hands the untalking head of Babo comes to represent the process by which white attempts at composing and authenticating narrative accounts of slavery (Stowe's *Key,* for example) render the black slave voiceless. For the text's use of Babo's untalking head embodies how the white appetite for slave "voice" objectified the black speaking subject by predetermining the parameters of that voice. Revealing all attempts at narrativizing slavery as inadequate, Melville's text recasts the reality of slavery as an unrepresentable myth produced by the very attempt at rendering slavery narratable, a myth that upholds the racial hierarchies on which slavery is founded. Hence the chronological ambiguity of the story's final paragraph: eschewing the neat narrativization of events in favor of the closing image of Babo's severed head, Melville's conclusion reveals to his reader how the desire for the narrative containment of slavery privileges the racial mythmaking on which slavery thrives, inventing both the category of genuine blackness and the mythic "voice" that promises to render this blackness meaningful for the white audience.

The authorial relationship to the reality of slavery on display here replaces Stowe's ideal of white abolitionist authorship—the author as purveyor of a kind of realism that can be fully authenticated—with Melville's own romantic ideal—the author as arbiter of reality, who conspicuously opposes Stowe's reader by locating the deeper truths of slavery in the "shadow" of narrative. By highlighting the narrative construction of both national and racial taxonomies, Melville articulates the "post-identity" space that today's critics understandably celebrate. As in his letter to Hawthorne, however, a fundamental paradox of "Benito Cereno" is that in Melville's imagination this was the space not only of ruthless democracy but also of ruthless individualism, a realm where the categories and practices of the masses could be seen for the delusions they are. Moreover, it is Melville's very desire to rhetorically transcend the empty signifiers of American culture that betrays the contingencies of his own subject position: while his invocation of a white "gaze" witnessing the severed head of "the black" quietly claims a foundational perspective outside slavery's binary racial logic, this imagined relationship to the question of slavery revises and reimagines a particular model of white authorial practice and, as such, reflects an ideal of authorship unavailable to nonwhite writers of the era.

But in order to understand this romantic logic as a racial privilege, we must be willing to apply to "Benito Cereno" the same critical paradigm that has long comprehended the storytelling forms of ex-slave authors as strategies of self-invention. A generation of critics has taught us that the slave writer's dual role as speaking subject and narrative object led to a slave narrative tradition rich in formal complexity. And so it no longer suffices to say that the slave narrative depicts a progression from captivity to freedom—from an oppressive and contingent identity violently shaped by the social practices underlying slavery to the narrator's discovery, upon escaping the South, of an autonomous selfhood in which the escaped slave partakes of a universal freedom. Certainly William Andrews is correct in arguing that for escaped slaves such as Frederick Douglass and William Wells Brown the writing of autobiography marked "the final, climactic act in the drama of [former slaves'] lifelong quests for freedom."[19] Yet the former slave's entrance into the antebellum print marketplace has more recently been understood as an arrival into a new network of social and economic contingencies.[20] Saidiya Hartman's description of the postbellum black experience can easily be applied to the predicament of the fugitive-slave abolitionist: "Emancipation appears less the grand event of liberation than a point of transition between modes of knowledge and racial subjection."[21]

By the early 1850s, black writers responded to abolitionism's demand for particular kinds of stories by departing from the conventions of traditional slave autobiography.[22] Frederick Douglass's revisions to his life story between 1845 and 1855, for example, suggest an increasingly complicated relationship between the author and abolitionism. In *My Bondage and My Freedom* (1855) Douglass famously attacks the expectations and demands placed upon him as an abolitionist lecturer.[23] Douglass's exposure of the abolitionist attempt to "pin me down to my simple narrative" highlights the relationship between the logic of storytelling and black commodification in the abolitionist marketplace that I have been describing.[24] The slave, Douglass implies, becomes a commodity at the precise moment when his life enters the marketplace—that is, when the life of Frederick Douglass becomes the "Life of Frederick Douglass." And underlying such a process, Douglass argues, is the merging of selfhood and narrativity that allowed white abolitionism to produce the black speaking and writing subject as "genuine." In a perfect illustration of this subtle merging of life and "life," John Collins tells Douglass, "Be yourself . . . and tell your story" (367)—as if the two were naturally synonymous. One could argue that Douglass's response to Collins was to write a second autobiography—so that in keeping more than one story of his life in public circulation the ex-slave writer could foreground the distance between the production(s) of his life and the Frederick Douglass who existed outside of the antebellum print marketplace.

One of the most significant responses to the dilemma of the ex-slave author was William Wells Brown's *Clotel; or, the President's Daughter,* which appeared in 1853 in England. As many critics have pointed out, the novel's mixing of fictional and nonfictional texts problematized the role of eyewitness imposed upon the black writer by white abolitionism.

In fact, Brown's evasion of the role of first-person storyteller began at least as far back as 1850, when he briefly toured England with a series of twenty-four paintings that were marketed as *William Wells Brown's Original Panoramic Views of the Scenes in the Life of an American Slave.*[25] In the published pamphlet that accompanied the panorama, Brown writes the following about his panorama's twelfth picture: "The view now before us is the first scene in which the writer is represented in this Panorama." His panorama included images based on the published narratives of other well-known escaped slaves (such as Henry Bibb), but by far the life most often represented in the panorama was his own. What is striking about these passages in the pamphlet is not his choice of subject matter but the rhetorical approach Brown takes in describing his own life. Eschewing the traditional autobiographical voice associated with slave eyewitness testimony, Brown writes about a representation of his own experiences under slavery in the third person. The decision to speak in third-person voice reveals the singular value a medium such as the panorama held for a black abolitionist like Brown. As an authentic former slave on the abolitionist lecture circuit, Brown was expected to speak in a first-person voice, one that could tell an autobiographical story of life in the American South. If the lived experience of the former slave was transformed into a commodity the moment it appeared in public—the moment, that is, when the slave's life became the "life" of an authentic slave—narrativizing the details of his own life meant putting into circulation (in lectures or in writing) a public version of himself that gained value solely from the meaning that white abolitionism found in his story. Thus the panorama afforded the former slave eyewitness a rhetorical means of physically removing himself from both the narrative machinery by which slavery was represented and the first-person voice by which the slave eyewitness was objectified and commodified.[26]

Nowhere concerned with opposing an "inmost Me" to the fictions of antebellum culture, Brown's reliance on representations of himself foregrounded and manipulated his status as an object in the public's eye. Pointing to someone else's visual representation of his own life (for he tells us that these scenes "have been copied by skilful artists in London") allowed Brown to exploit the physical distance between his body and the "life" that sat upon the abolitionist stage as a public commodity.[27] Similarly, when Brown published *Clotel* in 1853 the novel appeared with a strange prefatory autobiography, "Narrative of the Life and Escape of William Wells Brown," in which Brown again adopted a third-person perspective on his own life, even bringing in excerpted first-person passages from his 1847 autobiography and from his abolitionist lectures—so that Brown's authorial persona implied an editorial mastery over the public accounts of his life.[28] Such an editorial posture connected the prefatory "Life and Escape" with the narrative strategies of *Clotel,* which relied heavily on excerpts from newspaper extracts and legal documents and borrowed an entire plotline from Lydia Maria Child's story "The Quadroons."[29] Ultimately, the authorial self-portrait that emerges in both "Life and Escape" and *Clotel* rejects the notion of an authentic black voice, positing in its place a minstrel-like authorial figure who carefully manipulates public texts.[30] As an answer to white abolitionism's demand for a stable voice that embodied authentic blackness, the literary innovations of the 1853 text created a strange, hybrid text that flaunted the instability of its varied textual productions of black selfhood.

In the 1853 "Life and Escape," which continually frames and excerpts Brown's earlier first-person texts, Brown at once circulates competing stories of his life (à la Douglass) and reveals this self-mastery to be a form of economic control. Not allowing his reader to overlook the former slave's status as a commodity, Brown draws a parallel between his economic manipulation of whites (in the anecdotes excerpted from the autobiography and his lectures) and his manipulation of the (i.e., his) textual "life" from which he takes these very excerpts. In one of Brown's lectures excerpted by his third-person narrator, the lecture's first-person voice describes the process by which the young slave learned to read. Importantly, the later, third-person narrator picks up the first-person account at the moment when Brown enters the northern marketplace, having earned a shilling for an unnamed job—as if there is no textual "I" without a particular economy to render it meaningful:

> This was not only the only shilling I had, but it was the first I had received after obtaining my freedom, and that shilling made me feel, indeed, as if I had a considerable stock in hand. What to do with my shilling I did not know. . . . After considerable thinking upon the subject, I laid out 6*d.* for a spelling-book, and the other 6*d.* for sugar candy or barley sugar. Well, now, you will all say that the one 6*d.* for the spelling-book was well laid out; and I am of the opinion that the other was well laid out too; for the family in which I worked for my bread had two little boys, who attended the school every day, and I wanted to convert them into teachers; so I thought that nothing would act like a charm so much as a little barley sugar. (35–36)

Brown next describes how he manipulated the white children into teaching him all the letters of the alphabet. As in the above passage, here Brown highlights his economic mastery over the children: "I kept those two boys on my sixpenny worth of barley sugar for about three weeks. Of course I did not let them know how much I had" (37). Such a careful focus on economic manipulation allows Brown to foreground himself as an economic production: by the end of the excerpted section of his speech, Brown tells his audience, "I next obtained an arithmetic, and then a grammar, and I stand here tonight, without having had a day's schooling in my life" (38). While the first-person "William" of the lecture emerges as an economic production, the third-person narrator allows Brown to expose "voice" as one means by which this production is achieved—for Brown frames his own "I" to highlight the relationship between voice and the textual production of "William." "Voice," it seems, is not so much a means of expression as a mode of production.

This foregrounding of "William" as a textual production occurs from the opening paragraphs, in which our narrator introduces us to the region where William the slave grew up. The narrative of "Life and Escape" opens with the following statement: "William Wells Brown, the subject of this narrative, was born a slave in Lexington, Kentucky, not far from the residence of the late Hon. Henry Clay" (17). After describing William's move with his master to "a beautiful and fertile valley" in Missouri, Brown's second paragraph begins in the following way: "Here the slaves were put to work under a harsh and cruel overseer named Cook. A finer situation for a farm could not have been selected in the state. With climate favourable to agriculture, and soil rich, the products came in abundance. At an early age William was separated from his mother, she being worked in the field, and he as a servant in his master's medical department. When about ten years of age, the young slave's feelings were much hurt at hearing the cries of his mother, while being flogged for being a few minutes behind the other hands in reaching the field" (17–18). The striking contrast in tone between the first and second sentences—in which Brown describes the cruelty of slavery and then relies upon a picturesque mode of third-person description—highlights how abolitionist rhetoric objectifies the slave. If these ways of narrating strike the reader as paradoxical, that seems to be the very point: the narration moves back and forth between the disengaged stance of a tourist and sharp reminders of the violence of slavery to show how both narrative modes objectify their subjects. Brown cloaks his descriptions in the passive voice to make the language itself, with its indirect, distanced, even objective tone, echo the violence of the floggings Brown describes. By telling us that William "was separated," that his feelings "were much hurt," by saying only that his mother was "being worked in the field . . . [and] being flogged," Brown links the attempts of white abolitionism to contain slave experience to the violence of slavery itself: the passive voice literally makes William, "the subject of this narrative," into a grammatical object.

And throughout "Life and Escape" Brown's writing charts this very process. Almost immediately after the above passage, violence bursts through, shifting the tourist's passive voice to active. In the very next sentences, Brown states: "He heard her cry, 'Oh, pray! oh, pray! oh, pray!' These are the words which slaves generally utter when imploring mercy at the hands of their oppressors. The son heard it, though he was some way off. He heard the crack of the whip and the groans of his poor mother. The cold chill ran over him, and he wept aloud; but he was a slave like his mother, and could render her no assistance" (18). Here William-as-slave appears more directly, as the subject who hears and suffers. Framing slavery's violence with the narrator's explanatory commentary ("These are the words which slaves generally utter"), Brown's writing emulates the white attempt to determine the value of direct slave emotion. Such a narrative maneuver helps us understand Hartman's claim that the white attempt to imagine slave emotion is actually an act of distancing: "The gaze shifts from the spectacle to the inner recesses of feeling and desire—that is, the emotional substrate that presumably resides within the 'poor slave,' which mutes the shock of the scene and mitigates its ghastly incommensurability with the suggestion of containment."[31] In lieu of capturing (and thus containing) William's pain, Brown refuses to narrate in the first person—so that William's distance from his mother is paralleled by the narrator's distance from William. As the helplessness of William's position yanks the narrative back in the final sentence above, the narrator returns to the passive voice. "He was taught," the narrator tells us, "by the most bitter experience, that nothing could be more heart-rending than to see a dear and beloved mother or sister tortured by unfeeling men, and to hear her cries, and not be able to render the least aid" (18). William's experience of hearing his mother being whipped must capitulate to the meaning-making demands of storytelling; William's pain, it seems, must culminate in a lesson. And thus Brown reveals how abolitionism's demand for an authentic narrative account of slavery transforms the speaking slave as "expressive" subject into a narrative object.[32]

Herein lies the significance of what Andrews calls the "novelization" of slave writing at this moment.[33] *Clotel,* the first African American novel, emerged out of the ex-slave writer's singular position between the theoretical implications of the Uncle Tom debates on one hand and the commodifying threat of abolitionism on the other.[34] If a Stowe-like authorial distance from the goals of strict description was a marker of a productive abolitionist selfhood, the former slave's status as fetish object imposed a violent and paradoxical notion of individualism: slave subjectivity was only meaningful as a public text. In *Clotel*, then, the idea of a genuine black voice appears not as an authentic and liberating discovery on the part of the ex-slave writer but as a cultural product whose value was predetermined by abolitionism. Instead of giving Brown's own testimony as a former slave, *Clotel* exposes and undercuts the white attempt at commodifying black experience. Upon the death of Mr. Peck, a southern slaveholding parson, Peck's daughter Georgiana walks with Carlton, her suitor, as they overhear the singing of her father's slaves. In an oft-cited scene, Carlton is surprised to hear in the songs that the slaves "pretend" to grieve but are in fact "mighty glad" that their master "will no more trample on the neck of the slave." Georgiana, however, informs her suitor that "it is from these unguarded expressions of the feelings of the Negroes, that we should learn a lesson."[35]

Upon returning to their house, the couple encounters the same slave they had heard singing only moments earlier, now "looking as solemn and as dignified as if he had never sung or laughed in his life" (156). After Georgiana lectures Peck about the value of the slave songs, she goes on to philosophize about the universal faith in "the idea that [the slave] was born to be free" that survives in the slave's heart even in the face of oppression. By framing this white experience of black expression within Georgiana's arguments about slave humanity, Brown portrays the very category of the "genuine" as a function of white signification, for there is no place in the scene for slave utterance outside of the eyes of white characters: even when the slave thinks he is alone, the white Georgiana overhears him. While the scene looks on the surface like a somewhat typical rejection of apologist claims of slave contentment, Brown's careful avoidance here of slave subjectivity outside the ken of a white audience confronts the abolitionist appetite for a picture of genuine black expression—that is, for a trace of "black reality" outside of any white frame. By portraying (in Georgiana's lecture) this appetite and then refusing to give a glimpse of any slave utterance outside of the marketplace that demands it, Brown confronts the abolitionist marketplace with its own inescapable logic—and subtly associates the myth of pure self-expression with the terms of white narrativity. As Georgiana tells Peck, "It is from these unguarded expressions . . . that we should learn a lesson," as if black emotion exists solely for the production of white knowledge.

As in "Life and Escape," in *Clotel* Brown manipulates his own value as a genuine former slave to constantly flaunt the slave self's status as capital in the abolitionist marketplace. At one of the only moments in the entire novel where the author refers to himself explicitly, he appears with no voice at all. After excerpting a Boston church deed outlining its segregationist pewholder policy, Brown writes: "Such are the conditions upon which the Rowe Street Baptist Church, Boston, disposes of its seats. The writer of this is able to put that whole congregation, minister and all, to flight, by merely putting his coloured face in that church. We once visited a church in New York that had a place set apart for the sons of Ham. . . . It had two doors; over one was B. M.—black men; over the other B. W.—black women" (180–81). Brown's salient refusal here to write in the first-person singular—his move from "the writer of this" to "we"—signals a careful avoidance of an authorial voice that could be at all confused with the autobiographical writing associated with the slave eyewitness. While he uses his own position as the editor of a range of actual texts to validate one of his authenticating texts, he does so as a voiceless black body whose mere appearance "puts the whole congrega- tion . . . to flight." After referring to himself as "the writer of this," Brown places his body on display with the odd phrasing of "merely putting his coloured face in that church"—so that at the rare moment when Brown writes autobiographically, he simultaneously equates such a maneuver with his own self-objectification. Describing his body as something "put" before a white congregation, Brown confronts his reader with the striking contrast between the public roles of author and slave eyewitness.

Furthermore, Brown relies on fiction to fabricate a textual self-portrait in the pages of *Clotel* that flaunts its own contingent status, for the "Wil- liam Wells Brown" produced by *Clotel* (like the "William" who stands before an abolitionist audience in "Life and Escape") is largely a textual production. At the end of the novel, Brown includes a "Conclusion" in which he addresses the question of the reliability of his novel's account of slavery. Here Brown informs his reader that he has "personally partici- pated in many of these scenes" and has "derived" many of the other stories from various sources: "Having been for nearly nine years employed on Lake Erie, I had many opportunities for helping the escape of fugitives, who, in return for the assistance they received, made me the depositary of their suffering and wrongs. Of their relations I have made free use. To Mrs. Child, of New York, I am indebted for part of a short story. American Abolitionist journals are another source from whence some of the charac- ters appearing in my narrative are taken. All these have combined to make up my story" (245). The economic tone of Brown's conclusion (e.g., use of the words "depositary," "indebted," and, later, his "resources") under- scores the author's acknowledgment of his position within a marketplace and links his self-production here with the first-person William of "Life and Escape." If "Life and Escape" exposes abolitionism as the ultimate determinant of the value of slave utterance, *Clotel* further evades the promise of a genuine black voice within this marketplace. Brown's confession that "all these have combined to make up my story" is not what it appears to be: instead of undercutting his own authority as a creative author, the claim challenges the assumption of an autonomous selfhood on which the phrase "my story" relies. In place of the autobiographical writing expected of the black abolitionist, Brown has given his audience a hybrid text that has no "I" at the center. If "all these have combined" to make what must be called "my story," then the authorial self emerges as the product of storytelling, not as its source.[36]

As I have already suggested, Brown's flaunting of the self as a discursive product foregrounds both the romantic and the racialized dimensions of Melville's treatment of slavery. At its most basic level, Melville's deconstruction of racial and national taxonomies—his celebrated argument that these categories are largely the product of the (white American) appetite for an authentic story—was, like Brown's related project, a response to his own subject position: in pointing to white storytelling instead of embodying it, Melville, like Brown, sought to elude a model of antislavery authorship shaped by the intensifying debates over slavery. But while Brown responds to the demands on black authorship by inserting himself into his novel and flaunting the contingencies of black identity, Melville attributes the categories of "American," "Spanish," "black," and "white" to the narrative logic of Delano's mind—thereby distancing the text's authorial persona from Delano's white epistemology. When read alongside Brown's manipulation of those public masks that make up the spectacle of antebellum life, Melville's rhetorical flight from the surfaces of antebellum culture comes into focus as the calling card of white romanticism. As Paul Gilmore writes of *Clotel*, "Brown turns to fiction *not* to escape the problematic of stereotyped black representability, but to negotiate the objectification and commodification of the black image . . . thus opening up the possibility of a blackfaced version of literary manhood."[37] Instead of joining the game, Melville's response to the racial role-playing of slavery and abolitionism is to claim a foundational perspective that locates the romantic imagination outside the fictions of nation and race. The point is not that Melville is guilty of racism but that his desire for an authority over the racial role-playing of slavery, even as it frames and reject's Delano's model of white epistemology, cannot escape the whiteness of his ontological ideals.

Indeed, these racial contingencies of Melville's artistic ideals would reemerge two years later, in *The Confidence-Man,* his final novel and the last piece of his fiction that would appear during his lifetime. Much like "Benito Cereno," *The Confidence-Man* relies on the popular preoccupation with the criteria of authentication and documentation to articulate a totalizing vision of "America" on which the romantic author could look down. Relying on the status of the Mississippi River as a fluid, all-encompassing symbol that could contain the variety of the nation within a unifying representative logic—as it had, for example, in the various Mississippi River panoramas of the late 1840s—Melville portrays the nation as a collective ship of fools. Like Delano, those aboard the steamer *Fidèle* surrender their humanity not simply by being humbugged but by approaching reality exclusively through the question of confidence—so that their own identities are no more stable than the shape-shifting con man that preys on them. But while we might be tempted to agree with the popular critical assessment that in Melville's work the artist himself is a kind of confidence man, the romancer's presence in the novel appears to be defined *against* the superficial world of the *Fidèle,* where all identities depend on the public's confidence. Neither one of the masses nor confidence man (whose identity and financial well-being depend on the superficial practices of the public), the romantic author is perhaps most clearly aligned with the mysterious stranger of the final chapter, who overhears a conversation between two fellow travelers, and, still in darkness, asks, "Who's that describing the confidence-man?"[38] Out of view both to those aboard the ship and to the novel's reader, the author of *The Confidence-Man* hovers as a rhetorical presence whose ontological shape is defined against the fictional identities of a dehumanized America.

As in "Benito Cereno," this rhetorical distance from the logic of role-playing seems to quietly claim for Melville's authorial ideals an authority over the fiction of race itself. In one of the more famous moments in *The Confidence-Man,* "a grotesque negro cripple" named Black Guinea appears in the forward part of the boat, playing a tambourine and "raising a smile even from the gravest" of the crowd (10). As happens throughout the novel, a passenger begins "to croak out something about his deformity being a sham, got up for financial purposes" (12), and the crowd scrutinizes him for signs of impostery, asking him if he has "any documentary proof, any plain paper about him, attesting that his case was not a spurious one." Black Guinea responds by assuring his interrogators that there are several men aboard the ship who "knows me and will speak for me," including a "good ge'mman wid a weed" (13). While the boat is searched for the man with the weed, a country merchant hands him a half dollar as "some proof of [his] trust," making "the cripple's face" glow "like a polished copper saucepan" (17). Just as the spectacle of Babo's unspeaking head at the conclusion of "Benito Cereno" confronts the racial dynamics of mainstream white abolitionism (by refusing to ventriloquize for a black subject who can have no authentic voice), here Melville links the surface truths of racial difference with a broader cultural logic that renders identity dependent on the role-playing that emerges out of the pursuit of capital.

In both "Benito Cereno" and *The Confidence-Man,* Melville flees from the terms of this culture, staking out an authorial identity whose stability is offset by the "polished" surface of Black Guinea's black face and the arbitrary white authority of the man with the weed—whom the crowd searches out but of course will never find. According to *The Confidence-Man,* Brown (that is, the minstrel-like manipulator of images so aptly described by Paul Gilmore) and Stowe (the white authenticator of her own fictions in the *Key*) are not only dependent on one another for their fragile identities; by making both "Black Guinea" and the white man with the weed two incarnations of the confidence man, Melville seems to be telling us they are in fact the same person. As in the layered narrative approach of Hawthorne's *Story Teller* pieces, Melville carves out a romantic authorial identity predicated on exposing the contingent and ultimately interchangeable nature of all identities in the American marketplace.

The collectivizing logic of *The Confidence-Man,* according to which the romantic author seeks to portray American society *en masse,* helps us understand the centrality of the role played by Amasa Delano in Melville's literary imagination. By portraying the *San Dominick* through Delano's eyes, Melville connects the instability of national and racial taxonomies to the surface-oriented epistemology of those embodied by Delano's representativeness—not the American reader but the "American" reader. That is, Melville's text elevates the reader's relationship to the problem of reality as the defining characteristic of identity: to read surfaces is to be a mass subject; to understand the shadows and depths beyond the reach of language or storytelling is to be more genuinely human. Intriguingly, though, when we consider Melville's reliance on the Spanish Benito Cereno to offset Delano's delusional approach to reality, we are again reminded of the text's own location *within* the racial politics of 1850s America. For, as I will now suggest, Melville's distinction between the blunt-thinking American (who neatly falls under both national and racial logic) and the liminal Don Benito (who resides in the shadows of these distinctions) exploits the slippery nature of Spanish identity at the time Melville was writing, so that the novella's apparent quest for a postracial, postnational political space looks more like a different kind of racial logic, one that, even as "black" and "white" are recognized as biological and legal fictions, cannot escape the game of racial signification.

In the 1850s, in the wake of the U.S.-Mexican War and as American politicians and commentators debated the feasibility and desirability of annexing Cuba, the term "Spanish" occupied a singular discursive space, embodying an intriguing combination of national and racial significance. Antebellum accounts of American encounters with Mexico and Cuba provided an opportunity for writers to distinguish between "Anglo-Saxon" and Spanish-inflected identities. In a piece from the *United States Magazine and Democratic Review* written during the Mexican War, the prospect of annexing Mexico leads to a conception of "Spanish"-ness as an uncertain racial signifier:

> The very virtues of the Anglo-Saxon race make their political union with the degraded Mexican-Spanish impossible. . . . The Mexican race now see in the fate of the aborigines of the north, their own inevitable destiny. They must amalgamate and be lost, in the superior vigor of the Anglo-Saxon race, or they must utterly perish. They may postpone the hour for a time, but it will come, when their nationality shall cease. It is observable, that, while the Anglo-Saxon race have overrun the northern section, and purged it of a vigorous race of Indians, the Spaniards have failed to make any considerable progress at the south. . . . The proud, rapacious, and idle Spaniards have but poorly fulfilled their mission. . . . The progress of emigration on this continent has hitherto been peaceful;—but the Spanish race, to maintain their slothful possession of the country they hold, have, in the madness of their pride, attacked the colossal power that is about to overwhelm them.[39]

The above argument stakes its claim for the purity of "Anglo-Saxon" blood through a contrast with "the Spanish race," which has "failed to make any considerable progress" due to those qualities that are intrinsic to their nature. In a typical account of American-Mexican contact, the racial hybridity of the Mexican people is offset by the "Anglo-Saxon" identity of America.

As Julia Stern shows, the vagaries of Spanish racial identity provide an important context for the various invocations of the Spanish gentleman in passing novels: "Averting the dualism of black and white in his capacity as neither, the brown-skinned Spanish gentleman transmutes the problem of race by disputing its rigid terms. . . . Spanish masquerade obscures white supremacist fantasies about slaves in flight . . . [and]

thrusts a privileged and mysterious 'darkness' squarely in the face of a white racist patriarchy."[40] Discussing specifically the "Spanish masquerade" of George Harris in Stowe's *Uncle Tom's Cabin,* Stern reminds us that the racial ambiguity embodied by the figure of the Spaniard (an ambiguity with a history dating back several centuries) reemerges in the mid-nineteenth century to challenge the legal and cultural fictions of black and white. Similarly, in her discussion of George Lippard's *Legends of Mexico,* Shelley Streeby finds evidence that Lippard's writing extends the boundaries of American whiteness beyond "Anglo-Saxon" to include Germany, Scotland, Ireland, and other northern European countries; and yet, as Streeby makes clear, "this more expansive definition of white American unity crucially depends upon the construction of Mexicans as a [in Lippard's words] 'mongrel race, moulded of Indian and Spanish blood.'" Streeby also cites nativist writer Daniel Ullmann, who wrote in 1856 that the Spanish empire ultimately fell apart because it lacked the "real unity of race, language, and territory." Finally, Streeby illustrates how the antebellum fascination with "Spanish fantasy" novels provided a highly charged imaginative space in which American writers and readers could address the possibility of territories such as Mexico and especially Cuba becoming part of a "southern slave empire."[41]

Politicians, newspaper editors, and ordinary Americans debated the idea of taking over Cuba throughout the years leading up to the Civil War, and as such debates were taking place, popular novels such as Mary Denison's *The Prisoner of La Vintresse* worked through questions of race and slavery as they pertained to neighboring lands such as Cuba. At the same time, new illustrated periodicals such as *Frank Leslie's Illustrated Newspaper* depicted highly romanticized renderings of Havana, rural Cuba, and more distant lands such as Nicaragua—pictures that appeared alongside novels with titles such as *The Spanish Moor.* As Streeby points out in her discussion of *The Prisoner of La Vintresse,* these novels used the color line to debate the implications of Cuban annexation. Denison, Streeby writes, "racially 'darkens' Cuba in ways that echo the various antislavery but still racially phobic objections to the annexation of Cuba."[42] We see a similar reliance on the slipperiness of Spanish racial identity in Maturin Murray Ballou's *Miralda; or, the Justice of Taçon,* a melodramatic love story that takes place in Havana. The American character, Seth Swap, makes the following observations about the people he encounters on the island: "Thought I'd just stop a few weeks on this island of Cubey [on his way from Mexico to Maine] to see the folks. What a funny people they are! [T]wo fifths niggers, one fifth grandees, one fifth poll parrots and fireflies, and one fifth darnation pooty gals. The rest's pooty much sugar cane and merlasses."[43]

The story-seeking mind of Delano in "Benito Cereno" allows Melville to chart this slipperiness of "Spanish" as a racial and national signifier. On one hand, Delano's attitude toward Cereno exhibits the prominence of the "nation" as a marker of identity. As our narrator tells us, "as a nation . . . these Spaniards are all an odd set; the very word Spaniard has a curious, conspirator, Guy-Fawkish twang to it" (79). Indeed, throughout Melville's story, Delano attempts to make sense of Cereno's odd behavior by resorting to various narratives of Spanish national history. When he first encounters the *San Dominick,* for example, our narrator's description quietly attempts to explain the "slovenly" appearance of the ship by placing it within the larger story of Spanish decline: it was a "very large, and, in its time, a very fine vessel, such as in those days were at intervals encountered along that main; sometimes superceded Acapulco treasure-ships, or retired frigates of the Spanish king's navy, which, like superannuated Italian palaces, still, under a decline of masters, preserved signs of former state" (48). When Delano considers whether the Spanish captain is an "imposter," he soon dismisses the thought with an affirmation of the captain's genuineness: "He was a true off-shoot of a true hidalgo Cereno" (65).

What is perhaps more subtle about the text's invocation of Spanishness is the way in which Melville plays on the racial ambiguity of the Spanish throughout the text. At various moments the narration flaunts the slipperiness of its Spanish characters as they occupy the space between black and white—a space that typifies the unstable nature of Spanish identity at the time when Melville was writing. When Delano first boards the *San Dominick,* it is the American captain who is an outsider to the racially mixed and ambiguous population aboard the boat, as if the Spanish sailors are themselves opposed to the American's whiteness. It is not simply that the ship comprises both blacks and whites; rather, the Spanish characters seem to drift conspicuously between these two categories: Cereno is described as "the dark Spaniard" (69); another Spanish sailor, seated between two blacks, is described as "an old Barcelona tar" who seems at one point to merge into the blacks on either side, forming what our narrator calls a "centaur" (72); and soon after Cereno escapes into Delano's boat, we see the ship in chaos, with "the few Spanish sailors . . . helplessly mixed in, on deck, with the blacks" (99).

Once the battle to overtake the ship begins, and the Spaniards separate themselves physically from the blacks on board the *San Dominick* (either by leaping toward Delano's boat, or climbing the ship's masts, "just out of reach of the hurtling hatchets" [101]), the racial taxonomies fall into place, and the story becomes a clear battle between white and black. Indeed, once Cereno makes his escape, the Spaniards are at times no longer "Spaniards" at all; they are simply "whites." In one of the most intriguing sentences in Melville's narration, our narrator charts the return of the Spanish characters from the realm of racial ambiguity to the clarity that Delano so clearly desires: "Soon, in a reunited band, and joined by the Spanish seamen, the whites came to the surface, irresistibly driving the negroes toward the stern" (102). The "Spanish seamen" join the reunited whites, a formulation that at once implies their racial unity while also calling attention to the distance between the signifiers "Spanish" and "white." Melville thus links the narrative uncertainty of the first portion of the text, during which time Delano is attempting to figure out what has taken place aboard the ship, with the racial ambiguity of Delano's perceptions; when the narrative becomes a battle, though, and Delano and our narrator fully comprehend what is at stake, the racial categories fall into place, albeit uneasily. The Spaniards arise out of the murky depths and reunite with the whites, and the blacks quickly return to subjugation and racial caricature: "Their red tongues lolled, wolf-like, from their black mouths. But the pale sailors' teeth were set; not a word was spoken; and, in five minutes more, the ship was won" (102).

In one of the text's rare moments in which things proceed within a clear temporal progression, Melville connects such narrative clarity to a reassertion of the racial categories that had been challenged by Delano's inability to penetrate the narrative mystery. And yet if this interrogation of "Spanish" as a racial category preys on the slipperiness of race itself, the novella's concluding opposition—between a Spanish captain who dwells in "shadows" and a blunt-thinking American who can think only in the broadest cultural categories—seems to uphold the liminal status of Spanish identity in the popular imagination. As the textual representative of a racially hybrid people who fall short of the criteria of empire and nation, Cereno is more "human" than Delano precisely because he fits imperfectly into the categories of race or nation. In using the Spanish captain to make the point that such collective identities deform the individual, Melville's romantic ideal privileges antebellum race logic by making Don Benito representative of liminality.

Connecting "Benito Cereno" to Melville's subject position amid such subtle and inescapable racial politics, and reading the text alongside the contemporaneous writing of William Wells Brown, brings to light the important differences between the prevailing critical treatment of "Benito Cereno" as a text that verbalizes its author's moral beliefs and the long-standing sense of Brown's literary innovations as a way of carefully negotiating and manipulating identity. Despite the different ways they have typically been read, "Benito Cereno" and *Clotel* have a similar point to make about the instability of authenticating and documenting practices in the debates over slavery. Just as Brown's narrative maneuvers subtly mock the authenticating voice of white abolitionism, the court documents that conclude "Benito Cereno" exploit the textual surfaces that protect American slavery. If, by the time we encounter the legal extracts of "Benito Cereno," narrative has already been revealed as an inadequate and illusory mode of capture, we are clearly invited to turn to these documents with a suspicion toward their own storytelling machinery. We need not question the fact that Cereno's ship was actually overtaken by the slaves he was transporting; instead, we are asked to recognize that our experience of these events is merely the experience of texts. Cereno's deposition provides Melville with a link between his story's fictional narration and the rhetoric of factual writing that submerges the former mode's complexities and indeterminacies. When read as a rewriting of the events described in the earlier portion of the story, the deposition appears much like the excerpted bits of missionary writing in *Typee* in its subtle interest in smoothing over the difficulties of interpretation.

One need only look at Cereno's court-mandated account of the communications between the eighteen-year-old slave, José, and Babo before the revolt. While Cereno points to their "secret conversations . . . in which [José] was several times seen by the mate" (111) as evidence of their conspiracy, no direct account of the conversation is ever given. By relocating this impenetrable conversation to the context of his own narrative of events, though, Cereno's deposition makes meaning out of what cannot be read. Such a depiction of secret communication among the slaves essentially solves those various moments in the earlier portion of the narrative where our narrator suspects a similarly covert mode of communication on board the *San Dominick*, "as if silent signs of some Freemason sort had . . . been interchanged" (66). Resolving such moments of illegible signs with Cereno's legal narrative, the white witness makes meaning where before he was confronted with his own inability to know.

As far back as the Old Zack anecdotes, of course, Melville mocked the notion that the facts of nonfictional narrative could ever be certified in any reliable way. But in "Benito Cereno" the author connects the lie of authentication to the survival of American slavery in the 1850s. Near the end of Cereno's legal account of the events leading up to Delano's boarding the ship, he tells of the various acts of violence perpetrated by the rebelling slaves, including the murder of Don Alexandro Aranda. After describing the solemn songs and dances performed by the female slaves as the men

committed "the various acts of murder," Cereno claims that "this melancholy tone was more inflaming than a different one would have been, and
was so intended." The women, we are told, were bloodthirsty, using "their
utmost influence to have the deponent made away with." Finally, the
deposition points to black testimony to lend authority to this account: "All
this is believed," the narrative reads, "because the negroes have said it"
(112). The paradox of black testimony serving as the grounds on which a
white witness's deposition stands is striking, in part because the maneuver
calls to mind the manipulation of white texts that appear in Brown's 1853
rewriting of his autobiography and in *Clotel*. By inverting the traditional
relationship of black narrator/white authenticator, Melville, like Brown,
reveals the fictions on which narrative authentication was based.

And yet the respective critical fates of Melville and Brown suggest a
subtle but consequential double standard: Brown's narrative innovations,
which at once evade a first-person autobiographical voice and subvert
the logic of authentication, have long been understood as the product of
Brown's culturally specific status as a black eyewitness within an abolitionist movement that threatened to objectify black speaking subjects by
imposing upon the former slave a prefabricated "voice." Melville's invocation of slavery in "Benito Cereno," however, which similarly complicates
the logic of authentication, and which seeks to elude the *white* authorial voice sanctioned by Harriet Beecher Stowe's brand of abolitionism,
continues to be understood as evidence of its author's near-miraculous
sensitivity to timeless epistemological, linguistic, and moral truths. The
above account of William Wells Brown reminds us that we have long
read similar theoretical claims as a rhetorical by-product of historical
contingencies; it is just that we do not apply such criteria consistently.
For as the example of Brown makes clear, critics seem far more willing
to comprehend the deconstructive agenda of a literary text as a language
for imagining and communicating a certain kind of identity when that
author—a black slave, for example—writes from a subject position whose
contingencies are easily visible to our own eyes.

As I have attempted to illustrate, in this chapter and throughout my
readings of Hawthorne and Melville, the romantic deconstruction of
cultural facades was inextricable from the ongoing process of romantic
identity-making. To dig beneath the fraudulent surfaces of antebellum culture was not simply to model for American citizens an ideal of skeptical,
reflective civic participation; to foreground the artifice of narration and
language was not merely to provide a more genuine or more responsible
kind of national history. If these authors wrote as if they had access to a
more lasting authenticity than mass culture could ever provide, we have

also seen that such language was often most valuable to the romantic imagination for the ontological dimensions it afforded. This more rhetorical understanding of the romantic obsession with cultural surfaces suggests that maybe "Benito Cereno" is most valuable for the irresolvable contradiction at the heart of its authorial performance: is the text an attempt to rid America of the great social ill threatening its integrity and survival, or is it the invention of a fundamentally contrarian artist who valued his romantic autonomy more than anything else? The viability and importance of both ways of understanding "Benito Cereno" only reaffirms that the question of what constitutes genuine reality had penetrated to the very bone of antebellum being. Choosing one of these readings over another would be to isolate Melville's ethical and political beliefs from his ongoing negotiation of identity—and, in doing so, to elevate belief itself to a realm of impossible purity, above the contingencies of rhetoric and self-making. Instead, by interrogating the romantic worldview that sees culture as a realm of surfaces, by understanding how placing scare quotes around the word "reality" affords the romantic subject a foundation on which to build a self, we come to the more surprising conclusion that reality is a powerful but arbitrary way of understanding and communicating who we are.

CODA

FEW critics today would claim that what is commonly called American realism merely puts on display the realities of American social life. A generation of scholars has illustrated that understanding realism in all of its complexity as "a cultural practice within capitalism" requires an interrogation into *how* particular works theorize the task of representation itself.[1] As Amy Kaplan writes, "Realism cannot be understood only in relation to the world it represents; it is also a debate, within the novel form, with competing modes of representation."[2] But if we understand literary realism as a self-conscious representational practice (or rather, a range of practices) that speaks to the competing representational forms available in the popular marketplace, how do we reconcile this account of realist fiction with my project's view of romance as a similarly dialogic narrative form? After all, though different in important ways, a work such as *The House of the Seven Gables* shares with both William Dean Howells's *A Hazard of New Fortunes* and Charles Chesnutt's *The Marrow of Tradition* (among countless other realist novels) a suspicion regarding the modern technologies and journalistic practices that were transforming the nineteenth-century public realm into a spectacle manufactured for mass consumption. In these brief concluding paragraphs, I want to argue that the prevailing critical distinction between mid-nineteenth-century "romantic" fiction and late nineteenth-century "realist" fiction begins to fall apart when we approach the romance as a representational practice emergent out of the same economic, technological, and social conditions that shaped the rise of the institution of literary realism. Indeed, when we approach the romance as a way of witnessing modernization, the emergence of realism looks very much like the triumph of the romantic conception of reality.

In April of 1861, only months after the appearance of Hawthorne's last novel, the *Atlantic Monthly* published Rebecca Harding Davis's "Life in the Iron Mills," a text often described as the first major work of American realism.[3] Though Davis's story was published only a few years after the heyday of American romanticism, it is typically understood as belonging to an entirely different era.[4] Appearing only days before the start of the Civil War, "Iron Mills" provides an easy turning point for the long-standing narrative of nineteenth-century literary history in which "romance" is displaced by the postbellum "realism" of Twain, Howells, Chesnutt, Crane, and others. And yet, like Hawthorne and Melville, Davis foregrounds, even flaunts the distance between the journalistic stories that circulate in the popular marketplace and the kind of reality that can less easily be contained by storytelling. In fact, what is most striking about "Life in the Iron Mills," more striking even than the harshness of its titular setting, is the narrator's repeated insistence on the impossibility of her narrative task. The story begins with the difficulty of seeing, with the cloudiness both of the day itself and of the linguistic distance that lies between narrator and reader: "A cloudy day: do you know what that is in a town of iron-works? The sky sank down before dawn, muddy, flat, immovable. The air is thick, clammy with the breath of crowded human beings. It stifles me. I open the window, and, looking out, can scarcely see through the rain the grocer's shop opposite, where a crowd of drunken Irishmen are puffing Lynchburg tobacco in their pipes" (11). Confronting us immediately with a present-tense description of the world outside her room, Davis's narrator foregrounds the gap between narrator and subject, between reader and text, and between the social classes that define the audience and subject.

As she introduces her story to the reader, she further relies upon the cloudiness of the day to prevent her audience from composing too hastily in their minds a picture of what they expect to see: "Can you see how foggy the day is? As I stand here, idly tapping the window-pane, and looking out through the rain at the dirty back-yard and the coal-boats below, fragments of an old story float up before me,—a story of this old house into which I happened to come to-day. You may think it a tiresome story enough, as foggy as the day, sharpened by no sudden flashes of pain or pleasure.—I know: only the outline of a dull life, that long since, with thousands of dull lives like its own, was vainly lived and lost" (13). By placing her narrator on the same side of the window as the reader, Davis begins her story with two levels of narrative representation: the narrator sitting in an old house, which the reader is assumed to see vividly, and the reality that lies outside her window, which the narrator tells us is "as foggy as the day," and which is kept at a distance by our presumed preference for the "sudden flashes of pain or pleasure" of a more entertaining mode of storytelling. In the act of depicting her narrator "idly tapping on the window-pane," Davis draws our attention to the fictional lens through which we see reality. Telling us, "There is a secret down here, in this nightmare fog, that has lain dumb for centuries: I want to make it a real thing to you" (13–14), Davis's narrator simultaneously announces her desire to unveil a long-buried social reality and confesses that the story we are about to read is authentic precisely because it acknowledges the real as a category produced by the act of representation.

Like Hawthorne and Melville, Davis defines her text's own type of authenticity against competing accounts available in the mass marketplace, including both sentimental fiction and journalism.[5] Among the visitors who enter the mills with Kirby (one of the mill owners) and Doctor May is "a sharp peering little Yankee . . . a reporter for one of the city-papers, getting up a series of reviews of the leading manufactories" (27–28). By introducing the reporter briefly into the mills, Davis dramatizes the newspaper writer's exposure to the political machinations that keep Kirby's mill running smoothly: in the brief time the reporter appears, he is solely concerned with economic facts ("'Pig-metal,'—mumbled the reporter,—'um!—coal facilities,—um!—hands employed, twelve hundred,—bitumen,—um! all right, I believe, Mr. Clarke;—sinking-fund,— what did you say your sinking-fund was?'" [28]), as the other men discuss how Kirby "brought seven hundred votes to the polls for his candidate last November" (28). Davis's critique of the newspaper's complicity in the company's manipulations is perhaps obvious, but more significant is the way in which she carefully defines her own transparent agenda by opposing it to the submerged political and economic objectives of newspaper reporting.

As she asserts her own privileged understanding of reality, Davis also invites her audience to reject the reading practices of the mass consumer. The reporter's departure from the mills is followed closely by a fascinating scene in which, with Hugh Wolfe working nearby, Kirby "drew out a newspaper from his pocket and read aloud some article, which they discussed eagerly" (30). Coming on the heels of the reporter's superficial engagement with the workings of the mill, the newspaper here emerges as an important rhetorical device. As a political tool set up in opposition to journalism, Davis's narrative overturns the idea of newspaper writing as a vehicle for portraying working-class life. To the visitors discussing the newspaper article, Wolfe "listened more and more like a dumb, hopeless animal, with a duller, more stolid look creeping over his face, glancing

now and then at Mitchell, marking acutely every smallest sign of refine-
ment, then back to himself, seeing as in a mirror his filthy body, his more
stained soul" (30). By subtly linking the newspaper with this "mirror" that
embodies all that Wolfe is not, Davis places journalism entirely outside
the realm of the lower-class laborer and reveals its inability or unwillingness to acknowledge its own complicity in the plight of this class.

In a move that further distances newspaper reading from the reality
of Wolfe's plight, we learn of his arrest, conviction, and sentencing in
the strictly factual language of journalism. Before giving us these facts,
though, Davis taunts her reader: "What followed was mere drifting cir-
cumstance,—a quicker walking over the path,—that was all. Do you want
to hear the end of it? You wish me to make a tragic story out of it? Why,
in the police-reports of the morning paper you can find a dozen such
tragedies: hints of shipwrecks unlike any that ever befell on the high seas;
hints that here a power was lost to heaven,—that there a soul went down
where no tide can ebb or flow. Commonplace enough the hints are,—
jocose sometimes, done up in rhyme" (50). In other words, she connects
the narrative closure her audience presumably demands with the market-
oriented writing of popular journalism. Though she does indeed "make a
tragic story out of it," her constant acknowledgment of the artifice of storytelling shapes a narrative idiom—we might call it a realist idiom—that
continually highlights the distance between the stories that circulate in the
marketplace and the reality that exists beyond its reach.

Our narrator takes us from the above passage immediately to a conversation between Doctor May and his wife at the breakfast table: while the
realist author is defined in "Iron Mills" by her mastery over the fictions
of mass culture, the implied realist reader is defined against the popular
appetite for sentimentalism and narrative closure. May reads aloud a brief
newspaper account of Wolfe's arrest and sentencing, a story that wrongly
depicts Wolfe as responsible for stealing the money. The doctor moves
quickly from defining Wolfe by the details of the article ("Here he is;
just listen," he tells his wife) to moralizing upon the crime about which
he knows nothing ("Scoundrel! Serves him right!") (50).[6] Seated inside
their own home, the Mays inhabit a fictive, middle-class space outside
the mills, a position importantly analogous to the fictive library in which
Davis's narrator sits writing her story. But if all these figures are conspicuously removed from the reality that sits on the other side of the window,
only in the narrator's library is reality understood as the ever-shifting commodity of mass information culture.

Davis's story epitomizes realist fiction's desire to "juggle competing
visions of social reality . . . [and] encompass conflicting forms and narra-

tives which shape that reality."[7] But such a project should not only be read as a forward-looking introduction to late nineteenth-century fiction, for her preoccupation with the implications of a popular appetite for storytelling in the earliest days of modern journalism—Davis in fact sets her story in the first years of the penny press era—also brings us back to Hawthorne's early literary experiments, by which the young romantic author invoked the commercial nature of journalism to articulate a more foundational understanding of reality. If the literary interrogation of the relationship between language and the category of the real was, for Hawthorne, also a way of defining himself in the literary marketplace, the depiction of reality in "Iron Mills" similarly defines the literary as that which exists at arm's length from the commercialism of popular journalism and sentimental fiction.[8] And it is for this reason that "Iron Mills" serves as such a valuable bridge between my discussion of romantic fiction and the problem of reality in late nineteenth-century realism—not simply because Davis's story problematizes the task of representing reality but because this narrative agenda is so clearly aligned with the question of identity inside and outside of the text. If the rhetorical space of the library in which our narrator sits in "Iron Mills" acknowledges that we must first go through the realm of (a certain kind of) fiction to get to the "secret" reality of life in the mills, it is no doubt significant that this architecture looks a great deal like the room the story's nineteenth-century reader might be sitting in, perusing the latest issue of the *Atlantic Monthly* and looking out with Davis over the murky reality outside. To put this another way, the text's portrayal of a mass-produced, mass-consumed reality is the very means by which Davis communicates a particular kind of identity (for herself, her fiction, and the magazine in which "Iron Mills" appeared) against journalism and popular fiction—against, that is, mass culture.

Of course, it is not only in works of realism that we encounter arguments about the nature of reality, and so it was not only in late nineteenth-century America that such a project afforded authors an imagined autonomy from the masses.[9] Unlike the realist writer, Hawthorne and Melville often rejected the goal of depicting the world as it is. But this rejection was a way of speaking to mass culture—a way of recasting reality as that which cannot be genuinely represented, and a way of locating those who consume mere copies in a rhetorical world of lies. By the time Davis published "Life in the Iron Mills" in the *Atlantic Monthly,* of course, American periodical culture had begun carving out the kinds of cultural hierarchies that were not fully available to Hawthorne (and the editors of the *New-England Magazine*) in the earliest days of the penny press revolution. Each of these writers, I have argued, participated in antebellum debates about the problem of reality in a mass-mediated age while simultaneously asserting a romantic distance from the concerns and priorities of contemporary civic life. This mode of romantic self-invention would lose its cachet precisely because late nineteenth-century literary culture professionalized the role of the arbiter of reality, and thus what was a marker of autonomy became a preoccupation of authorship and readership on a mass scale. That is, the romancer's view of reality would become, over the final decades of the nineteenth century, a defining assumption of the age of realism.

NOTES

INTRODUCTION

1. *The American Notebooks*, vol. 7 of *The Centenary Edition of the Works of Nathaniel Hawthorne*, ed. Claude M. Simpson (Columbus: The Ohio State University Press, 1972), 244.

2. Herman Melville, "Hawthorne and His Mosses" (1850), in *The Piazza Tales and Other Prose Pieces, 1839–1860*, vol. 9 of *The Writings of Herman Melville*, ed. Harrison Hayford et al. (Evanston, IL: Northwestern University Press / Newberry Library, 1987), 244.

3. As countless commentators have pointed out, Melville's essay is as much about Melville as it is about Hawthorne. Edgar Dryden claims, "The assumptions which form the foundation of Melville's theory of the novel receive their most concise statement in his famous essay" (*Melville's Thematics of Form: The Great Art of Telling the Truth* [Baltimore: Johns Hopkins University Press, 1968], 21). Stephen Railton argues that Melville's essay "angrily dismisses popularity as crippling proof of artistic unworthiness" (*Authorship and Audience: Literary Performance in the American Renaissance* [Princeton, NJ: Princeton University Press, 1991], 161). Similarly, Michael Gilmore claims that it "insists that the author has to make himself inaccessible" (*American Romanticism and the Marketplace* [Chicago: University of Chicago Press, 1985], 60).

4. Even a glance at the titles of many of the most important discussions of nineteenth-century culture from recent decades reveals the collective story being told about the era: Neil Harris's *Humbug: The Art of P. T. Barnum* (Chicago: University of Chicago Press, 1973), Karen Halttunen's *Confidence Men and Painted Women: A Study of Middle-Class Culture in America, 1830–1870* (New Haven, CT: Yale University Press, 1982), Bluford Adams's *E Pluribus Barnum: The Great Showman and the Making of U.S. Popular Culture* (Minneapolis: University of Minnesota Press, 1997), Ronald Zboray's *A Fictive People: Antebellum Economic Development and the American Reading Public* (New York: Oxford University Press, 1993), Andie Tucher's *Froth and Scum: Truth, Beauty, Goodness, and the Ax Murder in America's First Mass Medium* (Chapel Hill: University of North Carolina Press, 1994), Paul Gilmore's *The Genuine Article: Race, Mass Culture, and American Literary Manhood* (Durham, NC: Duke University Press, 2001), Isabelle Lehuu's *Carnival on the Page: Popular Print Media in Antebellum America* (Chapel Hill: University of North Carolina Press, 2000), James Cook's *The Arts of Deception: Playing with Fraud in the Age of Barnum* (Cambridge, MA: Harvard University Press, 2004), Stephen John Hartnett's *Democratic Dissent and the Cultural Fictions of Antebel-

lum America (Urbana: University of Illinois Press, 2002). Each in its own compelling way, these works portray mid-nineteenth-century America as a time when capitalism and democracy conspired to exploit the slippery line between information and entertainment, between truth and fiction, reality and artifice.

5. Tucher, *Froth and Scum,* 46.

6. See Neil Harris, *Humbug.*

7. Cook, *Arts of Deception,* 13, 28.

8. Jonathan Elmer, *Reading at the Social Limit: Affect, Mass Culture, and Edgar Allan Poe* (Stanford, CA: Stanford University Press, 1995), 187.

9. Many historians have connected such a development to changes in print technologies, to the gradual urbanization of the American populace, and to an emerging market ethos. As Michael Schudson claims in *Discovering the News: A Social History of American Newspapers* (New York: Basic Books, 1978), it was during the early years of the 1830s that the very idea of the "news"—the elevation of reportage over editorializing, of facts over opinion—was invented. Of course (as Schudson himself has more recently acknowledged in "The Objectivity Norm in American Journalism," for example), the nonpartisanship of early penny papers such as James Gordon Bennett's *New York Herald* was to a great extent a rhetorical deception.

10. Quoted in Lehuu, *Carnival on the Page,* 37.

11. Tucher, *Froth and Scum,* 26.

12. Zboray, *A Fictive People,* 128.

13. Paul Gilmore, *Genuine Article,* 13.

14. In relying on the term "authenticity," then, my intent is not to challenge the critical view that traces the rise of authenticity as a philosophical and artistic ideal opposing a seemingly out-of-control American mass culture in the late nineteenth century. For two excellent accounts of how the category of authenticity emerges in the later nineteenth century as an antimarket mass ethos, see T. J. Jackson Lears, *No Place of Grace: Antimodernism and the Transformation of American Culture, 1880–1920* (New York: Pantheon, 1981), and Miles Orvell, *The Real Thing: Imitation and Authenticity in American Culture* (Chapel Hill: University of North Carolina Press, 1989).

15. As is perhaps already clear, this use of "romance" in describing the narrative modes of Hawthorne and Melville is (at least nominally) at odds with the current critical view that has largely accepted Nina Baym's claim that the words "novel" and "romance" were used interchangeably in nineteenth-century literary culture. See *Novels, Readers, and Reviewers: Responses to Fiction in Antebellum America* (Ithaca, NY: Cornell University Press, 1984), especially chapter 11. Not at all seeking to challenge Baym's careful and thoroughly convincing argument, I am embracing the term "romance" as a way of signifying Hawthorne's and Melville's shared view of their romantic fiction as a higher mode of truth-telling than the other representations available in the antebellum marketplace. In thus arguing that Hawthorne and Melville shared a theory of romantic fiction that saw their fiction as an escape from the unrealities of popular culture, I am, to a certain degree, reasserting the much-maligned view of Richard Chase and other mid-twentieth-century critics that the romance seeks "a world elsewhere." And yet, as I hope will be clear in my individual readings, I approach what I am calling "romance" as the artifact of a model of romantic individualism that was made possible by the economic, technological, and social dynamics of antebellum culture.

16. Because I am writing, almost exclusively, about two male authors, I will rely on the gendered pronoun "he" when referring either to one of my authors or to a general-

ized "romancer" or "romantic author" that is meant to stand in for both Hawthorne and Melville. In all other cases, I will try to remain gender-neutral.

17. Richard Chase, *Herman Melville: A Critical Study* (New York: Macmillan, 1949), 81.

18. Hawthorne, "The Artist of the Beautiful," *Tales and Sketches*, 908, 927 (hereafter cited parenthetically). For a fascinating account of the "Automaton Chess-Player," see chapter 1 of Cook's *Arts of Deception.*

19. Letter to John Murray, March 25, 1848, in *Correspondence*, vol. 14 of *The Writings of Herman Melville*, ed. Lynn Horth (Evanston, IL: Northwestern University Press / Newberry Library, 1993), 107.

20. Letter to Murray, September 2, 1846, in ibid., 65.

21. *Mardi and a Voyage Thither*, vol. 3 of *The Writings of Herman Melville*, ed. Harrison Hayford, Hershel Parker, and G. Thomas Tanselle (Evanston, IL: Northwestern University Press / Newberry Library, 1970), xvii.

22. In his masterful study of Melville and "the rhetoric of humor," John Bryant locates Melville in what he calls the highest "class" within "the culture of the liar" by virtue of his awareness that "our shared imaginative interplay is all of reality we can know" (*Melville and Repose: The Rhetoric of Humor in the American Renaissance* [New York: Oxford University Press, 1993], 85)—an understanding that elevates him over those who merely lie or expose the liar. I am interested in how this ideal of Melvillean truth-telling was fundamentally dependent on the competing forms of truth-telling in circulation during these years; unlike Bryant, however, I see Melville as an artist who continually seeks out a philosophical authority external to what Bryant calls "the culture of the liar." Thus while Bryant, like many other critics, suggests that Melville "tempts us to fall" (255) for the titular confidence man in his later novel, I disagree. Instead, I read the novel as an attempt at using the criterion of confidence to envision American society en masse—to portray the nation as a realm of con men and dupes—so as to imagine for the romantic artist an integrity untainted by the mass commodification of truth. As I suggest in chapter 6, Melville resembles not the con man but the unnamed figure in darkness at the novel's end, who alone recognizes the reversible nature of the linked identities of confidence man and mass public.

23. Neil Harris writes that Barnum's operational aesthetic "was served also by the 'Is it fact or is it fiction?' question Americans asked, not only of such Poe stories as 'The Facts in the Case of M. Valdemar' but of exotic travel narratives, like Melville's *Typee*" (*Humbug*, 88).

24. In a journal entry dated April 24, 1852, Thoreau writes that "men of society . . . live on the surface, they are interested in the transient & fleeting—they are like driftwood on the flood—They ask for ever & only the news—the froth & scum of the eternal sea" (486–87).

25. Thoreau, *Walden and Resistance to Civil Government*, 2nd ed., ed. William Rossi (New York: W. W. Norton, 1992), 66.

26. Mark Bauerlein, *Whitman and the American Idiom* (Baton Rouge: Louisiana State University Press, 1991), 5.

27. Lennard Davis, *Factual Fictions: The Origins of the English Novel* (New York: Columbia University Press, 1983), 12.

28. Elmer, *Reading*, 11.

29. See Terence Whalen, *Edgar Allan Poe and the Masses: The Political Economy of Literature in Antebellum America* (Princeton, NJ: Princeton University Press, 1999).

Like Whalen, Paul Gilmore argues that Poe's fiction ultimately upholds the marketplace's profit motive, even as Poe makes repeated attempts "at transcending and exploiting the market and fantasizing an alternative model of white literary manhood" (*Genuine Article*, 124). Writing before both Whalen and Gilmore, Jonathan Elmer explores how Poe's idiosyncratic literary art reflected the lack of highbrow/lowbrow distinctions in antebellum culture. Reading Poe as the ultimate "figure of mass culture" (*Reading*, 29), Elmer examines how "mass culture takes on its essential form in thematizing—and more especially, anathematizing—itself under the sign of unregulated affect" (8).

All three of these brilliant studies have greatly illuminated my own attempts at theorizing what Elmer calls the "co-implication of self and mass" (28). While Gilmore's reading of antebellum literature and culture shares with my own project an attention to the authorial manipulation and exploitation of mass cultural forms, he is less willing to see in Hawthorne's imagined relationship to these forms the romantic ideal of selfhood that I see as pervasive in his fiction. For example, Gilmore's reading of Hawthorne's *The House of the Seven Gables*—like my own reading of the novel, which concludes chapter 3—reads the text against the backdrop of daguerreotypy. In his account, "Hawthorne attempts to use daguerreotypy to reimagine the bourgeois family and literary manhood by cleansing them of the racialized taint of economic exploitation" (*Genuine Article*, 147–48). Because Gilmore assumes that Hawthorne uses the daguerreotype to accommodate himself to middle-class life, he can see the novel's conclusion only as evidence of an incomplete project of social amelioration: "The artistic failure of his novel's conclusion then rests on his failure to imagine the possibility of more fluid racial boundaries, a possibility at once presented and denied in both minstrelsy and daguerreotypy" (148). In my own reading of the novel's conclusion, however, I argue that Hawthorne's ultimate objective is not to locate middle-class respectability for himself but to use Holgrave's domestication into the middle class (the artifice of which is echoed in the novel's contrived ending) to offset his own imagined *autonomy from* the terms of the middle class.

30. Michael Gilmore, *Surface and Depth: The Quest for Legibility in American Culture* (Oxford: Oxford University Press, 2003), 78 (hereafter cited parenthetically).

31. Hawthorne, letter to William D. Ticknor, February 2, 1855, in *Letters, 1853–56*, vol. 17 of *The Centenary Edition of Nathaniel Hawthorne*, ed. Thomas Woodson, James A. Rubino, L. Neal Smith, and Norman Holmes Pearson (Columbus: The Ohio State University Press, 1987), 308.

32. This reading of "The Custom-House," which is expanded in chapter 3, sees a more romantic Hawthorne than that described by Lauren Berlant, who argues in *The Anatomy of National Fantasy: Hawthorne, Utopia, and Everyday Life* (Chicago: University of Chicago Press, 1991) that the "relation of personal experience to public form" in "The Custom-House" is not "a relation of the 'real' to the 'inauthentic'" (3). In Berlant's reading, Hawthorne engages in "the fantasy-work of national identity," accepting each stage of his personal transformations as "a fundamental condition of identity" (2). While Hawthorne indeed writes autobiographically in "The Custom-House," Berlant points out that "he reveals not 'the inmost Me' detached from social inscription but speaks in an exemplary way, as a citizen, taking care to play out the complex games of knowledge, power, and desire that transform him into a being intimate somehow with mass political culture" (3). As should already be clear, I am more interested in how the very shape of that unrepresented "inmost Me" depends on the public aspects of identity that Hawthorne clearly foregrounds. Significantly, my own portrayal of Hawthorne and Melville can be said to fall into what Berlant calls a more "symptomatic" school of romanticist scholar-

ship (she invokes the critical examples of Myra Jehlen and Sacvan Bercovitch), while her own work (like that of Donald Pease and Jonathan Arac, she notes) sees Hawthorne as "more powerfully registering and contesting" the "fractures" of American "social hierarchy" by "aligning with populist sentiments and insisting on the productive indeterminacy of national, personal, juridical, and political identity" (*Anatomy*, 9).

33. Part of my goal in the following chapters will be to unveil how the romancer's self-conception as an arbiter of reality depended upon each author's status as a white, northern, American male. Most significantly, chapter 6 will argue that Melville's critique of the racial role-playing of American slavery in "Benito Cereno" reflected the binary racial logic of progressive authorship in the wake of Harriet Beecher Stowe's *Uncle Tom's Cabin*.

34. Quotations from Lionel Trilling, *The Liberal Imagination: Essays on Literature and Society* (New York: Harcourt Brace Jovanovich, 1978), 4, 198, 200, 8–9. Trilling's language of morality demands some clarification. As Trilling writes in "Manners, Morals, and the Novel," what he calls moral realism (epitomized in the nineteenth century by Henry James) involves the reader "in the moral life, inviting him to put his own motives under examination, suggesting that reality is not as his conventional educations has led him to see it" (209). In other words, the acknowledgment of reality as a problem was for Trilling a moral project—involving, he tells us at the end of the essay, the very fate of human freedom.

35. Richard Chase, *The American Novel and Its Tradition* (London: G. Bell and Sons, 1957), 12.

36. Michael Davitt Bell, *The Development of American Romance: The Sacrifice of Relation* (Chicago: University of Chicago Press, 1980), xiv; Evan Carton, *The Rhetoric of American Romance: Dialectic and Identity in Emerson, Dickinson, Poe, and Hawthorne* (Baltimore: Johns Hopkins University Press, 1985), 1; Walter Benn Michaels, *The Gold Standard and the Logic of Naturalism: American Literature at the Turn of the Century* (Berkeley: University of California Press, 1987), 101; Emily Miller Budick, *Fiction and Historical Consciousness: The American Romance Tradition* (New Haven, CT: Yale University Press, 1989), ix; G. R. Thompson and Eric Carl Link, *Neutral Ground: New Traditionalism and the American Romance Controversy* (Baton Rouge: Louisiana State University Press, 1999), 20; Peter J. Bellis, *Writing Revolution: Aesthetics and Politics in Hawthorne, Whitman, and Thoreau* (Athens: University of Georgia Press, 2003), 7.

37. Throughout the 1990s, a new generation of "new Americanists" endeavored to "desublimate" the romance as a literary genre by reconnecting those critics most responsible for the romance thesis (namely Trilling, Chase, and F. O. Matthiessen) to the political contexts out of which their readings emerged. Donald Pease, in his introduction to *Revisionary Interventions into the Americanist Canon* (Durham, NC: Duke University Press, 1994), uses the phrase "desublimation" to describe the critical process by which new Americanist criticism has come to explore the "overdetermination" of romance as a "field-imaginary" that names "at once the genre within the field, the means of producing and interpreting its canonical objects, the relations between the field's practitioners, the mediation between the field and its culture, and the means of separating culture from politics" (30). By uncovering the ideological assumptions and motivations underlying this account of American literary history, the new Americanists explored how the romance thesis has shaped our critical understanding of literature in the nineteenth century. At the heart of the new Americanist project was (and continues to be) a skepticism regarding the romance's sense of itself as a "neutral territory" that exists in the realm of pure fancy, an

ethereal place "having a great deal more to do with the clouds overhead, than with any portion of the actual soil." As John McWilliams writes, "Insisting upon the removal of the Romance world from political and social contexts, Chase's followers treated American Romances as instances of psychological modernity, thereby slighting their historical import for the world around them" ("The Rationale for 'The American Romance,'" in Pease, *Revisionary Interventions*, 74). For the most sustained and eloquent response to the new Americanist desublimation of romance, see Thompson and Link.

38. John Carlos Rowe, "Melville's *Typee:* U.S. Imperialism at Home and Abroad," in *National Identities*, ed. Donald L. Pease (Durham, NC: Duke University Press, 1994), 258.

39. Peter Coviello, "The American in Charity: 'Benito Cereno' and Gothic Anti-Sentimentality," *Studies in American Fiction* 30, no. 2 (2002): 171. My emphasis.

40. Joel Pfister, "Hawthorne as Cultural Theorist," in *The Cambridge Companion to Nathaniel Hawthorne*, ed. Richard Millington (Cambridge: Cambridge University Press, 2004), 37.

41. Richard Millington, *Practicing Romance: Narrative Form and Cultural Engagement in Hawthorne's Fiction* (Princeton, NJ: Princeton University Press, 1992), 3.

42. Millicent Bell, "Hawthorne and the Real," in *Hawthorne and the Real: Bicentennial Essays*, ed. Millicent Bell (Columbus: The Ohio State University Press, 2005), 19 (hereafter cited parenthetically).

43. My desire to disrupt the line between the romance's critique of mass culture and romantic identity-making responds to what Winfried Fluck, in "'The American Romance' and the Changing Functions of the Imaginary" (*New Literary History* 27, no. 3 [1996]) sees as a misguided critical commitment to a neatly oppositional view of the romantic artist as either conformer or reformer: "Traditional theories of the American romance . . . are locked in a basic, restricted, and basically ahistorical opposition between conformism and rebellion and, hence, argue along the reductive semantic lines of society/conformism/realism on the one side versus individual/nonconformism/romance on the other" (444–45). Indeed, Fluck's excellent essay argues that even the "radical revisionists" of new Americanism perpetuate this mythic oppositionalism by quietly privileging the dream of noncontingent selfhood. In discussing Michaels's reading of *The House of the Seven Gables*, Fluck writes, "Where it 'unmasks' the romance as complicitous, it does so in the name of its own political romance of a society without coercion and restraints" (447).

44. Letter to Allan Melville, February 20, 1849, in *Correspondence*, 116. For a thorough book-length discussion of this letter, see Hennig Cohen and Donald Yannella, *Herman Melville's Malcolm Letter: "Man's Final Lore"* (New York: Fordham University Press and the New York Public Library, 1992). Among other insights, Cohen and Yannella tell us that the "Lambert" to which Melville refers is Daniel Lambert, a 739-pound member of the "Lambert Family," or "the Highland Mammoth Boys," who were exhibited by Barnum from 1846 to 1849.

45. Letter to Sophia Peabody, September 3, 1841, in *The Letters, 1813–1843*, vol. 15 of *The Centenary Edition of Nathaniel Hawthorne*, ed. Thomas Woodson, L. Neal Smith, and Norman Holmes Pearson (Columbus: The Ohio State University Press, 1984), 565.

46. Letter to Sophia Peabody, October 4, 1840, in ibid., 495.

47. Letter to Sophia Peabody, [October 4, 1841?], in ibid., 584.

48. Hawthorne, *American Notebooks*, 334.

49. Letter to Sophia Peabody, July 29, 1839, in *Letters, 1813–1843*, 330.

50. *Albany Weekly Herald,* May 31, 1845, 6.
51. Thompson and Link, *Neutral Ground,* 43.

CHAPTER 1

1. On April 12, 1830, the *Boston Daily Commercial Gazette* reported on a town hall meeting in Salem that was attended by two thousand people. At this meeting, "A committee of vigilance, consisting of seven for each ward was raised, with full power to search every house, and interrogate every person, on any point that could lead to the detection of the murderer."
2. *Salem Gazette,* April 8, 1830.
3. Ibid., April 20, 1830.
4. Ibid., June 1, 1830.
5. See Karen Halttunen, *Murder Most Foul: The Killer and the American Gothic Imagination* (Cambridge, MA: Harvard University Press, 1998).
6. *Salem Gazette,* August 20, 1830.
7. Ibid., October 5, 1830.
8. Ibid., January 5, 1831. While the charges that the committee of vigilance might have acted too rashly and with too much power appear nowhere in the early local coverage of the case, such suggestions were so widespread that Webster himself felt compelled to "defend . . . the Committee of Vigilance, and the citizens of Salem at large, from the imputations which he said learned counsel on the other side had attempted to cast upon them for the interest they had taken in bringing the perpetrators of so atrocious a crime to justice" (ibid., August 20, 1830). Other papers, such as the *Boston Daily Commercial Gazette,* defended in print "the conduct of the citizens of Salem, against the charges made against them in some of the many foolish and exaggerated statements, which have, from time to time, been published, of the various proceedings in reaction to the arrest and trials of [Frank Knapp]" (*Daily Commercial Gazette,* September 2, 1830). In condoning the second jury's conviction of Frank Knapp, the writer was careful to attribute the "universal satisfaction" not to "any feelings of revenge" but "on account of the moral effect which the detection and punishment of such evil" carries with it.
9. *Essex Register,* June 10, 1830.
10. Ibid., November 11, 1830.
11. Ibid., September 30, 1830.
12. Reprinted in *Salem Gazette,* August 17, 1830.
13. *Marblehead Register,* May 8, 1830.
14. Ibid., July 24, 1830.
15. Ibid., July 31, 1830.
16. *Boston Courier,* August 11, 1830.
17. Ibid., August 3, 1830; *New York Enquirer for the Country,* August 3, 1830.
18. *Boston Daily Commercial Gazette,* August 10, 1830.
19. Bennett himself reported this on August 17 in the *Morning Courier and New York Enquirer for the Country.*
20. Reprinted in Newburyport *Herald,* August 13, 1830.
21. In the days leading up to the first trial, for example, Bennett wrote of the rivalry between Salem and nearby Marblehead: "There was a species of rejoicing by firing off guns at Marblehead when these persons were set at liberty." Continuing, Bennett claimed

that "secret and under-current attempts have been making to oppose the course of that committee, and to stem the torrent of public opinion. . . . Some few sparks of opposition to the committee have been struck out on the rocks of Marblehead" (*Morning Courier and New York Enquirer for the Country,* July 27, 1830).

22. *Morning Courier and New York Enquirer for the Country,* August 16, 1830.

23. See *Boston Daily Commercial Gazette,* August 27, 1830, for an excerpt from this pamphlet and an excerpted response from the *Essex Register.*

24. *Rhode Island American, Statesman,* and *Providence Gazette,* December 24, 1830.

25. *Salem Gazette,* November 23, 1830.

26. See, for example, James L. Crouthamel, *Bennett's* New York Herald *and the Rise of the Popular Press* (Syracuse, NY: Syracuse University Press, 1989), 12–13.

27. Whalen, *Poe,* 24, 57, 272. Emphasis in original.

28. Hawthorne, letter to J. S. Dike, September 1, 1830, in *Letters, 1813–1843,* 207–8.

29. Margaret B. Moore, *The Salem World of Nathaniel Hawthorne* (Columbia: University of Missouri Press, 1998), 166–67.

30. Hawthorne, letter to Sophia Peabody, May 1, 1841, in *Letters, 1813–1843,* 538.

CHAPTER 2

1. Hawthorne, *Tales and Sketches* (New York: The Library of America, 1982), 152 (hereafter cited parenthetically).

2. For a fascinating analysis of the role of the book peddler in early-nineteenth-century literary dissemination, see Zboray, *Fictive People,* chapter 3. Zboray notes that the traditional view casts the book peddler "in the role of an unwary facilitator of national communication" (38), an image that Hawthorne's tale seems to be invoking. As we shall see, by contrasting the face-to-face gossiping of Pike with the transatlantic communication of the story of Higginbotham's (rumored) death, Hawthorne relies on the quaintness of the peddler stereotype to portray the looming menace of modern journalism.

3. Hawthorne, letter to Elizabeth C. Hawthorne, March 13, 1821, in *Letters, 1813–1843,* 138–39.

4. For a discussion of how Irish whiteness is constructed in "Mr. Higginbotham's Catastrophe," see Monika Elbert, "Nathaniel Hawthorne, The Concord Freeman, and the Irish 'Other,'" *Eire-Ireland: A Journal of Irish Studies* 29, no. 3 (1994): 60–73.

5. "Mr. Higginbotham's Catastrophe" has received remarkably little critical attention. Michael Colacurcio, in *The Province of Piety: Moral History in Hawthorne's Early Tales* (Cambridge, MA: Harvard University Press, 1984), typifies one stream of critical thought in reading the tale as a religious allegory. And Nina Baym argues that the story of the rumored murder, in its status as "a fantasy that realizes itself," epitomizes the author's sense of reality as a composite of imagination and actuality (*The Shape of Hawthorne's Career* [Ithaca, NY: Cornell University Press, 1976], 48). See below for a brief discussion of G. R. Thompson's account of the tale.

6. "Hints to Newspaper Editors," *New-England Magazine,* May 1832: 361, 367.

7. John Neal, "Story-telling," *New-England Magazine* (Jan. 1835): 1, 4. It is worth pointing out that Brenda Wineapple, in *Hawthorne: A Life* (New York: Alfred A. Knopf, 2003), argues that Neal's fiction from the 1820s was a major influence on the young Haw-

thorne. Neal, Wineapple writes, "loudly banged the drum for American literature without frills, a literature of democratic spunk, and he practiced what he preached in a spate of sensationalistic novels intended to shock the complacent bourgeoisie" (59).

8. "History and Biography," *New-England Magazine*, March 1834: 199.

9. "Loose Thoughts on Plagiarism," *New-England Magazine*, May 1832: 333.

10. G. R. Thompson has highlighted the "parallel between the conditions of the Higginbotham narrative and the frame narrative" (*The Art of Authorial Presence: Hawthorne's Provincial Tales* [Durham, NC: Duke University Press, 1993], 225). In addressing the misleading advertisements of the storyteller's fame, Thompson argues that "the parallels have the effect of blurring the distinction between the 'fictive' and the 'real' in the frame fiction (in addition to the blurring of these in the tale proper), an effect that is lost when 'Mr. Higginbotham's Catastrophe' is printed separate from the frame" (225–26).

11. Whalen, *Poe*, 229.

12. "Old News" is in fact three sketches, which were published from February to May of 1835 in the *New-England Magazine*.

13. As Walter Benjamin writes in describing the difference between storytelling and information, "The value of information does not survive the moment in which it is new" ("The Storyteller," in *Illuminations*, ed. Hannah Arendt (New York: Schocken Books, 1968), 90, hereafter cited parenthetically).

14. *Salem Gazette*, May 25, 1830.

15. Ibid., February 21, 1834.

16. Ibid., April 14, 1834.

17. Letter to *Boston Courier*, September 9, 1826. Reprinted in Kenneth Walter Cameron, *Genesis of Hawthorne's "The Ambitious Guest"* (Hartford, CT: Transcendental Books, 1955), 4. In choosing not to portray the discovery of the family's remains, Hawthorne left out one of the most compelling details of the story. As many newspaper accounts reported, the Willey family dog survived the catastrophe and assisted rescuers in locating the corpses.

18. *Essex Register*, September 11, 1826. Reprinted in Cameron, *Genesis of Hawthorne's "The Ambitious Guest,"* 5–6.

19. Hawthorne's and Poe's symbolic use of the individual letter actually reflects the rhetorical complexity of this mode of correspondence throughout the antebellum information revolution. Two months after the sweeping postal reforms of 1845 went into effect, an article appeared in *The New Englander and Yale Review* that outlined the implications and limitations of the new law. In attacking the drastically reduced rates charged to newspaper bundles that emerged out of the 1845 law, the author of this piece links such a practice to "a tax on the writers and receivers of letters" that is used to fund the "privileged class" of newspaper editors ("The New Post-Office Law," 540). Against this depiction of the profit-driven, amoral newspaper, the author turns to the rhetorical object that, according to the logic of the essay, epitomizes "real" information—the individual letter: "We believe that the influence of an unlimited epistolary correspondence as would gradually yet rapidly spring up under the lowest possible uniform postage . . . would be worth more than all the influence of the newspapers in diffusing knowledge, in stimulating enterprise, in facilitating commerce, in promoting good morals, in educating the people, and in binding the country together as one body, and sending the pulsations of one heart and the glow of one life to its uttermost extremities" (542). Finally, the writer argues that the cost of sending a letter should not be "what the writer or receiver of a letter

or anything else can afford to pay or can be induced to pay without complaining"—that is, not a price that answers to the laws of supply and demand—but what the "operation of receiving, conveying, and delivering this particular article costs the government." The post office should not follow "the rule by which prices are determined in trade," for, as we are later reminded, "the post-office department is not a trading concern in respect to the assessment of postage" (544). On the most basic level, the essay suggests how the development of a not-for-profit system of information exchange would fuel economic expansion and centralization in the age of manifest destiny. But here we also see the individual letter invoked as a privileged ideal of information exchange that opposed the corruption of a commercial newspaper culture—even as it is seen as a way of "stimulating enterprise" and "facilitating commerce." In other words, the individual letter was at once the marker of a prelapsarian ideal of authentic information and the rhetorical tool of a capitalist logic that saw information as an economic commodity.

20. Poe, *Poetry and Tales* (New York: Library of America, 1984), 682.

CHAPTER 3

1. Hawthorne, *The House of the Seven Gables*, vol. 2 of *The Centenary Edition of Nathaniel Hawthorne* (Columbus: The Ohio State University Press, 1965), 91 (hereafter cited parenthetically).

2. M. A. Root, "The Daguerreotypic Art," Appendix to *Photographic Researches and Manipulations*, ed. Levi L. Hill (Philadelphia: Myron Shew, 1854), 176 (hereafter cited parenthetically).

3. Dewy, "Remarks," Appendix to Hill, 179, 180 (hereafter cited parenthetically).

4. Cathy Davidson argues that in this passage "the daguerreotype aligns with the fluidity of the romance form in contrast to the mimetic rigidity required by the novel," thereby allowing Hawthorne "to define the extrarepresentational responsibilities of the romance" ("Photographs of the Dead: Sherman, Daguerre, Hawthorne," *South Atlantic Quarterly* 89 [1990]: 686, 687).

5. Hawthorne, *American Notebooks*, 491 (hereafter cited parenthetically).

6. Susan S. Williams, "'The Aspiring Purpose of an Ambitious Demagogue': Portraiture and *The House of the Seven Gables*," *Nineteenth-Century Literature* 49 (1994): 236.

7. Dana Brand, "The Panoramic Spectator in America: A Re-Reading of Some of Hawthorne's Sketches," *American Transcendental Quarterly* 59 (1986): 11–12.

8. Certainly these moments from the notebooks (as well as sketches like "Sights from a Steeple" and "The Old Apple-Dealer") should also be considered in the broader context of the figure of the *flâneur*. For an excellent overview of this tradition as it relates to Hawthorne and other nineteenth-century authors, see Dana Brand, *The Spectator and the City in Nineteenth-Century American Literature* (Cambridge: Cambridge University Press, 1991).

9. This is a reference to Helen Jewett, the New York prostitute who had been murdered two years earlier in one of the most famous crimes in American history up to that point. See Patricia Cline Cohen, *The Murder of Helen Jewett* (New York: Vintage, 1998), and Tucher, *Froth and Scum*.

10. Hawthorne, *The Scarlet Letter*, vol. 1 of *The Centenary Edition of Nathaniel Hawthorne*, ed. William Charvat, Roy Harvey Pearce, and Claude M. Simpson (Columbus: The Ohio State University Press, 1962), 42–43.

11. It should be evident that my reading of "The Custom-House" disagrees with the

scholarly view of Hawthorne as a citizen who saw the romance as a way of encouraging what Donald Pease calls "civic virtue" (*Visionary Compacts: American Renaissance Writings in Cultural Context* [Madison: University of Wisconsin Press, 1987], 74). Pease reads "The Custom-House" as a text by which Hawthorne "turned his writing into a means of letting others live through him, even as he came into full life through them. Writing became an occasion to sacrifice his self-interest for the interest of an entire community of persons. What resulted was what he called a republic of letters—'somewhere else'" (76).

12. Richard Walsh, "Fictionality and Mimesis: Between Narrativity and Fictional Worlds," *Narrative* 11, no. 1 (January 2003): 115.

13. Intriguingly, Walsh points to two thinkers often associated with the idea of mimesis—Georg Lukács and Eric Auerbach—as largely responsible for its critical redefinition.

14. Walsh, "Fictionality and Mimesis," 119.

15. Dana Brand suggests that "Main Street" allowed Hawthorne to express "his frustration about the cultural conditions under which, as an American writer, he was expected to write" ("Panoramic Spectator," 13).

16. If all texts were also commodities in Hawthorne's world, the romancer vouchsafed his own artistic purity by pointing to the mercenary approach to storytelling as anathema to the romancer's castles in the air. It is not surprising, then, that his fiction often turns to the figure of the showman to offset his own preoccupation with the higher truths of romance. In "Ethan Brand," for example, Hawthorne describes a Jew who goes through life "eking out the profits of the day" from a diorama whose illusions are marred by a "gigantic, Brown, hairy hand" belonging to the showman himself (*Tales*, 1060, 1061). When Brand reveals the unpardonable sin that has kept him away, the money-minded lime-burner rejects it as "humbug," as if the depth of Brand's (and the romancer's) truths are defined by the shallowness of a public that prefers dioramas to moral insight. As Stephen Railton has argued about the story, Hawthorne performs his own literariness both by contrasting his tale with the Jew's thrown-together panorama and by presenting the characters of "Ethan Brand" as more interested in the diorama than in Brand's own story. See Railton, *Authorship*, 111–14.

17. Panoramas relied upon the invisibility of their machinery. As Joseph Moldenhauer tells us in "Thoreau, Hawthorne, and the Seven-Mile Panorama" (*ESQ: A Journal of the American Renaissance* 44, no. 4 [1998]), the operators and the various machinery (which included reels to unfurl and collect the enormous canvases, along with the gears used to turn each scroll) "could be hidden from the audience by theater curtains or some similar visual barrier that simultaneously framed the image" (229). Thus the showman of "Main Street" undercut the authority of his own panoramic exhibition by repeatedly drawing attention to the machinery on which it relied.

18. Jeffrey H. Richards, "The Showman as Romancer: Theatrical Presentation in Hawthorne's 'Main Street,'" *Studies in Short Fiction* 21 (1984): 53.

19. *Description of Bayne's Gigantic Panorama of a Voyage to Europe* (Boston: Printed by William Chadwick, 1848).

20. As Moldenhauer points out, panoramists sought various ways of enhancing "the sense that the two-hour illusion was above all else truthful, and that the artistry lay not in the painter's selection, composition, and emphasis but in minute fidelity to 'naturally beautiful' material. The mirror metaphor so often adopted by the painters and impresarios of panoramas . . . announces the aesthetic standard by which the paintings were measured" ("Seven-Mile Panorama," 232).

21. *Burr's Pictorial Voyage* (Boston: Dutton and Wentworth, 1850), 43.

22. *Hudson's Great National Painting of the Ohio and Mississippi Rivers* (New Haven, CT: J. H. Benham, printer, 1848), 17.

23. From an advertising sheet entitled *Lane's Mammoth Panorama of the Hudson, or North River . . .* , announcing an exhibition of the panorama at Lynde Hall in Salem, on September 18, 1848. Found inside *Description of Lane's Panorama of the Hudson River* (New York, 1848), at the American Antiquarian Society (Worcester, MA).

24. John Rowson Smith, *Descriptive Book of the Tour of Europe* (New York: Pattinger and Gray, 1855), 26.

25. My reading of the balcony scene is informed by Michael Warner's lucid discussion, in "The Mass Public and the Mass Subject" (in *Publics and Counterpublics* [New York: Zone Books, 2002]) of the "self-abstraction" that defines the mass subject against the republican self. While the ideal of republican virtue, Warner argues, "was designed exactly to avoid any rupture of self-difference between ordinary life and publicity" (160), the "mass public sphere tries to minimize the difference between . . . positivity and self-abstraction" (176).

26. As Tom Standage writes in *The Victorian Internet: The Remarkable Story of the Telegraph and the Nineteenth Century's On-line Pioneers* (New York: Walker and Company, 1998), "The trouble with the electric telegraph was that, compared to the optical telegraphs that came before it, it seemed more like a conjuring trick than a means of communication" (41). In *Haunted Media: Electronic Presence from Telegraphy to Television* (Durham, NC: Duke University Press, 2000), Jeffrey Sconce has argued that in its earliest years Morse's technology was seen by many to have supernatural implications. Because the telegraph "made possible the instantaneous exchange of messages in the complete absence of physical bodies," many commentators considered the telegraph "the most momentous innovation in human history" (21–22). Sconce describes the famous case of the Fox family, whose daughters claimed to hear rapping sounds that constituted messages from the world of the dead, sent to them through a "spiritual telegraph" (22). Antebellum Spiritualists, who believed that the dead could communicate with the living through living mediums, "eagerly linked Spiritualist phenomena with the similarly fantastic discourses of electromagnetic telegraphy" (24). Even those who were skeptical of such attitudes were fascinated by the technology's "apparent ability to separate consciousness from the body" (25). Thus, "more than an arbitrary, fanciful, and wholly bizarre response to the innovation of a technological marvel, the spiritual telegraph's contact with the dead represented, at least initially, a strangely 'logical' application of telegraphy consistent with period knowledges of electromagnetic science" (28–29).

27. In *News Over the Wires: The Telegraph and the Flow of Public Information in America, 1844–1897* (Cambridge, MA: Harvard University Press, 1994), Menahem Blondheim writes, "The function of the AP in the news industry may be likened to that of a giant funnel. From the vast network of wires of the nation's telegraph monopoly it gathered information from all over the country in its headquarters. There, the news was consolidated to a single report and . . . distributed throughout the country. Not all information that reached those headquarters went out, and what did was necessarily transformed in the process" (174).

28. E. L. McCallum, "Hawthorne and Pynchon on the Line," *Arizona Quarterly* 56, no. 2 (2000): 69.

29. Lawrence Buell describes the novel's willingness to suspend time, to ignore the conventions of narrative writing, as "symptomatic of contemporary distrust of narrative

invention as against informational or moralistic content" (*New England Literary Culture: From Revolution Through Renaissance* [Cambridge: Cambridge University Press, 1986], 356).

30. Ronald Thomas, "Double Exposures: Arresting Images in *Bleak House* and *The House of the Seven Gables,*" *Novel: A Forum on Fiction* 31 (1997): 103. As Alan Trachtenberg writes, "A visibility incomplete in itself, the daguerrean image Holgrave offers to Phoebe's eyes is in search of an explanatory narrative" ("Seeing and Believing: Hawthorne's Reflections on the Daguerreotype in *The House of the Seven Gables,*" *American Literary History* 9 [1997]: 468).

31. As Ronald Thomas writes, "the novel reminds its readers that, like the narrative that contains these images, the photograph is a representation of a thing in need of interpretation. It is not the thing itself" ("Double Exposures," 110).

32. Trachtenberg, "Seeing and Believing," 472, 477.

33. Ned Buntline, *Love at First Sight: or, The Daguerreotype* (Boston: Lerow and Co., 1848[?]), 6 (hereafter cited parenthetically).

34. And so it should not come as a surprise that when Hawthorne wrote to his publisher about the troubles he was having concluding *Seven Gables,* he did so in the language of the daguerreotypist: "It darkens damnably towards the close, but I shall try hard to pour some setting sunshine over it" (letter to J. T. Fields, December 1, 1850, in *The Letters, 1843–1853,* vol. 16 of *The Centenary Edition of Nathaniel Hawthorne,* ed. Thomas Woodson, L. Neal Smith, and Norman Holmes Pearson [Columbus: The Ohio State University Press, 1985], 376). Holgrave, Cathy Davidson reminds us, is described by Hawthorne's narrator as a proletarian wanderer who has bounced from job to job—including, not surprisingly, newspaper editor and peddler. Intriguingly, however, Holgrave is also an author, one who has published in both *Graham's* and *Godey's.* Perhaps, then, Hawthorne is attempting to define the autonomy of the romancer over the magazine writer that he used to be. So when Holgrave finally gives up his writing career for domestic life at the novel's end, the character's entry into the middle class offsets the romantic autonomy that Hawthorne, by this time a husband and father, implicitly claims. In Meredith McGill's excellent reading of the novel, she charts how *Seven Gables* participated in the process by which Hawthorne sought to extricate himself from "his many years of publishing anonymous, pseudonymous, and authored tales and sketches" and reposition himself as "a major author" (*American Literature and the Culture of Reprinting, 1834–1853* [Philadelphia: University of Pennsylvania Press, 2003], 219, 220).

35. I would suggest that the reader, at the conclusion of *Seven Gables,* is in a position also analogous to that of Annie and Danforth in the concluding moments of "The Artist of the Beautiful." Like those characters, the reader is left with a work of fiction in her hands—as the romancer occupies a more genuine reality.

36. In one of the earliest and most influential new historicist treatments of Hawthorne's fiction, Brook Thomas wrote, "Closer to the foundation of his society, Hawthorne was in a better position than his British counterparts were to see that social reality is a construct, that to be interested in society is not necessarily to describe what is already there but to show how a possible world would be organized if human beings had the freedom to choose" ("*The House of the Seven Gables:* Reading the Romance of America," *PMLA* 97, no. 2 [1982]: 196). Thomas argues that the romance's unwillingness to shape "the social contradictions it explores [into] . . . unities and harmonies," a view of romance he takes from Richard Chase's famous account of the form, makes it a dynamic vehicle for "imagining an alternative to the society the romancer inherits" (195, 196). Thomas's excellent

reading reveals how Hawthorne's novel "questions the impersonal, rational authority of a democracy's most sacred texts—its legal documents" (199). While his reading of *Seven Gables* highlights the limitations of Hawthornean romance as an agent of moral reform—"the reformer seems capable of offering only a system that, like a romance, is an extension of his imagination" (203)—Thomas never falters from the basic assumption that Hawthorne's goal is such reform: his Hawthorne "asks not for assent [from his reader] but for participation and consent. Authority becomes intersubjective, not subjective. The basis for a community is thus established" (207).

More recently, Grantland Rice has charted how the commercialization of American print culture in the eighteenth and early nineteenth centuries threatened to replace the civic dimensions of authorship with more professional, market-oriented concerns. Rice's meticulous account of the evolution of the early American print culture, and of the effect of this transformation on the category of the "author" through the mid-nineteenth century, opens up the study of antebellum literature by inviting us to comprehend the work of an author such as Hawthorne as a response to the commercialization of American print culture. In his concluding discussion of *The House of the Seven Gables,* Rice writes that Hawthorne confronted "a commercial print culture which threatened to rob the individual of his or her capacity to participate in public affairs and his or her ability to envision a world different than that which was rendered by custom and tradition" (*The Transformation of Authorship in America* [Chicago: University of Chicago Press, 1997], 177). In the face of such a challenge, Rice argues, Hawthorne "translated the disinterested civic conscience of the classical citizen into the disinterested aesthetic conscience of the modern author," a move marked by the conception of "romance" as a neutral territory that could connect the contemporaneous present with a particular past. While Rice's work makes possible a view of Hawthornean romance as a response to changing print conditions, his Hawthorne reaches out to a reading public that was increasingly exploited and corrupted by the underwriters of a new mass print culture. Privileging Hawthorne's commitment to a "disinterested social activism" that was rapidly receding into the past (even as he acknowledges how the romancer "idealized" such a past), Rice attends to Hawthorne's critique of antebellum commercialism as if it were grounded in the author's disinterested concern for the fate of his reading public.

37. See, for example, Lauren Berlant's important work on Hawthorne's engagement with what she calls "the fantasy-work of national identity" (*Anatomy,* 2).

CHAPTER 4

1. In his biography of Melville, *Melville: His World and Work* (New York: Alfred A. Knopf, 2005), Andrew Delbanco devotes an entire chapter to the often-overlooked impact of mid-1840s New York City on the young author's life and work. As Delbanco tells us, in early 1845 Melville was in New York often, stopping in at the law firm of his brothers Allan and Gansevoort regularly enough that he was apparently known as the "runaway brother" (87). Delbanco writes that by the summer of 1847 (when Melville and his new wife made the decision to move full time to the city), "Melville had become a figure on the New York literary scene" (91). For an excellent book-length discussion of Melville's relationship to New York culture, see Bergmann, *God in the Street: New York Writing from the Penny Press to Melville* (Philadelphia: Temple University Press, 1995).

2. Dryden, *Thematics,* 21. Richard Brodhead has argued that "Melville does not have

a well-defined philosophy—or rather he has a hundred of them. But what all his formulations have in common is a sense of reality as something finally mysterious or unknowable" (*Hawthorne, Melville, and the Novel* [Chicago: University of Chicago Press, 1976], 126). Just as significantly, Brodhead connects Melville's desire to "challeng[e] the credentials of any representational art" (129) with Hawthorne's own rejection of perfect representation—so that these two romantic authors are ultimately defined in his book, as in my own, by a shared sense of reality as something that cannot be adequately reproduced or captured.

3. For the definitive study on twentieth-century media events, see Daniel Dayan and Elihu Katz, *Media Events: The Live Broadcasting of History* (Cambridge, MA: Harvard University Press, 1992).

4. *Albany Weekly Herald*, May 31, 1845, 6.

5. For a detailed discussion of the role of the telegraph in the Mexican War, see Blondheim, *News Over the Wires*, chapter 3. For an account of the role of journalistic correspondents in the war, see Robert Desmond, *The Information Process: World News Reporting to the Twentieth Century* (Iowa City: University of Iowa Press, 1978), chapter 10.

6. See Robert Johannsen, *To the Halls of the Montezumas: The Mexican War in the American Imagination* (Oxford: Oxford University Press, 1985), especially chapter 1. As Johannsen writes, "The press's 'telegraphic era' began with the Mexican War" (19). In a brief discussion of the use of war correspondents and news expresses during the war, Johannsen illustrates that "the war coincided with the era of the penny press, a time when technology, marketing innovations, and a dramatic increase in literacy all combined to produce a veritable 'print explosion'" (18).

7. "Annexation," *U.S. Magazine and Democratic Review*, July/August 1845: 9.

8. "Mexico—The Church, and Peace," *U.S. Magazine and Democratic Review*, August 1847: 101.

9. An article from the *New York Herald* on June 27, 1846, was typical in its expansionist imagining of a time when the telegraph wires "may yet extend . . . to the halls of Montezuma."

10. *New York Herald*, April 3, 1847.

11. Reported in ibid., May 5, 1847.

12. *Albany Argus*, December 13, 1844, 3 (hereafter cited parenthetically).

13. Shelley Streeby, in *American Sensations: Class, Empire, and the Production of Popular Culture* (Berkeley: University of California Press, 2002), argues that this unifying of "America" into a single body elided the question of difference as a threat to national unity in part by isolating an external enemy—Mexico—that reinforced the cohesiveness of the American body. Reading George Lippard's *Legends of Mexico*, Streeby outlines Lippard's vision of individual American bodies reacting in unison to war news from Mexico, a vision in which "the national community as a collective body . . . convulses, quivers, and thrills to the news of the U.S.-Mexican War" (54).

14. *Albany Argus*, September 12, 1844.

15. Reprinted as "A Game of Drafts" in ibid., November 29, 1844, 1.

16. "The Magnetic Telegraph—Some of Its Results," *Living Age* 26 (July 1845): 194.

17. Note the parallels between this piece and the satirical poem "The Last Newsboy," which appeared in *Yankee Doodle* and which I discuss below. In the poem, the magazine's editors seem to mock the popular idea that the telegraph would soon make newspapers

obsolete.

18. See, for example, "The American Electric Telegraph" (*New York Observer,* July 24, 1847).

19. Alfred Vail, *The American Electric Telegraph with the Reports of Congress* (Philadelphia: Lea and Blanchard, 1845), vii.

20. For a thorough account of the Young America movement, see Edward L. Widmer, *Young America: The Flowering of Democracy in New York City* (Oxford: Oxford University Press, 1999). Widmer makes clear the complexity of the movement, in part by challenging the popular view that O'Sullivan was its most significant spokesperson.

21. Reprinted as "Morse's Magnetic Telegraph," *New York Weekly Tribune,* June 15, 1844, 6.

22. Streeby, *American Sensations,* 55. While Streeby reveals how Lippard's fiction "could be said to incorporate marginal whites such as the Irish into the American 'race'" (60), she reads the dime novels of Augustine Joseph Hickey Duganne to illustrate the popular conception of Mexico as both similar to the United States and somewhat alien— "largely because of the mixtures of multiple 'races' and the persistence of feudalism and colonial institutions" (195).

23. Indeed, these anecdotes were so popular that *The Taylor Anecdote Book* appeared in 1848.

24. "A little more grape, Captain Bragg," *New York Herald,* September 8, 1847.

25. "Old Zack," *New York Atlas,* July 4, 1847.

26. *New York Atlas,* July 18, 1847, 2.

27. Ibid., July 25, 1847, 2.

28. One obvious reason Barnum might be called a "necromancer" is the case of Joice Heth, with whom Barnum toured in 1835, claiming that the elderly slave was the former nurse of George Washington. See Reiss, *The Showman and the Slave: Race, Death, and Memory in Barnum's America* (Cambridge, MA: Harvard University Press, 2001).

29. *New York Atlas,* April 18, 1847.

30. Ibid., April 25, 1847.

31. *New York Tribune,* July 3, 1847.

32. Ibid., July 15, 1847.

33. Reprinted in ibid. as "Authentic News from the Army," March 31, 1847.

34. Newspapers were not the only places where this contrast of American and Mexican dispatches appeared. In his *A Complete History of the Mexican War* (Baltimore: Hutchinson and Seebold, 1849), N. C. Brooks juxtaposes Taylor's official account of Palo Alto with that of General Mariano Arista. Between Taylor's and Arista's dispatches, Brooks writes the following: "In striking contrast with this plain statement is the account of the vanquished Arista, addressed to the Mexican Minister of War and Marine, and dated, 'In sight of the enemy, May 8.' Though in sight of the enemy, the Mexican commander was at the time in *retreat.* This omission, however, is of little moment, when we consider the many misstatements of his dispatch" (134).

35. Of course, the very myth of a unified American identity was itself a response to an era that, as Shelley Streeby points out, was "marked by increasing sectionalism, struggles over slavery, the formation of an urban industrial working class, and nativist hatred directed at the new, mostly German and Irish, immigrants whose numbers increased rapidly after 1845" (*American Sensations,* 39).

36. Timothy Brennan, "The National Longing for Form," in *Nation and Narration,* ed. Homi Bhabha (London: Routledge, 1990), 49.

37. *New York Atlas*, September 19, 1847, 2.

38. Corydon Donnavan, *Adventures in Mexico* (Cincinnati: Robinson and Jones, 1847), 67 (hereafter cited parenthetically). The emphases are Donnavan's.

39. *New York Tribune*, April 8, 1846.

40. *New York Atlas*, January 10, 1847.

41. By the end of the decade, writers were attacking even authorized journalistic use of the telegraph as a means of manipulating information for financial gain—so that the line between news and speculation became increasingly hard to distinguish. When the Associated Press was established at the end of the 1840s as a way of consolidating various newspaper interests into one centralized organization, opponents claimed that this consolidation of news transmission was nothing short of fraudulent. One opponent of such press associations, writing in 1850, argued to the commissioners of the Nova Scotia Telegraph that the agreement between the AP and their telegraph company unfairly benefited the publishers of morning newspapers in Boston by exclusively transmitting the news for an organization that excluded evening papers. The writer, in addressing the "inequity of control" over the news, describes such as practice as a "fraud" played upon the people of Boston. The fact that the author of this attack was himself a publisher of an evening paper in Boston only underscores how intertwined business and information had become in such a short period of time.

42. "Fraud on the Press and on the Public," *New York Tribune*, January 20, 1846, 2.

43. *New York Tribune*, March 21, 1846.

44. Melville, *Correspondence*, 40. While he does go on, as Edward Widmer points out, to claim that "something great is impending" (*Flowering*, 87) (which Widmer reads as a hint by Melville that "a final struggle against England is in the air"), what is probably more meaningful is the very tension in this one letter between his nationalistic dreaming and the rejection of the war as mere spectacle. Crucial to any reading of this letter is the fact of Gansevoort's political involvement and of Herman's awareness of their differences in this regard. Lynn Horth, in the note introducing this letter, argues that the letter is "clearly intended to distract Melville's ailing brother" (*Correspondence*, 39).

45. One piece on the questionable authenticity of the Chinese junk that appeared in *Yankee Doodle* has been attributed by many scholars to Melville himself. See "On the Chinese Junk" and the accompanying note (beginning on page 784) in *Piazza Tales* (hereafter cited parenthetically).

46. "Watching the Telegraph" (*Yankee Doodle* 1, no. 11 [December 19, 1846]: 158); "Telegraph Office" (*Yankee Doodle* 1, no. 11 [December 19, 1846]: 72); and "The Last Newsboy" (*Yankee Doodle* 1, no. 7 [November 21, 1846]: 72).

47. Another attack on the myth of telegraphic authenticity can be found in the 1848 story "News from Mexico," from Anne W. Abbot's *How to Spoil a Good Citizen; and Other Stories* (Boston: Crosby and Nichols, and S. G. Simkins, 1848). Abbot's story, in which two characters debate the merits of the war, begins with the patriotic Jonathan teasing his friend, John Hammond, for subscribing to a paper too worried about being hoaxed to report the latest news from the front lines. Ultimately, "News from Mexico" allows the author to give voice (in the character of John) to the argument that Mexican lands are being unjustly annexed by the United States. But what is most fascinating about the story is the way its author attacks the newspaper's role in the "great talk about patriotism," which the story describes as an "old cloak" that is covering up the country's moral wrongdoing. While Jonathan claims throughout the story to merely report on the latest news taken from his paper, the way our author presents his character's recounting of the

news suggests that the story of the American victory of Mexico had already been written, even before the details arrived in print.

48. Dryden, *Thematics*, 117, 137.

49. For a fascinating account of Melville's debt in *Moby-Dick* to antebellum popular culture, see David Reynolds, "'Its wood could only be American!': *Moby-Dick* and Antebellum Popular Culture," in *Critical Essays*, ed. Brian Higgins and Hershel Parker (New York: G. K. Hall and Co., 1992), as well as his groundbreaking *Beneath the American Renaissance: The Subversive Imagination in the Age of Emerson and Melville* (Cambridge, MA: Harvard University Press, 1988). While Reynolds has convincingly argued in both works that "Melville's narrative art was one of wide-ranging assimilation and literary transformation" ("'Its wood,'" 523), I see Melville as more of an ironic, even hostile, borrower from mass culture—often invoking its terms only to assert the supremacy of his own art. In this way, my Melville is closer to the one described in Railton, *Authorship*, chapter 8.

50. For the authoritative account of the relationship of the early English novel to truth-telling discourses, see Lennard Davis, *Factual Fictions*. In opposing *Roxana* to *Don Quixote*, for example, Davis argues that Defoe's reliance on an authenticating document is "uniquely novelistic" (16).

51. Melville, *Pierre; or the Ambiguities*, vol. 7 of *The Writings of Herman Melville*, ed. Harrison Hayford, Hershel Parker, and G. Thomas Tanselle (Evanston, IL: Northwestern University Press / Newberry Library, 1971), 141 (hereafter cited parenthetically).

52. Quoted in Elmer, *Reading*, 13.

CHAPTER 5

1. Geoffrey Sanborn, *The Sign of the Cannibal: Melville and the Making of a Postcolonial Reader* (Durham, NC: Duke University Press, 1998). As Sanborn writes of Tommo's discovery of what appear to be human bones, "even if we accept that there are human bones in the vessel, we cannot take it for granted that the flesh missing from these bones has been eaten." Sanborn reveals that "it was widely recognized throughout the early nineteenth century that the discovery of human remains did not count as evidence of cannibalism" (111).

2. Samson has written that in *Typee* Melville rewrites his own textual sources by making such "perceptual conflict" a subject of his own narratives. See *White Lies: Melville's Narratives of Facts* (Ithaca, NY: Cornell University Press, 1989). But Samson's approach, as Elizabeth Renker points out, "is meant to bolster his ultimate argument that Melville was politically forward-thinking and engaged in a deliberate and conscious critique of his sources as representations of 'white' ideology" ("Melville's Spell in *Typee*," *Arizona Quarterly* 51, no. 2 [1995]: 4).

3. Melville, *Typee: A Peep at Polynesian Life*, vol. 1 of *The Writings of Herman Melville*, ed. Harrison Hayford, Hershel Parker, and G. Thomas Tanselle (Evanston, IL: Northwestern University Press / Newberry Library, 1968), 74 (hereafter cited parenthetically).

4. In addition to Sanborn, see Paul Lyons, "From Man-Eaters to Spam-Eaters: Literary Tourism and the Discourse of Cannibalism from Herman Melville to Paul Theroux" (*Arizona Quarterly* 51, no. 2 [Summer 1995]: 33–62), and Alex Calder, "'The Thrice Mysterious Taboo': Melville's *Typee* and the Perception of Culture" (*Representations* 67 [1999]: 27–43).

5. For two excellent discussions of the fate of *Typee* as text, see John Bryant, "Manuscript, Edition, Revision: Reading *Typee* with Trifocals," in *Melville's Evermoving Dawn: Centennial Essays*, ed. John Bryant and Robert Milder (Kent, OH: Kent State University Press, 1997), and Leon Howard's "Historical Note" in *Typee*.

6. For a full account of Toby's emergence, see Hershel Parker, *Herman Melville*, vol. 1 (Baltimore: Johns Hopkins University Press), chapter 22.

7. For two lucid discussions of the place of travel writing in Western imperialism, see Mary Louise Pratt, *Imperial Eyes: Travel Writing and Transculturation* (London: Routledge, 1992), and David Spurr, *The Rhetoric of Empire: Colonial Discourse in Journalism, Travel Writing, and Imperial Administration* (Durham, NC: Duke University Press, 1993).

8. Rowe, "Melville's *Typee*," 258. Rowe argues that "*Typee* is one of the first U.S. literary texts to establish a connection between the institutions of slavery in the United States and the Euroamerican colonialism in Polynesia" (255). While Rowe does not address Melville's pro-England sentiment in the appendix that was published in the book's first American and British editions, he suggests that Melville's text argues "that the domestic sins of slavery and westward expansion were already finding their equivalents in foreign policies just as insidious" (256).

9. Railton, *Authorship*, 153.

10. Spurr, *Rhetoric of Empire*, 15, 127.

11. "The South Seas," in *Piazza Tales*, 419–20 (hereafter cited parenthetically).

12. Douglas Ivison, "'I Saw Everything but Could Comprehend Nothing': Melville's *Typee*, Travel Narrative, and Colonial Discourse," *American Transcendental Quarterly* 16, no. 2 (2002): 115. See also Justin Edwards, "Melville's Peep-Show: Sexual and Textual Cruises in 'Typee,'" *ARIEL: A Review of International English Literature* 30, no. 2 (1999): 61–74.

13. Wai Chee Dimock, "*Typee*: Melville's Critique of Community," *ESQ* 30 (1984): 31.

14. In his brilliant reading of Melville's treatment of cannibalism, Geoffrey Sanborn unveils the truth of cannibalism in *Typee* to be its very status as a sign—that is, Sanborn argues that cannibalism's theatricality is the aspect of it that is most real. Sanborn's Melville is a theorist of the highest order, one whose interest in the "articulation of dynamics of anxiety and menace in the colonial encounter" (xiii) anticipates the work of both Homi Bhabha and Slavoj Žižek. He sees in Melville's writing a fascination with the dynamics of colonial contact, which anticipates Bhabha's work on the same subject, and an awareness of cannibalism as "a screen masking a void," which adumbrates Žižek's ideas (*Sign of the Cannibal*, xiv). Specifically, Sanborn points to the moment near the end of *Typee*, when Tommo finally sees what appear to be human bones, to suggest that Melville's use of this evidence of cannibalism highlights how the bones are most real in their theatricality. In another excellent reading, Leonard Cassuto asks that we read *Typee* in the context of antebellum racial freak shows, which provided an outlet for national doubts regarding racial essentialism. Like Sanborn, Cassuto recognizes cannibalism in Melville's narrative to be a titillating presence, but his reading reveals how Melville's Tommo resists being made into a freak show exhibit—specifically, by refusing to be tattooed. The whole book, Cassuto argues, may be read as a "tattooing narrative" (in which highly tattooed sailors would reveal the stories behind each marking) without the tattoos; Tommo "fears being imprisoned inside the narrative of a freak show exhibit pamphlet" ("'What an object he would have made of me!': Tattooing and the Racial Freak in Melville's *Typee*," in *Freak-*

ery: Cultural Spectacles of the Extraordinary Body, ed. Rosemarie Garland-Thomson [New York: New York University Press, 1996], 241). In his own account of the book's depiction of cannibalism, Alex Calder argues that Melville relies upon the concept of "taboo" to allow a place for "a remainder . . . something more than can be said" in the author's narrative account. In Calder's reading, Melville relinquishes the need to access all meaning, turning instead to narrative "mimicry" of the Typee. Finally, Calder writes, such mimicry becomes "a camouflage one adopts in response to a perceived disjunction between self and milieu . . . a quasi-automatic but potentially strategic response to ambiguity" ("Melville's *Typee*," 39).

15. Lyons, "From Man-Eaters to Spam-Eaters," 47–48.

16. Brook Thomas writes that *Typee* "lays bare the imperialistic motives behind the introduction of Christianity to non-Western cultures, the savagery it causes rather than eliminates. Most important, if opponents of slavery think the eradication of slavery from America's shores will finally make America the land of the free, Melville's works offer example after example demonstrating exploitation in the 'free' states" (*Cross-Examinations of Law and Literature: Cooper, Hawthorne, Stowe, and Melville* [Cambridge: Cambridge University Press, 1987], 137).

17. In a later rhetorical use of telegraphy that illustrates what Melville was writing against, Ezra Gannett in 1858 saw in Morse's technology the promise of a Christianity-based imperialism: "The most remarkable effect [of the telegraph], if I may judge from my own narrow thought, will be the approach to a practical unity of the human race; of which we have never yet had a foreshadowing, except in the gospel of Christ. Actually, the race has been divided into as distinct portions as if they lived on separate planets. Jealous of one another, or mutually unknown, they have exchanged no sympathies, united in no common labors, recognized no obligations of kindred blood. . . . The death-blow has been struck to barbarism. An exclusive policy must yield to the universal solvent. . . . It is an institution for the people. Its office is to diffuse intelligence; its effect, to allay differences" ("The Oceanic Telegraph," *North American Review* 87, no. 181 [October 1858]: 543–44). In descriptions such as this, the logic of the telegraphic metaphor entirely overshadows the reality of the technology as a means of linguistic communication. Gannett's faith in the technology's ability to "diffuse intelligence" and "allay differences" rests on the assumption that Western modes of information exchange are a "universal solvent"—that is, that the telegraph as a method of disembodied communication is an impartial, apolitical ideal.

18. For discussions of the significance of tattooing in *Typee*, see Cassuto; Otter, *Melville's Anatomies* (Berkeley: University of California Press, 1999), chapter 1; and Sanborn, chapter 2.

19. Letter to Duyckinck, February 12, 1851, in *Correspondence*, 180.

20. Letter to Hawthorne, November [17?] 1851, in ibid., 212–13 (hereafter cited parenthetically).

21. Letter to Lemuel Shaw, October 6, 1849, in ibid., 139.

22. Quoted in Dryden, *Thematics*, vii.

23. In truth, of course, Melville's and Hawthorne's imaginations were different in some rather fundamental ways. Though the two authors shared a sense of the inauthenticity of mid-nineteenth-century life, each differed in the way he imagined the relationship between his romantic fiction and what I have called the problem of reality. Against the lies of antebellum life, Hawthorne was able to articulate the more authentic "reality" he shared with Sophia, or the "free air" of romance, both rhetorical realms that could be positively

imagined and communicated. But if Hawthorne was a citizen of somewhere else, Melville seems more often an eternal noncitizen—of whatever culture he found himself in, in the United States or abroad. Thus the telegraph, the antebellum avatar of informational timeliness and reliability, appears in Melville's imagination as a powerful symbol by which the romancer can distance his own art of telling the truth from the truth-telling ideals of antebellum culture.

CHAPTER 6

1. See Coviello, "The American in Charity." In a provocative reading of Melville's text, Dana Luciano argues that the novella's exploration of historical memory "can best be understood in light of the cultural work performed by the contemporary [i.e., early twenty-first-century] counter-monument, which Melville's narrative anticipates and elucidates" ("Melville's Untimely History: 'Benito Cereno' as Counter-Monumental Narrative," *Arizona Quarterly: A Journal of American Literature, Culture, and Theory* 60, no. 3 [2004]: 34). Maurice S. Lee has recently pointed out how many twentieth-century critics claimed for "Benito Cereno" an uncanny relevance to particular twentieth-century cultural moments—as if, Lee writes, Melville "apparently speaks to *us* at the expense of an earlier *them*" ("Melville's Subversive Political Philosophy: 'Benito Cereno' and the Fate of Speech," *American Literature: A Journal of Literary History, Criticism, and Bibliography* 72, no. 3 [2000]: 513). In attempting to make sense of this critical phenomenon, Lee argues that "the story anticipates our reactions. It is sensitive to the psychology of Otherness" (512). In his final paragraph, Lee concludes, "Melville's hermeneutics lean more toward new than old, more toward a differentially interpreted past than any recoverable history." As Lee tells us, "one province of literature, and one labor of those who would read it, is to seek and imagine an honest speech—in the antebellum then, in our present now, and in the ongoing talk over 'Benito Cereno' from which . . . something further will follow" (514).

2. Christopher Castiglia and Russ Castronovo, "A 'Hive of Subtlety': Aesthetics and the End[s] of Cultural Studies," *American Literature* 76, no. 3 (September 2004): 433, 432, 427.

3. Carolyn Karcher, *Shadow Over the Promised Land: Slavery, Race, and Violence in Melville's America* (Baton Rouge: Louisiana State University Press, 1980), 128.

4. Letter to Nathaniel Hawthorne, [1 June?] 1851, in *Correspondence*, 190, 192 (hereafter cited parenthetically).

5. Sundquist, *To Wake the Nations: Race in the Making of American Literature* (Cambridge, MA: Harvard University Press, 1993).

6. Luciano, "Untimely History," 54.

7. Melville, "Benito Cereno," in *Piazza Tales,* 116 (hereafter cited parenthetically).

8. Sundquist describes the complicated narrative voice of "Benito Cereno" in the following way: "The difficulty with judging Delano's perceptions lies in the complex relationship between him and the narrative voice, which moves silently in and out of the captain's point of view, engaging and promoting his suspicions, then retracting them in sudden dismissals. . . . It would be appropriate to speak of the narrative voice, which dictates to Babo as surely as Babo does to Benito Cereno, as itself a kind of 'shadow,' at once merged with but partially suspended above or outside his conscious point of view" ("Suspense and Tautology in 'Benito Cereno,'" *Glyph: Textual Studies* 8 [1981]: 109).

9. Critics have long recognized the ways in which Melville's invocation of slavery critiques sentimental fiction and reading. Most recently, Peter Coviello has illustrated how "'Benito Cereno' . . . pits gothic occlusion and opacity against sentimental modes of reading and response, and sentimental readers, the better to show how easily sentimentality consorts with a particularly American racism" ("The American in Charity," 157). Like my own reading, Coviello's approaches "Benito Cereno" as a response to Stowe's "signature locutions of knowingness" (171). But I do not share the critical assumption that Melville's subversion of mass reading practices stemmed from a civic-minded belief that "a wise and healthy republic *demands* good readers" (175).

10. "Lecture on Slavery," from Len Gougeon and Joel Myerson, eds., *Ralph Waldo Emerson: Emerson's Antislavery Writings* (New Haven, CT: Yale University Press, 1995), 91. "Endless negation" posed a problem greater than flatness, of course; it became a formidable political obstacle. Stowe responded to accusations of exaggeration and misrepresentation with her now-famous *The Key to Uncle Tom's Cabin,* in which she provided documentation for her various portraits of life in the South. Such a defense, however, could never rise above the debate over whose picture of slavery was ultimately truthful. Soon after her "key" was published, in fact, Reverend E. J. Stearns published his *Notes on Uncle Tom's Cabin* (Philadelphia: Lippincott, Grambo and Co., 1853), in essence a response to Stowe's response, in which he sought to call further into question the accuracy of Stowe's account. Some Northern apologists for slavery went south, including Nehemiah Adams, who propped himself up as a firsthand observer in his 1854 *South-Side View of Slavery* (Boston: Ticknor and Fields, 1860).

11. As Len Gougeon tells us, Emerson's lecture was greeted warmly by most New England abolitionists, who tended to see the 1855 lecture as a major step into political advocacy for an author who had previously been considered more interested in the "upper sphere" of American culture. See Gougeon, "Historical Background," in *Emerson's Antislavery Writings,* xliii–xliv.

12. See Thomas F. Gossett, *Uncle Tom's Cabin and American Culture* (Dallas, TX: Southern Methodist University Press, 1985), especially chapters 10 and 11. Many attacked Stowe for being too much of a "storyteller" and for her "fictional facts."

13. Peter Dorsey argues that "attacks on Stowe's novel caused her to formulate a realistic ethics of fiction" ("De-authorizing Slavery: Realism in Stowe's *Uncle Tom's Cabin* and Brown's *Clotel,*" *ESQ* 41 [1995]: 258).

14. Harriet Beecher Stowe, *The Key to Uncle Tom's Cabin* (Salem, NH: Ayer Company, 1987), 90 (hereafter cited parenthetically).

15. Stowe was regularly attacked for being too far from the reality of slavery. In his *Notes on Uncle Tom's Cabin,* E. J. Stearns argues that the "personal observations" that Stowe points to in the *Key* are (at least in one case) letters handed to her by former slaves.

16. Dwight McBride, *Impossible Witnesses: Truth, Abolitionism, and Slave Testimony* (New York: New York University Press, 2001), 4–5.

17. F. C. Adams, *Uncle Tom at Home* (Philadelphia: Willis Hazard, 1853), 123.

18. As Sheila Post-Lauria has convincingly argued in *Correspondent Colorings: Melville in the Marketplace* (Amherst: University of Massachusetts Press, 1996), writers in *Putnam's,* where "Benito Cereno" was first published in the 1850s, consistently challenged the "truth of facts," searching instead for a means of exploring those circumstances that lead to the creation of any totalizing narrative. Post-Lauria writes that *Putnam's* "articles, essays, and stories analyzed and evaluated the variety of perspectives

that comprised a particular issue" (204).

19. William Andrews, *To Tell a Free Story: The First Century of Afro-American Auto-biography, 1760–1865* (Urbana: University of Illinois Press, 1986), xi.

20. See, as just a few examples, the work of Saidiya Hartman, Dwight McBride, Carla Peterson, and Paul Gilmore.

21. Hartman, *Scenes of Subjection: Terror, Slavery, and Self-Making in Nineteenth-Century America* (New York: Oxford University Press, 1997), 6. For the most compelling account of the commodification of black literacy and subjectivity, see Henry Louis Gates, *Figures in Black: Words, Signs, and the "Racial" Self* (New York: Oxford University Press, 1989).

22. William Andrews has famously written of the "novelization of voice" in black writing of the 1850s. See "The Novelization of Voice in Early African American Narrative," *PMLA: Publications of the Modern Language Association* 105 (1990): 23–34.

23. In discussing Frederick Douglass's revisions to his 1845 narrative in the 1855 *My Bondage and My Freedom*, Eric Sundquist argues that the 1855 autobiography constituted "a sign of Douglass's recognition that in the [1845] *Narrative* he stood 'within the circle'—not of the total institution of slavery . . . but of Garrison's radical antislavery and the defined self of the platform storyteller it provided" (*To Wake the Nations*, 92). Andrews reminds us, however, that "it may be . . . that Douglass learned from [William Wells] Brown the advantages of self-revision for a fugitive slave who aspired to a career as a writer" ("Introduction" to *From Fugitive Slave to Free Man: The Autobiographies of William Wells Brown* [Columbia: University of Missouri Press, 2003], 3).

24. Frederick Douglass, *Autobiographies* (New York: Library of America, 1994), 366 (hereafter cited parenthetically).

25. The panorama was Brown's response to a visit he made (in Boston) to a panorama of the Mississippi River. "Amazed at the very mild manner in which the 'Peculiar Institution' of the Southern States was there represented," Brown "succeeded in obtaining a series of sketches of beautiful and interesting American scenery, as well as of many touching incidents in the lives of Slaves" (*A Description of William Wells Brown's Original Panoramic Views of the Scenes in the Life of an American Slave* [London: Charles Gilpin, 1849?], 3)

26. For an excellent recent discussion of the former slave's use of moving panoramas, see Daphne A. Brooks, *Bodies in Dissent: Spectacular Performances of Race and Freedom, 1850–1910* (Durham, NC: Duke University Press, 2006), chapter 2.

27. Brown, *Panoramic Views*, 3–4. In her discussion of Henry "Box" Brown's *Panorama of Slavery* (which premiered in America in April 1850), Cynthia Griffin Wolff argues that the panorama afforded "Box" Brown an "almost anti-autobiographical" form that "turned the tables" on abolitionism. See "Passing Beyond the Middle Passage: Henry 'Box' Brown's Translations of Slavery," *Massachusetts Review: A Quarterly of Literature, the Arts, and Public Affairs* 37, no. 1 (1996): 5, 1.

28. "Life and Escape" actually first appeared a year earlier as an introduction to Brown's series of travel sketches. Parenthetical citations here refer to the version that appears in William Wells Brown's *Clotel; or, The President's Daughter.*

29. John Ernest argues that the excerpt-filled *Clotel* most resembles not *Uncle Tom's Cabin* (as other critics have argued) but a contemporary antislavery journal. See *Resistance and Reformation in Nineteenth-Century African-American Literature: Brown, Wilson, Jacobs, Delany, Douglass, and Harper* (Jackson: University of Mississippi Press, 1995), 33.

30. Paul Gilmore locates parallels between black abolitionists such as Brown and the racial role-playing of antebellum minstrelsy. "Putting on the blackface of the minstrel show," Gilmore writes, "Brown creates himself as a self-sufficient manipulator of the literary marketplace and its dependence on mass cultural images of blackness, thus authorizing himself as a black model of literary manhood" (*Genuine Article,* 41). One of the few critics to take into account Brown's prefatory autobiography in his reading of the novel, Gilmore argues that "Life and Escape" both "authorizes Brown as a writer of fiction" and "places Brown in a position of literary authority . . . through his ability to put on multiple masks" (42). Gilmore convincingly points to the character of George from *Clotel* as an example of Brown "using . . . masquerade to create a representative black manhood" (63).

31. Hartman, *Scenes of Subjection,* 33.

32. As John Ernest reminds us, and as the above reading of "Life and Escape" suggests, Brown sought to "reconfigure the terms of the cultural arguments about slavery, terms that implicitly either denied Brown's own authority or limited his voice to that of a witness" ("Resistance and Reformation," 47).

33. William Andrews argues that "during the 1850s, when black as well as white American literature underwent a renaissance . . . the voice of black narrative broke most profoundly with discursive conventions and white expectations in an attempt to find new ways of authorizing itself ("Novelization," 24).

34. In an excellent essay linking the emergence of African American fiction in the early 1850s to the limitations imposed upon ex-slave writers by white abolitionism, Carla Peterson argues that "In writing slave autobiographies under the aegis of white abolitionism, black writers all too often found themselves producing conventionalized narratives that offered increasingly stereotyped images of the slave both as narrated and narrating *I*" ("Capitalism, Black [Under]Development, and the Production of the African American Novel in the 1850s," in *Postcolonial Theory and the United States: Race, Ethnicity and Literature,* ed. Amritjit Singh and Peter Schmidt [Jackson: University Press of Mississippi, 2000], 178). As a response to such pressures, Peterson argues, black authors "hoped that novelization would enable them to avoid the self-commodification of the slave narrative by disguising those traces of the self they desired to keep hidden." Peterson's account of the "split between narrating and narrated personae" suggests that "fictional characterization encouraged these writers to dismantle essentialized notions of black subjectivity, conceptualize identity as socially constructed, and explore the multiple facets of African-American experience" (179).

35. William Wells Brown, *Clotel; or, The President's Daughter,* ed. William Edward Farrison (New York: Carol Publishing Group, 1995), 156.

36. Approaching the authorial performances of "Life and Escape" and *Clotel* as Brown's attempt at evading the subject position prescribed for the former slave by abolitionism recasts the various excerpts that mark the idiosyncratic form of *Clotel.* If the narrative containment of slave experience guaranteed the former slave's objectification and commodification, and if Brown's refusal to inhabit a fixed first-person narratorial posture performed his own refusal to be so contained, the journalistic excerpts and fictional borrowings that appear throughout *Clotel* are the textual markers against which Brown defines his distance from the fixed subject positions shaped by abolitionist discourse.

37. Paul Gilmore, *Genuine Article,* 39.

38. Melville, *The Confidence-Man: His Masquerade,* ed. Harrison Hayford, Hershel Parker, and G. Thomas Tanselle (Evanston, IL: Northwestern University Press / New-

berry Library, 1984), 242 (hereafter cited parenthetically).

39. "The War," 100.

40. Julia Stern, "Spanish Masquerade and the Drama of Racial Identity in *Uncle Tom's Cabin*," in *Passing and the Fictions of Identity*, ed. Elaine K. Ginsberg (Durham, NC: Duke University Press, 1996), 108–10.

41. Streeby, *American Sensations*, 55, 113, 235.

42. Ibid., 245.

43. Maturin Murray Ballou, *Miralda; or, the Justice of Taçon* (Boston: W. V. Spencer, [1858?]), 8. It is worth pointing out that when Brown published a revised version of *Clotel* at the end of the decade, he decided to change its title to *Miralda*. Importantly, Brown was living and writing (probably working on the revisions that would lead to his own *Miralda*) in Boston at the time that Ballou's play of the same name appeared there. Brown's decision to rename his play (he would change the name back, with a revised spelling, to *Clotelle* in later versions) would seem to link his work's obvious interest in the slipperiness of racial categorization to the slipperiness of Spanish identity during these years.

CODA

1. The phrase comes from Keith Gandal, *The Virtues of the Vicious: Jacob Riis, Stephen Crane, and the Spectacle of the Slum* (New York: Oxford University Press, 1997), 17.

2. Amy Kaplan, *The Social Construction of American Realism* (Chicago: University of Chicago Press, 1988), 13. Kaplan's work made possible the somewhat later argument of Nancy Glazener, who meticulously reveals how the editorial decisions and strategies of a periodical such as the *Atlantic Monthly* shaped the category of the literary and thus the very concept of what came to be known as "realism." Understanding how realism was produced by late nineteenth-century print culture, and how realism itself produced cultural stratifications such as class distinctions, Glazener's work illustrates how the elusive nature of reality as a subject of writing leads to a whole range of textual modes of truth-telling, each with its own set of assumptions about the relationship between writing and what Kaplan calls the "world 'out there'" (*Reading for Realism: The History of a U.S. Literary Institution, 1850–1910* [Durham, NC: Duke University Press, 1997], 9).

3. Rebecca Harding Davis, "Life in the Iron Mills," in *Life in the Iron Mills and Other Stories*, ed. Tillie Olsen (New York: The Feminist Press at the City University of New York, 1985). Parenthetical citations refer to this edition.

4. For example, Morris Dickstein's *A Mirror in the Roadway: Literature and the Real World* (Princeton, NJ: Princeton University Press, 2005), his account of the relationship between "literature and the real world," opens with a discussion of Whitman, Melville, and Henry James. But Dickstein's Melville (whose cameo lasts for only two pages) is interested in reality only so far as he brings the "real world" into urban tales such as "Bartleby, the Scrivener" and "The Two Temples."

5. For an intriguing discussion of Davis's use of sentimental language in "Life in the Iron Mills," see Amy Schrager Lang's "Class and the Strategies of Sympathy," in *The Culture of Sentiment: Race, Gender, and Sentimentality in Nineteenth-Century America*, ed. Shirley Samuels (Oxford: Oxford University Press).

6. Sharon M. Harris has suggested that at this moment the reader "is now required

to translate Doctor May's telegraphic language. Since his language removes the details the reader has been forced to observe, Dr. May can no longer be viewed as presenting a version of 'reality'" [*Rebecca Harding Davis and American Realism* (Philadelphia: University of Pennsylvania Press, 1991], 40).

7. Kaplan, *Reading for Realism*, 13.

8. Kaplan acknowledges the performative dimension of the realist project when she writes, "In this competition with other cultural practices, realism also becomes a strategy for defining the social position of the author. To call oneself a realist means to make a claim not only for the cognitive value of fiction but for one's own cultural authority both to possess and to dispense access to the real" (ibid.).

9. To remind ourselves that the contextual status of reality is relevant to even the most counterrealist works of fiction, we need only turn to Erich Auerbach's landmark study, *Mimesis: The Representation of Reality in Western Literature,* trans. Willard R. Trask (Princeton, NJ: Princeton University Press, 1953).

BIBLIOGRAPHY

Abbot, Anne W. *How to Spoil a Good Citizen; and Other Stories*. Boston: Crosby and Nichols, and S. G. Simkins, 1848.

Adams, Bluford. *E Pluribus Barnum: The Great Showman and the Making of U.S. Popular Culture*. Minneapolis: University of Minnesota Press, 1997.

Adams, F. C. *Uncle Tom at Home*. Philadelphia: Willis Hazard, 1853.

Adams, Nehemiah. *South-Side View of Slavery*. 4th ed. Boston: Ticknor and Fields, 1860.

Anderson, Benedict. *Imagined Communities: Reflections on the Origins and Spread of Nationalism*. Rev. ed. London: Verso, 1991.

Andrews, William, ed. *African American Autobiography: A Collection of Critical Essays*. Englewood Cliffs, NJ: Prentice Hall, 1993.

———. "The 1850s: The First Afro-American Literary Renaissance." In *Literary Romanticism in America*, ed. William Andrews. Baton Rouge: Louisiana State University Press, 1981. 38–60.

———, ed. and intro. *From Fugitive Slave to Free Man: The Autobiographies of William Wells Brown*. Columbia: University of Missouri Press, 2003.

———, ed. *Literary Romanticism in America*. Baton Rouge: Louisiana State University Press, 1981.

———. "Mark Twain, William Wells Brown, and the Problem of Authority in New South Writing." In *Southern Literature and Literary Theory*, ed. Jefferson Humphries. Athens: University of Georgia Press, 1990. 1–21.

———. "The Novelization of Voice in Early African American Narrative." *PMLA: Publications of the Modern Language Association* 105 (1990): 23–34.

———. *To Tell a Free Story: The First Century of Afro-American Autobiography, 1760–1865*. Urbana: University of Illinois Press, 1986.

"Annexation." *U.S. Magazine and Democratic Review*, July/August 1845: 5–10.

Armstrong, Nancy. *Fiction in the Age of Photography: The Legacy of British Realism*. Cambridge, MA: Harvard University Press, 1999.

Auerbach, Erich. *Mimesis: The Representation of Reality in Western Literature*. Trans. Willard R. Trask. Princeton, NJ: Princeton University Press, 1953.

Baldasty, Gerald J. *The Commercialization of News in the Nineteenth Century*. Madison: University of Wisconsin Press, 1992.

Ballou, Maturin Murray. *Miralda; or, The Justice of Taçon*. Boston: W. V. Spencer, [1858?].

Bauerlein, Mark. *Whitman and the American Idiom*. Baton Rouge: Louisiana State University Press, 1991.

Baym, Nina. *Novels, Readers, and Reviewers: Responses to Fiction in Antebellum America*. Ithaca, NY: Cornell University Press, 1984.

————. *The Shape of Hawthorne's Career*. Ithaca, NY: Cornell University Press, 1976.

Bell, Michael Davitt. *The Development of American Romance: The Sacrifice of Relation*. Chicago: University of Chicago Press, 1980.

Bell, Millicent. "Hawthorne and the Real." In *Hawthorne and the Real: Bicentennial Essays*, ed. Millicent Bell. Columbus: The Ohio State University Press, 2005. 1–21.

Bellis, Peter J. *Writing Revolution: Aesthetics and Politics in Hawthorne, Whitman, and Thoreau*. Athens: University of Georgia Press, 2003.

Benjamin, Walter. "The Storyteller: Reflections on the Works of Nikolai Leskov." In *Illuminations*, ed. and introd. Hannah Arendt. New York: Schocken Books, 1968. 83–109.

Bercovitch, Sacvan. *The Office of the Scarlet Letter*. Baltimore: Johns Hopkins University Press, 1991.

Bergmann, Hans. *God in the Street: New York Writing from the Penny Press to Melville*. Philadelphia: Temple University Press, 1995.

Berlant, Lauren. *The Anatomy of National Fantasy: Hawthorne, Utopia, and Everyday Life*. Chicago: University of Chicago Press, 1991.

Bhabha, Homi K., ed. *Nation and Narration*. London: Routledge, 1990.

Bisbee, A. *The History and Practice of Daguerreotyping*. Dayton, OH: L. F. Claplin and Co., 1852.

Blondheim, Menahem. *News Over the Wires: The Telegraph and the Flow of Public Information in America, 1844–1897*. Cambridge, MA: Harvard University Press, 1994.

Boorstin, Daniel J. *The Image: A Guide to Pseudo-Events in America*. New York: Atheneum, 1961.

Bourdieu, Pierre. *The Field of Cultural Production: Essays on Art and Literature*. Ed. and introd. Randal Johnson. New York: Columbia University Press, 1993.

Brand, Dana. "The Panoramic Spectator in America: A Re-Reading of Some of Hawthorne's Sketches." *American Transcendental Quarterly* 59 (1986): 5–17.

————. *The Spectator and the City in Nineteenth-Century American Literature*. Cambridge: Cambridge University Press, 1991.

Brennan, Timothy. "The National Longing for Form." In *Nation and Narration*, ed. Homi Bhabha. London: Routledge, 1990. 44–70.

Brodhead, Richard H. *Cultures of Letters: Scenes of Reading and Writing in Nineteenth-Century America*. Chicago: University of Chicago Press, 1993.

————. *Hawthorne, Melville, and the Novel*. Chicago: University of Chicago Press, 1976.

Brooks, Daphne A. *Bodies in Dissent: Spectacular Performances of Race and Freedom, 1850–1910*. Durham, NC: Duke University Press, 2006.

Brooks, N. C. *A Complete History of the Mexican War*. Baltimore: Hutchinson and Seebold, 1849.

Brown, William Wells. *Clotel; or, The President's Daughter*. 1853. Ed. William Edward Farrison. New York: Carol Publishing Group, 1995.

————. *Clotelle; or, the Colored Heroine: A Tale of the Southern States*. Boston: Lee and Shepard, 1867.

———. *A Description of William Wells Brown's Original Panoramic Views of the Scenes in the Life of an American Slave*. London: Charles Gilpin, [1849?].

———. "A Lecture Delivered Before the Female Anti-Slavery Society of Salem." 1847. In *The Narrative of William W. Brown, a Fugitive Slave*, by William Brown. Reading, MA: Addison-Wesley Publishing Company, 1969. 81–98.

———. *Miralda; or, the Beautiful Quadroon. A Romance of American Slavery, Founded on Fact. Weekly Anglo-African*, 1 Dec. 1860–16 Mar. 1861.

———. *My Southern Home: or, the South and Its People*. Boston: A. G. Brown, 1880.

———. "Narrative of the Life and Escape of William Wells Brown." 1853. In *Clotel; or, The President's Daughter*.

———. *The Narrative of William W. Brown, a Fugitive Slave*. 1847. Reading, MA: Addison-Wesley Publishing Company, 1969.

———. *Sketches of Places and People Abroad; The American Fugitive in Europe*. 1854. Freeport, ME: Books for Libraries Press, 1970.

Bryant, John. "Manuscript, Edition, Revision: Reading *Typee* with Trifocals." In *Melville's Evermoving Dawn: Centennial Essays*, ed. John Bryant and Robert Milder. Kent, OH: Kent State University Press, 1997. 297–306.

———. *Melville and Repose: The Rhetoric of Humor in the American Renaissance*. New York: Oxford University Press, 1993.

Budick, Emily Miller. *Fiction and Historical Consciousness: The American Romance Tradition*. New Haven, CT: Yale University Press, 1989.

———. *Nineteenth-Century American Romance: Genre and the Construction of Democratic Culture*. New York: Twayne Publishers, 1996.

Buell, Lawrence. *New England Literary Culture: From Revolution Through Renaissance*. Cambridge: Cambridge University Press, 1986.

Buntline, Ned. *Love at First Sight: or, The Daguerreotype*. Boston: Lerow and Co., 1848[?].

Burr's Pictorial Voyage to Canada, American Frontier, and the Saguenay. Boston: Dutton and Wentworth, 1850.

Calder, Alex. "'The Thrice Mysterious Taboo': Melville's *Typee* and the Perception of Culture." *Representations* 67 (1999): 27–43.

Cameron, Kenneth Walter. *Genesis of Hawthorne's "The Ambitious Guest."* Hartford, CT: Transcendental Books, 1955.

Carton, Evan. *The Rhetoric of American Romance: Dialectic and Identity in Emerson, Dickinson, Poe, and Hawthorne*. Baltimore: Johns Hopkins University Press, 1985.

Cassuto, Leonard. "'What an object he would have made of me!': Tattooing and the Racial Freak in Melville's *Typee*." In *Freakery: Cultural Spectacles of the Extraordinary Body*, ed. Rosemarie Garland-Thomson. New York: New York University Press, 1996. 234–47.

Castiglia, Christopher, and Russ Castronovo. "A 'Hive of Subtlety': Aesthetics and the End[s] of Cultural Studies." *American Literature* 76, no. 3 (September 2004): 423–35.

Chandler, Alfred D., Jr., and James W. Cortada, eds. *A Nation Transformed by Information: How Information Has Shaped the United States from Colonial Times to the Present*. Oxford: Oxford University Press, 2000.

Chase, Richard. *The American Novel and Its Tradition*. London: G. Bell and Sons, 1957.

———. *Herman Melville: A Critical Study*. New York: Macmillan, 1949.

Chew III, William C., ed. *Images of America: Through the European Looking Glass.* Brussels: VUBPress, 1997.

Cohen, Hennig, and Donald Yannella. *Herman Melville's Malcolm Letter: "Man's Final Lore."* New York: Fordham University Press and The New York Public Library, 1992.

Cohen, Patricia Cline. *The Murder of Helen Jewett: The Life and Death of a Prostitute in Nineteenth-Century New York.* New York: Vintage, 1998.

Colacurcio, Michael J. *The Province of Piety: Moral History in Hawthorne's Early Tales.* Cambridge, MA: Harvard University Press, 1984.

Cook, James W. *The Arts of Deception: Playing with Fraud in the Age of Barnum.* Cambridge, MA: Harvard University Press, 2004.

Coviello, Peter. "The American in Charity: 'Benito Cereno' and Gothic Anti-Sentimentality." *Studies in American Fiction* 30, no. 2 (2002): 155–80.

Crouthamel, James L. *Bennett's New York Herald and the Rise of the Popular Press.* Syracuse, NY: Syracuse University Press, 1989.

Davidson, Cathy. "Photographs of the Dead: Sherman, Daguerre, Hawthorne." *South Atlantic Quarterly* 89 (1990): 667–701.

———, ed. *Reading in America: Literature and Social History.* Baltimore: Johns Hopkins University Press, 1989.

Davis, Lennard. *Factual Fictions: The Origins of the English Novel.* New York: Columbia University Press, 1983.

Davis, Rebecca Harding. *Life in the Iron Mills and Other Stories.* 1861. Ed. Tillie Olsen. New York: The Feminist Press at the City University of New York, 1985.

Dayan, Daniel, and Elihu Katz. *Media Events: The Live Broadcasting of History.* Cambridge, MA: Harvard University Press, 1992.

Delbanco, Andrew. *Melville: His World and Work.* New York: Alfred A. Knopf, 2005.

Description of Bayne's Gigantic Panorama of a Voyage to Europe. Boston: Printed by William Chadwick, 1848.

Description of Lane's Panorama of the Hudson or North River. New York: [s.n.], 1848.

Descriptive and Historical View of Burr's Moving Mirror, of the Lakes, the Niagara, St. Lawrence, and Saguenay Rivers. Boston: Dutton & Wentworth, printers, 1850.

Desmond, Robert W. *The Information Process: World News Reporting to the Twentieth Century.* Iowa City: University of Iowa Press, 1978.

Dewy, George W. "Remarks." Appendix to *Photographic Researches and Manipulations,* by Levi L. Hill. Philadelphia: Myron Shew, 1854.

Dicken-Garcia, Hazel. *Journalistic Standards in Nineteenth-Century America.* Madison: University of Wisconsin Press, 1989.

Dickstein, Morris. *A Mirror in the Roadway: Literature and the Real World.* Princeton, NJ: Princeton University Press, 2005.

Dimock, Wai Chee. *Empire for Liberty: Melville and the Poetics of Individualism.* Princeton, NJ: Princeton University Press, 1989.

———. "*Typee*: Melville's Critique of Community." *ESQ* 30 (1984): 27–39.

Donnavan, Corydon. *Adventures in Mexico.* Cincinnati: Robinson and Jones, 1847.

Dorsey, Peter A. "De-authorizing Slavery: Realism in Stowe's *Uncle Tom's Cabin* and Brown's *Clotel.*" *ESQ* 41 (1995): 257–88.

Douglass, Frederick. *Autobiographies.* New York: Library of America, 1994.

Dryden, Edgar. *Melville's Thematics of Form: The Great Art of Telling the Truth.* Baltimore: Johns Hopkins University Press, 1968.

DuCille, Ann. "Where in the World Is William Wells Brown?: Thomas Jefferson, Sally Hemings, and the DNA of African-American Literary History." *American Literary History* 12 (2000): 443–62.

Dunne, Michael. *Hawthorne's Narrative Strategies.* Jackson: University Press of Mississippi, 1995.

Eaton, Mark. A. "'Lost in Their Mazes': Framing Facts and Fictions in *Benito Cereno.*" *Journal of Narrative Technique* 24 (1994): 212–36.

Edwards, Justin D. "Melville's Peep-Show: Sexual and Textual Cruises in 'Typee.'" *ARIEL: A Review of International English Literature* 30, no. 2 (1999): 61–74.

Elbert, Monika. "Nathaniel Hawthorne, *The Concord Freeman,* and the Irish 'Other.'" *Eire-Ireland: A Journal of Irish Studies* 29, no. 3 (1994): 60–73.

Elmer, Jonathan. *Reading at the Social Limit: Affect, Mass Culture, and Edgar Allan Poe.* Stanford, CA: Stanford University Press, 1995.

Ernest, John. *Resistance and Reformation in Nineteenth-Century African-American Literature: Brown, Wilson, Jacobs, Delany, Douglass, and Harper.* Jackson: University of Mississippi Press, 1995.

Fabi, M. Giulia. "Representing Slavery in Nineteenth Century Britain: The Anxiety of Non/Fictional Authorship in Charles Dickens' *American Notes* (1842) and William Wells Brown's *Clotel* (1853)." In Chew, *Images of America.* 125–40.

———. "The 'Unguarded Expressions of the Feelings of the Negroes': Gender, Slave Resistance, and William Wells Brown's Revisions of *Clotel.*" *African American Review* 27 (1993): 639–64.

Fern, Fanny [Sara Payson Willis Parton]. *Ruth Hall and Other Writings.* Ed. Joyce W. Warren. New Brunswick, NJ: Rutgers University Press, 1986.

Fisch, Audrey. "'Negrophilism' and British Nationalism: The Spectacle of the Black American Abolitionist." *Victorian Review* 19, no. 2 (1993): 20–47.

———. "Uncle Tom in England." *Victorian Literature and Culture* 22 (1994): 23–53.

Fluck, Winfried. "'The American Romance' and the Changing Functions of the Imaginary." *New Literary History* 27, no. 3 (1996): 415–57.

Fretz, Eric. "P. T. Barnum's Theatrical Selfhood and the Nineteenth-Century Culture of Exhibition." In *Freakery: Cultural Spectacles of the Extraordinary Body,* ed. Rosemarie Garland-Thomson. New York: New York University Press, 1996. 97–107.

Gandal, Keith. *The Virtues of the Vicious: Jacob Riis, Stephen Crane, and the Spectacle of the Slum.* New York: Oxford University Press, 1997.

Gannett, Ezra. "The Oceanic Telegraph." *North American Review* 87, no. 181 (October 1858): 532–44.

Gates, Henry Louis. *Figures in Black: Words, Signs, and the "Racial" Self.* Reprint ed. New York: Oxford University Press, 1989.

———. *The Signifying Monkey: A Theory of African-American Literary Criticism.* New York: Oxford University Press, 1988.

Gilmore, Michael T. *American Romanticism and the Marketplace.* Chicago: University of Chicago Press, 1985.

———. *Surface and Depth: The Quest for Legibility in American Culture.* Oxford: Oxford University Press, 2003.

Gilmore, Paul. *The Genuine Article: Race, Mass Culture, and American Literary Manhood.* Durham, NC: Duke University Press, 2001.

Gilmore, William J. *Reading Becomes a Necessity of Life: Material and Cultural Life in Rural New England, 1780–1835.* Knoxville: University of Tennessee Press, 1989.

Ginsberg, Elaine K., ed. *Passing and the Fictions of Identity.* Durham, NC: Duke University Press, 1996.

Glazener, Nancy. *Reading for Realism: The History of a U.S. Literary Institution, 1850–1910.* Durham, NC: Duke University Press, 1997.

Gossett, Thomas F. *Uncle Tom's Cabin and American Culture.* Dallas, TX: Southern Methodist University Press, 1985.

Gougeon, Len, and Joel Myerson, eds. *Ralph Waldo Emerson: Emerson's Antislavery Writings.* New Haven, CT: Yale University Press, 1995.

Halttunen, Karen. *Confidence Men and Painted Women: A Study of Middle-Class Culture in America, 1830–1870.* New Haven, CT: Yale University Press, 1982.

———. *Murder Most Foul: The Killer and the American Gothic Imagination.* Cambridge, MA: Harvard University Press, 1998.

Harris, Neil. *Humbug: The Art of P. T. Barnum.* Chicago: University of Chicago Press, 1973.

Harris, Sharon M. *Rebecca Harding Davis and American Realism.* Philadelphia: University of Pennsylvania Press, 1991.

Hartman, Saidiya. *Scenes of Subjection: Terror, Slavery, and Self-Making in Nineteenth-Century America.* New York: Oxford University Press, 1997.

Hartnett, Stephen John. *Democratic Dissent and the Cultural Fictions of Antebellum America.* Urbana: University of Illinois Press, 2002.

Hawthorne, Nathaniel. *The American Notebooks.* Vol. 8 of *The Centenary Edition of Nathaniel Hawthorne,* ed. Claude M. Simpson. Columbus: The Ohio State University Press, 1972.

———. *The House of the Seven Gables.* Vol. 2 of *The Centenary Edition of Nathaniel Hawthorne.* Columbus: The Ohio State University Press, 1965.

———. *The Letters, 1813–1843.* Vol. 15 of *The Centenary Edition of Nathaniel Hawthorne,* ed. Thomas Woodson, L. Neal Smith, and Norman Holmes Pearson. Columbus: The Ohio State University Press, 1984.

———. *The Letters, 1843–1853.* Vol. 16 of *The Centenary Edition of Nathaniel Hawthorne,* ed. Thomas Woodson, L. Neal Smith, and Norman Holmes Pearson. Columbus: The Ohio State University Press, 1985.

———. *The Letters, 1853–1856.* Vol. 17 of *The Centenary Edition of Nathaniel Hawthorne,* ed. Thomas Woodson, James A. Rubino, L. Neal Smith, and Norman Holmes Pearson. Columbus: The Ohio State University Press, 1987.

———. *Mosses from an Old Manse.* Vol. 10 of *The Centenary Edition of Nathaniel Hawthorne,* ed. William Charvat, Roy Harvey Pearce, and Claude M. Simpson. Columbus: The Ohio State University Press, 1974.

———. *The Scarlet Letter.* Vol. 1 of *The Centenary Edition of Nathaniel Hawthorne,* ed. William Charvat, Roy Harvey Pearce, and Claude M. Simpson. Columbus: The Ohio State University Press, 1962.

———. *Tales and Sketches.* New York: The Library of America, 1982.

———. *Twice-Told Tales.* Vol. 9 of *The Centenary Edition of Nathaniel Hawthorne,* ed. William Charvat, Roy Harvey Pearce, and Claude M. Simpson. Columbus: The Ohio State University Press, 1974.

Higgins, Brian, and Hershel Parker, eds. *Critical Essays on Herman Melville's* Moby-Dick. New York: G. K. Hall and Co., 1992.

———, eds. *Herman Melville: The Contemporary Reviews.* Cambridge: Cambridge University Press, 1995.

Hill, Levi L. *Photographic Researches and Manipulations: including the author's former*

Treatise on daguerreotype. Philadelphia: Myron Shew, 1854.

"Hints to Newspaper Editors." *New-England Magazine,* May 1832: 361–67.

"History and Biography." *New-England Magazine,* March 1834: 197–200.

Hudson's Great National Painting of the Ohio and Mississippi Rivers. New Haven, CT: J. H. Benham, printer, 1848.

Humphrey, S[amuel]. D[wight]. *American Hand Book of the Daguerreotype.* New York: S. D. Humphrey, 1853.

Humphries, Jefferson, ed. *Southern Literature and Literary Theory.* Athens: University of Georgia Press, 1990.

Huntzicker, William E. *The Popular Press, 1833–1865.* Westport, CT: Greenwood Press, 1999.

Idol, John L., Jr., and Buford Jones, eds. *Nathaniel Hawthorne: The Contemporary Reviews.* Cambridge: Cambridge University Press, 1994.

Ivison, Douglas. "'I Saw Everything but Could Comprehend Nothing': Melville's *Typee,* Travel Narrative, and Colonial Discourse." *American Transcendental Quarterly* 16, no. 2 (2002): 115–30.

Jehlen, Myra. *American Incarnation: The Individual, the Nation, and the Continent.* Cambridge, MA: Harvard University Press, 1986.

Johannsen, Robert. *To the Halls of the Montezumas: The Mexican War in the American Imagination.* Oxford: Oxford University Press, 1985.

John, Richard R. "Recasting the Information Infrastructure for the Industrial Age." In *A Nation Transformed by Information: How Information Has Shaped the United States from Colonial Times to the Present,* ed. Alfred D. Chandler, Jr. and James W. Cortada. Oxford: Oxford University Press, 2000. 55–105.

Kaplan, Amy. *The Social Construction of American Realism.* Chicago: University of Chicago Press, 1988.

Karcher, Carolyn. *Shadow Over the Promised Land: Slavery, Race, and Violence in Melville's America.* Baton Rouge: Louisiana State University Press, 1980.

Kielbowicz, Richard B. *News in the Mail: The Press, Post Office, and Public Information, 1700–1860s.* New York: Greenwood Press, 1989.

Lang, Amy Schrager. "Class and the Strategies of Sympathy." In *The Culture of Sentiment: Race, Gender, and Sentimentality in Nineteenth-Century America,* ed. Shirley Samuels. Oxford: Oxford University Press. 128–42.

"The Last Newsboy." *Yankee Doodle,* November 21, 1846: 72.

Lears, T. J. Jackson. *No Place of Grace: Antimodernism and the Transformation of American Culture, 1880–1920.* New York: Pantheon, 1981.

Lee, Maurice S. "Melville's Subversive Political Philosophy: 'Benito Cereno' and the Fate of Speech." *American Literature: A Journal of Literary History, Criticism, and Bibliography* 72, no. 3 (2000): 495–519.

Lehuu, Isabelle. *Carnival on the Page: Popular Print Media in Antebellum America.* Chapel Hill: University of North Carolina Press, 2000.

"Loose Thoughts on Plagiarism." *New-England Magazine,* May 1832: 333–36.

Luciano, Dana. "Melville's Untimely History: 'Benito Cereno' as Counter-Monumental Narrative." *Arizona Quarterly: A Journal of American Literature, Culture, and Theory* 60, no. 3 (2004): 33–60.

Lyons, Paul. "From Man-Eaters to Spam-Eaters: Literary Tourism and the Discourse of Cannibalism from Herman Melville to Paul Theroux." *Arizona Quarterly* 51, no. 2 (Summer 1995): 33–62.

Machor, James L., ed. *Readers in History: Nineteenth-Century American Literature and the Contexts of Response.* Baltimore: Johns Hopkins University Press, 1993.

"The Magnetic Telegraph—Some of Its Results." *Living Age* 26 (July 1845): 194–95.

McBride, Dwight. *Impossible Witnesses: Truth, Abolitionism, and Slave Testimony.* New York: New York University Press, 2001.

McCallum, E. L. "Hawthorne and Pynchon on the Line." *Arizona Quarterly* 56, no. 2 (2000): 65–96.

McDowell, Deborah E., and Arnold Rampersad, eds. *Slavery and the Literary Imagination.* Baltimore: Johns Hopkins University Press, 1989.

McGill, Meredith L. *American Literature and the Culture of Reprinting, 1834–1853.* Philadelphia: University of Pennsylvania Press, 2003.

McWilliams, John. "The Rationale for 'The American Romance.'" In *Revisionary Interventions into the Americanist Canon,* ed. Donald E. Pease. Durham, NC: Duke University Press, 1994. 71–82.

Melville, Herman. *The Confidence-Man: His Masquerade,* Vol. 10 of *The Writings of Herman Melville,* ed. Harrison Hayford, Hershel Parker, and G. Thomas Tanselle. Evanston, IL: Northwestern University Press / Newberry Library, 1984.

———. *Correspondence.* Vol. 14 of *The Writings of Herman Melville,* ed. Lynn Horth. Evanston, IL: Northwestern University Press / Newberry Library, 1993.

———. *Mardi and a Voyage Thither.* Vol. 3 of *The Writings of Herman Melville,* ed. Harrison Hayford, Hershel Parker, and G. Thomas Tanselle. Evanston, IL: Northwestern University Press / Newberry Library, 1970.

———. *Moby-Dick; or, the Whale.* Vol. 6 of *The Writings of Herman Melville,* ed. Harrison Hayford, Hershel Parker, and G. Thomas Tanselle. Evanston, IL: Northwestern University Press / Newberry Library, 1988.

———. *The Piazza Tales and Other Prose Pieces, 1839–1860.* Vol. 9 of *The Writings of Herman Melville,* ed. Harrison Hayford, Hershel Parker, and G. Thomas Tanselle. Evanston, IL: Northwestern University Press / Newberry Library, 1987.

———. *Pierre; or the Ambiguities.* Vol. 7 of *The Writings of Herman Melville,* ed. Harrison Hayford, Hershel Parker, and G. Thomas Tanselle. Evanston, IL: Northwestern University Press / Newberry Library, 1971.

———. *Redburn: His First Voyage.* 1849. Vol. 4 of *The Writings of Herman Melville,* ed. Harrison Hayford, Hershel Parker, and G. Thomas Tanselle. Evanston, IL: Northwestern University Press / Newberry Library, 1969.

———. *Typee: A Peep at Polynesian Life.* 1846. Vol. 1 of *The Writings of Herman Melville,* ed. Harrison Hayford, Hershel Parker, and G. Thomas Tanselle. Evanston, IL: Northwestern University Press / Newberry Library, 1968.

"Mexico—The Church, and Peace." *U.S. Magazine and Democratic Review,* August 1847: 93–102.

Michaels, Walter Benn. *The Gold Standard and the Logic of Naturalism: American Literature at the Turn of the Century.* Berkeley: University of California Press, 1987.

Millington, Richard H. *Practicing Romance: Narrative Form and Cultural Engagement in Hawthorne's Fiction.* Princeton, NJ: Princeton University Press, 1992.

———, ed. *The Cambridge Companion to Nathaniel Hawthorne.* Cambridge: Cambridge University Press, 2004.

Mindich, David T. Z. *Just the Facts: How "Objectivity" Came to Define American Journalism.* New York: New York University Press, 1998.

Moldenhauer, Joseph. "Thoreau, Hawthorne, and the Seven-Mile Panorama." *ESQ: A*

Journal of the American Renaissance 44, no. 4 (1998): 227–74.

Moore, Margaret B. *The Salem World of Nathaniel Hawthorne.* Columbia: University of Missouri Press, 1998.

Neal, John. "Story-telling." *New-England Magazine,* January 1835, 1–12.

"The New Post-Office Law." *New Englander and Yale Review* 3, no. 12 (October 1845): 536–48.

Newberry, Michael. *Figuring Authorship in Antebellum America.* Stanford, CA: Stanford University Press, 1997.

Orvell, Miles. *The Real Thing: Imitation and Authenticity in American Culture.* Chapel Hill: University of North Carolina Press, 1989.

Otter, Samuel. *Melville's Anatomies.* Berkeley: University of California Press, 1999.

Parker, Hershel. *Herman Melville: A Biography, Volume 1, 1819–1851.* Baltimore: Johns Hopkins University Press, 1996.

Pease, Donald E., ed. *National Identities and Post-Americanist Narratives.* Durham, NC: Duke University Press, 1994.

———. "New Americanists: Revisionist Interventions into the Canon." In *Revisionary Interventions,* ed. Donald Pease. Durham, NC: Duke University Press, 1994. 1–37.

———, ed. *Revisionary Interventions into the Americanist Canon.* Durham, NC: Duke University Press, 1994.

———. *Visionary Compacts: American Renaissance Writings in Cultural Context.* Madison: University of Wisconsin Press, 1987.

Peterson, Carla. "Capitalism, Black [Under]Development, and the Production of the African American Novel in the 1850s." In *Postcolonial Theory and the United States: Race, Ethnicity and Literature,* ed. Amritjit Singh and Peter Schmidt. Jackson: University Press of Mississippi, 2000. 176–95.

Pfaelzer, Jean. *Parlor Radical: Rebecca Harding Davis and the Origins of American Social Realism.* Pittsburgh: University of Pittsburgh Press, 1996.

Pfister, Joel. "Hawthorne as Cultural Theorist." In *The Cambridge Companion to Nathaniel Hawthorne,* ed. Richard H. Millington. Cambridge: Cambridge University Press, 2004.

Poe, Edgar Allan. *Poetry and Tales.* New York: Library of America, 1984.

Post-Lauria, Sheila. *Correspondent Colorings: Melville in the Marketplace.* Amherst: University of Massachusetts Press, 1996.

Pratt, Mary Louise. *Imperial Eyes: Travel Writing and Transculturation.* London: Routledge, 1992.

Railton, Stephen. *Authorship and Audience: Literary Performance in the American Renaissance.* Princeton, NJ: Princeton University Press, 1991.

Reiss, Benjamin. *The Showman and the Slave: Race, Death, and Memory in Barnum's America.* Cambridge, MA: Harvard University Press, 2001.

Renker, Elizabeth. "Melville's Spell in *Typee.*" *Arizona Quarterly* 51, no. 2 (1995): 1–31.

Reynolds, David. *Beneath the American Renaissance: The Subversive Imagination in the Age of Emerson and Melville.* Cambridge, MA: Harvard University Press, 1988.

———. "'Its wood could only be American!': *Moby-Dick* and Antebellum Popular Culture." In *Critical Essays,* ed. Brian Higgins and Hershel Parker. New York: G. K. Hall and Co., 1992. 523–44.

Rice, Grantland. *The Transformation of Authorship in America.* Chicago: University of Chicago Press, 1997.

Richards, Jeffrey H. "The Showman as Romancer: Theatrical Presentation in Hawthorne's 'Main Street.'" *Studies in Short Fiction* 21 (1984): 47–55.

Robinson, Amy. "It Takes One to Know One: Passing and Communities of Common Interest." *Critical Inquiry* 20 (1994): 715–36.

Rogin, Michael Paul. *Subversive Genealogy: The Politics and Art of Herman Melville.* New York: Alfred A. Knopf, 1983.

Root, M. A. "The Daguerreotypic Art." Appendix to *Photographic Researches and Manipulations,* ed. Levi L. Hill. Philadelphia: Myron Shew, 1854.

Rowe, John Carlos. "Melville's *Typee:* U.S. Imperialism at Home and Abroad." In *National Identities,* ed. Donald L. Pease. Durham, NC: Duke University Press, 1994. 255–78.

Samson, John. *White Lies: Melville's Narratives of Facts.* Ithaca, NY: Cornell University Press, 1989.

Samuels, Shirley, ed. *The Culture of Sentiment: Race, Gender, and Sentimentality in Nineteenth-Century America.* Oxford: Oxford University Press, 1992.

Sanborn, Geoffrey. *The Sign of the Cannibal: Melville and the Making of a Postcolonial Reader.* Durham, NC: Duke University Press, 1998.

Schudson, Michael. *Discovering the News: A Social History of American Newspapers.* New York: Basic Books, 1978.

———. "The Objectivity Norm in American Journalism." *Journalism* 2, no. 2 (2000): 149–70.

Schwarzlose, Richard A. *The Nation's Newsbrokers: Volume I, The Formative Years, from Pretelegraph to 1865.* Evanston, IL: Northwestern University Press, 1989.

Sconce, Jeffrey. *Haunted Media: Electronic Presence from Telegraphy to Television.* Durham, NC: Duke University Press, 2000.

Sekora, John. "Black Message/White Envelope: Genre, Authenticity, and Authority in the Antebellum Slave Narrative." *Callaloo* 10 (1987): 482–515.

Singh, Amritjit, and Peter Schmidt, eds. *Postcolonial Theory and the United States: Race, Ethnicity, and Literature.* Jackson: University Press of Mississippi, 2000.

Smith, John Rowson. *Descriptive Book of the Tour of Europe.* New York: Pattinger and Gray, 1855.

Spurr, David. *The Rhetoric of Empire: Colonial Discourse, Travel Writing, and Imperial Administration.* Durham, NC: Duke University Press, 1993.

Standage, Tom. *The Victorian Internet: The Remarkable Story of the Telegraph and the Nineteenth Century's On-line Pioneers.* New York: Walker and Company, 1998.

Stearns, Rev. E. J. *Notes on Uncle Tom's Cabin: Being a Logical Answer to Its Allegations and Inferences against Slavery as an Institution.* Philadelphia: Lippincott, Grambo and Co., 1853.

Stepto, Robert B. *From Behind the Veil: A Study of Afro-American Narrative.* Urbana: University of Illinois Press, 1979.

———. "Narration, Authentication, and Authorial Control in Frederick Douglass' *Narrative* of 1845." In *African American Autobiography,* ed. William Andrews. Englewood Cliffs, NJ: Prentice Hall. 26–35.

Stern, Julia. "Spanish Masquerade and the Drama of Racial Identity in *Uncle Tom's Cabin.*" In *Passing and the Fictions of Identity,* ed. Elaine K. Ginsberg. Durham, NC: Duke University Press, 1996. 103–30.

Stowe, Harriet Beecher. *The Key to Uncle Tom's Cabin.* 1854. Salem, NH: Ayer Company, 1987.

Streeby, Shelley. *American Sensations: Class, Empire, and the Production of Popular Culture.* Berkeley: University of California Press, 2002.

Sundquist, Eric. "Suspense and Tautology in 'Benito Cereno.'" *Glyph: Textual Studies* 8 (1981): 103–26.

———. *To Wake the Nations: Race in the Making of American Literature.* Cambridge, MA: Harvard University Press, 1993.

Tanner, Laura E. "Self-Conscious Representation in the Slave Narrative." *Black American Literature Forum* 21 (1987): 415–24.

"Telegraph Office." *Yankee Doodle,* December 19, 1846: 217.

Thomas, Brook. *Cross-examinations of Law and Literature: Cooper, Hawthorne, Stowe, and Melville.* Cambridge: Cambridge University Press, 1987.

———. "*The House of the Seven Gables:* Reading the Romance of America." *PMLA* 97, no. 2 (1982): 195–211.

Thomas, Ronald R. "Double Exposures: Arresting Images in *Bleak House* and *The House of the Seven Gables.*" *Novel: A Forum on Fiction* 31 (1997): 87–113.

Thompson, G. R. *The Art of Authorial Presence: Hawthorne's Provincial Tales.* Durham, NC: Duke University Press, 1993.

Thompson, G. R., and Eric Carl Link. *Neutral Ground: New Traditionalism and the American Romance Controversy.* Baton Rouge: Louisiana State University Press, 1999.

Thoreau, Henry David. *Journal,* Vol. 4, 1851–52. Edited by Leonard N. Neufeldt and Nancy Craig Simmons. Princeton, NJ: Princeton University Press, 1971.

———. *Walden and Resistance to Civil Government.* 2nd ed. Edited by William Rossi. New York: W. W. Norton, 1992.

Tower, Rev. Philo. *Slavery Unmasked.* Rochester, NY: E. Darrow and Brother, 1856.

Trachtenberg, Alan. "Seeing and Believing: Hawthorne's Reflections on the Daguerreotype in *The House of the Seven Gables.*" *American Literary History* 9 (1997): 460–81.

Trilling, Lionel. *The Liberal Imagination: Essays on Literature and Society.* New York: Harcourt Brace Jovanovich, 1978.

Tucher, Andie. *Froth & Scum: Truth, Beauty, Goodness, and the Ax Murder in America's First Mass Medium.* Chapel Hill: University of North Carolina Press, 1994.

Vail, Alfred. *The American Electric Telegraph with the Reports of Congress. . . .* Philadelphia: Lea and Blanchard, 1845.

Walsh, Richard. "Fictionality and Mimesis: Between Narrativity and Fictional Worlds." *Narrative* 11, no. 1 (January 2003): 110–21.

"The War." *U.S. Magazine and Democratic Review,* February 1847, 99–102.

[Warland, John H.] "The Devil among the Books." *New-England Magazine,* August 1833, 100–106.

Warner, Michael J. "The Mass Public and the Mass Subject." In *Publics and Counterpublics.* New York: Zone Books, 2002. 159–86.

"Watching the Telegraph." *Yankee Doodle,* December 19, 1846: 158.

Weber, Alfred. "The Outlines of 'The Story Teller,' The Major Work of Hawthorne's Early Career." *Nathaniel Hawthorne Review* 15, no. 1 (1989): 14–19.

Weiner, Susan. "'Benito Cereno' and the Failure of Law." *Arizona Quarterly* 47, no. 2 (1991): 1–28.

Weinstein, Cindy. *The Literature of Labor and the Labors of Literature: Allegory in Nineteenth-Century American Fiction.* Cambridge: Cambridge University Press, 1995.

Weld, Theodore. *American Slavery as It Is: Testimony of a Thousand Witnesses*. New York: American Anti-Slavery Society, 1839.

Whalen, Terence. *Edgar Allan Poe and the Masses: The Political Economy of Literature in Antebellum America*. Princeton, NJ: Princeton University Press, 1999.

Whitman, Walt. *Poetry and Prose*. New York: The Library of America, 1996.

Widmer, Edward L. *Young America: The Flowering of Democracy in New York City*. Oxford: Oxford University Press, 1999.

Williams, Susan S. "'The Aspiring Purpose of an Ambitious Demagogue': Portraiture and *The House of the Seven Gables*." *Nineteenth-Century Literature* 49 (1994): 221–44.

Wineapple, Brenda. *Hawthorne: A Life*. New York: Alfred A. Knopf, 2003.

Wolff, Cynthia Griffin. "Passing Beyond the Middle Passage: Henry 'Box' Brown's Translations of Slavery." *Massachusetts Review: A Quarterly of Literature, the Arts, and Public Affairs* 37, no. 1 (1996): 23–44.

Zboray, Ronald J. *A Fictive People: Antebellum Economic Development and the American Reading Public*. New York: Oxford University Press, 1993.

INDEX

CPSIA information can be obtained
at www.ICGtesting.com
Printed in the USA
FFOW04n0143220316
22496FF